Journeys under the Moon

Writing
and the
Hero's Quest

Ill. 0-1: *Jason employed the Argos to aid him in building a vessel capable of sustaining fifty men during a time when the only type of navigation known to the Greeks was small boats or hollowed out tree trunks resembling canoes. The Argonauts would go on to have one of the greatest hero's journeys ever: their mission—to find the Golden Fleece. Their story is told in two ancient works, a Greek classical poem called Argonautica written by Apollonius Rhodius in the 3rd century BCE and the play Medea, an ancient Greek tragedy, written by Euripides in 431 BCE. Much of the structure of these works is exactly the same as the three act structure you'll learn in this book (also known as Mythic Structure). There have been some refinements over the years, but the basic building blocks have remained the same.*

Journeys under the Moon

Writing
and the
Hero's Quest

Michael Hiebert

DangerBoy Books
British Columbia, Canada

Journeys under the Moon: Writing and the Hero's Quest
Published by DangerBoy Books

Copyright © 2013 by Michael Hiebert
All rights reserved.
Printed in the United States.

No part of this book may be reproduced in any form or by any means without prior written consent of the Publisher, excepting brief quotes used in reviews.

Special book excerpts or customized printings can be created to fit specific needs and special quantity discounts are available for bulk purchases for sales promotion, premiums, fund-raising, and educational or institutional use. For information on this or to attend workshops or lectures based on the topics discussed within this book, please contact Michael Hiebert through by email at michael.hiebert@aol.com, or by visiting his website located at www.michaelhiebert.com.

Hiebert, Michael [1967-]

Includes bibliographical references.

ISBN-13: 978-1-927600-04-7
ISBN-10: 1-927600-04-9

  1. Writing, non-fiction, English. 2. Hiebert, Michael. 1697- . *Journeys Under the Moon: Writing and the Hero's Quest*. 3. Carrol, Lewis, 1832-1898. *Alice's Adventures in Wonderland*. 4. Carrol, Lewis, 1832-1898. *Through the Looking-Glass*. 5. Twain, Mark, 1835-1910. *The Adventures of Tom Sawyer*.

DangerBoy Books, Chilliwack, British Columbia, Canada, V2R 0B4
www.michaelhiebert.com/fiction/dangerboy-books

First trade paperback edition. May 2013.

To everyone who's ever had a dream . . .

Other Books by Michael Hiebert

Close to the Broken Hearted
Kensington Publishing Corp. New York, 2014.

Darkstone: The Perfection of Wisdom
DangerBoy Books for Children British Columbia, Canada, 2013.

Dream with Little Angels
Kensington Publishing Corp. New York, 2013.

Sometimes the Angels Weep
DangerBoy Books. British Columbia, Canada, 2013.

Dolls
DangerBoy Books for Children British Columbia, Canada, 2012.

The Hyperbole Engine
DangerBoy Books. British Columbia, Canada, 2012.

Dust
DangerBoy Books. British Columbia, Canada, 2012.

Edges
DangerBoy Books. British Columbia, Canada, 2012.

Not Forgotten
DangerBoy Books. British Columbia, Canada, 2012.

TABLE OF CONTENTS

TABLE OF ILLUSTRATIONS	xiii
ACKNOWLEDGEMENTS	xv
PREFACE	xvii
INTRODUCTION	xix

PART I: THE HERO'S JOURNEY

Chapter One—Structure

1.	THREE ACT STRUCTURE	5
2.	STRUCTURE IS FORM, NOT FORMULA	7
3.	STUDYING STRUCTURE	10
4.	FORM FOLLOWS FUNCTION	12
5.	THE STRUCTURE IS FLEXIBLE	12
6.	BEGINNINGS, MIDDLES, AND ENDINGS	16
	KEY POINTS	18

Chapter Two—A Brief Look at the Path

1.	RITES OF PASSAGE	19
2.	FROM THE WOMB TO THE TOMB	21
3.	BECOMING A HERO	23
4.	MYTHOLOGICAL JOURNEYS	24
5.	FAIRYTALE JOURNEYS	28
	EXERCISES	33
	KEY POINTS	34

Chapter Three—The Basics — 35

FIRST PIVOT POINT	39
SECOND PIVOT POINT	39
KEY POINTS	41

Chapter Four—Act I: The Beginning	42
1. SETUP	43
2. THE INCITING EVENT	44
3. DEBATE	45
4. PIVOT POINT I: ENTERING ACT II	46
EXERCISES	48
KEY POINTS	50
Chapter Five—Act II: The Barren Wasteland	51
1. YOUR PROTAGONIST AGAINST OPPOSING FORCES	52
2. SUBPLOTS	52
3. ACT II MIDPOINT CLIMAX	55
4. THE REST OF ACT II: RAISING THE STAKES	57
5. DARKNESS CLOSES IN	58
6. ALL IS LOST	58
7. DARK NIGHT BEFORE DAWN	59
8. PIVOT POINT II: ENTERING ACT III	61
EXERCISES	62
KEY POINTS	65
Chapter Six—Act III: The End of the Story	
1. SUBPLOTS INTERTWINE	67
2. CHASE SCENES	68
3. THE CLIMAX	68
4. CHARACTER ARCS	75
5. THE RESURRECTION	76
6. ENDINGS	77
7. THE DENOUEMENT: THE NEW OLD WORLD	78
8. RETURNING WITH THE ELIXIR	81
EXERCISES	83
KEY POINTS	86

Chapter Seven—Studying Structure
1. PICKING UP THAT PEN ... 88
2. MOTION PICTURE BREAKOUTS ... 89
CASABLANCA ... 91
JUNO ... 96
STAR WARS: A NEW HOPE ... 103
THE HELP ... 109
TOY STORY ... 116

PART II: WRITING WELL

Chapter One—Some Notes on Style & Etiquette
1. GETTING OUT THE WORDS ... 123
2. AUTHOR/READER TRUST ... 126
3. START WITH SOMETHING INTERESTING ... 131
EXERCISES ... 132
KEY POINTS ... 133

Chapter Two—Building Scenes ... 134
1. POINT OF VIEW ... 136
2. CONFLICT ... 138
3. USING INDEX CARDS ... 138
4. SCENE ENERGY ... 139
5. HERO'S JOURNEY: MAIN PLOT POINTS ... 141
6. GIVING CREATIVITY BLOCK A SWIFT KICK ... 144
7. COMPOSITION ... 151
EXERCISES ... 158
KEY POINTS ... 160

Chapter Three—Voice
1. CHARACTER VOICE ... 162
2. AUTHORIAL VOICE ... 180
EXERCISES ... 183

ix

KEY POINTS	184
Chapter Four—Action	
1. ACTIVE VOICE VERSUS PASSIVE VOICE	186
2. BEWARE NEEDLESS STAGE DIRECTION	194
EXERCISES	196
KEY POINTS	198
Chapter Five—Description & Setting	
1. BE SPECIFIC	199
2. ADJECTIVES, ADVERBS, AND CONCRETE NOUNS	201
3. WHEN TO USE DESCRIPTION	202
EXERCISES	208
KEY POINTS	209

PART III: ARCHETYPES

Chapter One—How to Use Archetypes	
1. WHAT ARE ARCHETYPES?	213
2. ARCHETYPES ARE NOT STEREOTYPES	216
3. LIGHT SIDES AND SHADOW SIDES	216
4. CHARACTERS MAY HAVE MULTIPLE ARCHETYPES	217
5. SOME BASIC ARCHETYPES	217
KEY POINTS	224
Chapter Two—Getting More Out of Archetypes	
1. A JOURNEY THROUGH ARCHETYPES	225
2. MORE ESOTERIC ARCHETYPES	230
EXERCISES	241
KEY POINTS	243
Chapter Three: Animal Archetypes	
1. FINDING YOUR STORY'S THEME	244
2. COMBINING THEMES	269
EXERCISES	270
KEY POINTS	272

APPENDICIES
I.	BIBLIOGRAPHY	275
II.	GLOSSARY	279
III.	CONTACT	285

TABLE OF ILLUSTRATIONS

Ill. 0-1	**The Argos.** Thomas Bulfinch, *The Age of Fable* (Philadelphia: Henry Altemus Company, 1897) 163	ii
Ill. 0-2	**Alice and the Rabbit.** *Harper's Young People* (New York: Harper and Brothers, 1889) Vol.XI No. 544.374	2
Ill. 1-1	**Greek Soldiers.** Webster, Hutton, *Ancient History* (Boston, MA: D.C. Heath & Co., 1913)	14
Ill. 1-2	**Cupid and Venus.** Richard Ford Heath, *Illustrated Biographies of the Great Artists Tiziano Vecelli* (London: Samrson Low, Marston and Company, 1985) 70	25
Ill. 1-3	**Siegfried Slays the Dragon.** Klugh, Maria, *Tales from the Far North* (Chicago, IL: A. Flanagan Company, 1909)	27
Ill. 1-4	**Jack and the Beanstalk.** Charles H. Sylvester, *Journeys Through Bookland* (Chicago: Bellows-Reeve Company, 1909) 1:170	29
Ill. 1-5	**Pandora.** Thomas Bulfinch, *The Age of Fables* (Philadelphia: Henry Altemus Company, 1897) 19	40
Ill. 1-6	**The Little Mermaid.** Hans Christian Anderson, *Fairy Tales* (Dayton: R. Worthington, 1884) 33	46
Ill. 1-7	**Arthur and Guinevere.** Charles H. Sylvester, *Journeys Through Bookland* (Chicago: Bellows-Reeve Company, 1909) 294	53
Ill. 1-8	**Sleeping Beauty.** Crane, Walter, *The Decorative Illustration of Books Old and New* (New York, NY: G. Bells and Sons Ltd., 1905)	63
Ill. 1-9	**The Death of Hamlet.** Charles and Mary Lamb, *Tales from Shakespeare* (Philadelphia: Hentry Altemus Company, 1901) 151	80
Ill. 1-10	**Jason and the Golden Fleece.** 1600-1610 Chiaroscuro Woodcut.	81
Ill. 2-1	**Sir Galahad.** Ginn and Company, *The Common School Catalogue* (Boston, MA: Ginn & Company Publishing, 1906)	130
Ill. 2-2	**The Banquet of Damocles.** Ridpath, John Clark, *Cyclopedia of Universal History* (Cincinnati, OH: The Jones Brothers Publishing Co., 1885)	137
Ill. 2-3	**Index Card.** Copyright © 2013 Michael Hiebert. All rights reserved.	142

Ill. 2-4	**The Tea Party.** *Harper's Young People* (New York: Harper and Brothers, 1889) Vol.XI No. 544.377	174
Ill. 2-5	**The Mad Hatter.** *Harper's Young People* (New York: Harper and Brothers, 1889) Vol.XI No. 544.377	176
Ill. 3-1	**Merlin.** Charles H. Sylvester, *Journeys Through Bookland* (Chicago: Bellows-Reeve Company, 1909) 300	219
Ill. 3-2	**Poseidon.** Mara L. Pratt, *Myths of Old Greece* (New York: Educational Publishing Company, 1896) 16	230
Ill. 3-3	**Apollo.** Mara L. Pratt, *Myths of Old Greece* (New York: Educational Publishing Company, 1896) 72	231
Ill. 3-4	**Hades and Cerberus.** Charles Mills Gayley, *The Classic Myths in English Literature and in Art* (Boston: Ginn and Company, 1893) 53	235
Ill. 3-5	**Osiris.** Thomas Bulfinch, *The Age of Fables* (Philadelphia: Henry Altemus Company, 1897) 359	236
Ill. 3-6	**Isis.** Thomas Bulfinch, *The Age of Fables* (Philadelphia: Henry Altemus Company, 1897) 359	186

ACKNOWLEDGEMENTS

Knowledge is in the end based on acknowledgement.
—Ludwig Wittigenstein[1]

Thanks goes out to those who helped me get my original workshop on the Hero's Journey off the ground. Originally, this entire book was one complete workshop. I'm not sure what I was thinking—it would have taken an entire weekend to give it. It was my friend and colleague Annie Daylon who suggested I trim it down into three or four separate workshops, the first one being on the Hero's Journey. Her advice turned out to be sage advice, which is always what I seem to get from Annie.

She sat through my entire presentation of that workshop not just once, but twice, and for that I cannot thank her enough. Especially when I consider that the first time was so rough it was painful for *me*.

Annie was also one of the early readers of this manuscript and her suggestions for improvements made the book all that better.

Other people who suffered through early performances of my workshop and others that led to the creation of this book are my son Sagan Hiebert, Shannon Mairs, Abe Hiebert, Ann Hiebert, and, believe it or not, my dog Chloe.

Chloe has seen them all more than anyone.

To all those other early readers, especially those who worked so hard at finding mistakes that I inevitably missed, I give a dear thanks. Thanks

---

[1] Ludwig Josef Johann Wittgenstein (April 26, 1889 - April 29, 1951). Austrian-British philosopher working primarily in logic, the philosophy of mathematics, the philosophy of the mind, and the philosophy of language.

for your time and for questioning me on my methods and ideas. At the very top of this list is Yvonne Rupert, who did more to turn this book into what it is today than anyone. It was she who suggested the exercises and, before Yvonne got a hold of it, I had sections mixed up and information out of order and a slew of other "unmentionables" that are better left that way. Yvonne also did an over-the-top magnificent editing job. I don't think I can thank her enough. Funny, the people you meet through the Internet.

Also to Johanne Sauvé for taking time not only to read this book, but nearly every book I've ever published. Thanks for your excitement about the little things in life, Joanne. It's quite contagious.

Two more people I am in need of thanking are Garth Pettersen and Ken Loomes who both critique my work with great passion on a regular basis and keep me honest by forcing me to make sure my chops are up to snuff. Ken, especially, has saved me from embarrassment a few times by catching factual errors that somehow always seem to slip by me unnoticed. Luckily, he catches them before those manuscripts see the light of my editor's office.

I have to send a big shout out to the Federation of BC Writers for giving me a voice in the British Columbia writing community and helping me in finding a home for my workshops and, ultimately, homes for this book.

Finally, I would like to thank the Chilliwack Writers' Group—Garth Pettersen, Lori Christie, Mary Keane, and Terri McKee—a fine bunch of folks who listen to and critique my work every fortnight.

PREFACE

A man who carries a cat by the tail learns something he can learn in no other way.

—Mark Twain[2]

I wrote this book as an accompaniment for a series of workshops I designed on three act structure techniques, archetypes, and story theme based on animal archetypes. In every way, the book goes into much greater detail than the workshops. In most cases, the workshops are confined to a time limit of an hour, maybe an hour and thirty minutes. This book provides me with the opportunity and versatility to explain these subjects in as much depth as I want, and include everything I know about writing well and writing on target. With the information included, you'll gain self-confidence in your own skills, be able to write to deadlines, and obtain the ability to dissect and discuss other works in a way that makes sense. This book gives people a common language; a grounding point, if you will; a foundation to stand on.

It's also a way for me to reach writers who can't attend my workshops due to time or distance constraints. This book is a viable alternative, although you miss the one-on-one interaction and the ability to ask me questions directly. So best situation is still to par-

---

[2] Born Samuel Langhorne Clemens (November 30, 1835 - April 21, 1910), Mark Twait was an American author and humorist most noted for his novels *The Adventures of Tom Sawyer* (1876) and its sequel, *Adventures of Huckleberry* Finn (1885).

ticipate in a workshop and then take the book home with you to act as a supplement to the material given.

There's nothing here that hasn't been said before in other books. The strength of this text lies in its simplicity. For a writer looking to bring his work to a professional level, this book contains a complete course on how to do it. I have taken some needlessly complicated concepts and broken them down into simpler forms so that you can learn them quickly and concentrate on what's important: your writing.

This book is not meant as a replacement for other books on writing. Indeed, I have included a fairly thorough bibliography in Appendix II of writing books that I think are extremely valuable and also a great place to continue your study once you've mastered the techniques presented here.

Within these pages lie the secrets to improving your work dramatically. This book will make your writing more professional, more presentable, and above all, more reachable to a general readership—agents and editors included.

I wish you all the best in your writing endeavors. The writing life is not an easy one. It's a constant struggle and balancing act between time, energy, creativity, and imagination. But if you persevere, like the protagonist moving through his journey of trials and tests, the rewards are great.

And always remember, if you keep at it, returning home as the Hero is not a long way off.

In fact, it might be just over that next horizon, beyond those distant hills . . .

INTRODUCTION

> *Life is a series of natural and spontaneous changes. Don't resist them—that only creates sorrow. Let reality be reality. Let things flow naturally forward in whatever way they like.*
>
> —Lao Tzu[3]

This book, like the set of workshops I developed that go with it, are for people who are tired of rejection letters from agents and editors. It's also for those Indy authors who are sick of writing novels that just lie there listlessly on Amazon making no sales, while other authors around them are making the bestseller lists (and no, it's not about using some esoteric KDP scheme to get your numbers up or anything like that).

I wrote this book to help good authors become great authors in as little time as possible—to take writers whose work is "really not that bad" and skyrocket them to a new level by using a few tried and true techniques that "the professionals" are already using on a day-to-day basis.

It's for people who want to create sellable, professional, and, above all, commercial fiction. By commercial fiction, I mean sellable fiction that people buy on a regular basis. Think about James Patterson. Clive Cussler. Nora Roberts. Jonathon Kellerman. People like that. They're writing commercial fiction.

---

[3] Lao Tzu was the father of Taoism, an ancient philosophy from the 6th century BCE. He's best known as the author of the *Tao Te Ching*.

The book is divided into three separate parts, with a set of Appendices at the end. The parts are: The Hero's Journey; Writing Well; and Archetypes.

In "The Hero's Journey", I break down the complete journey—the quest the protagonist takes through a story as he moves from an Initiate toward the Climax, until he finally overcomes his adversary and becomes the Hero. Learning the Hero's Journey will take your writing to brand new levels practically overnight, and, although many books have been written about the Hero's Journey, I take a different tactic than most. My journey is a scaled down version that includes only what I consider to be absolutely necessary.

It doesn't bog the writer down with more than he needs to worry about. You can learn this structure quickly, committing it to memory so that you can concentrate on the actual craft of writing.

If you *do* want to learn more about the intricacies of the Hero's Journey that I've left out—those little subtleties that you might wish to one day draw upon—there are many books out there that can supply that information. I've included a list of some great ones in the Bibliography.

This section ends with a small discussion of some popular movies which I break out into the three act structure to show concrete examples.

"Writing Well" talks about some common issues I've run into while critiquing manuscripts for other people. I do a lot of manuscript critiques and encounter the same problems again and again. Things like trouble with scene construction, bad or stilted dialogue, problems with conflict, and point of view issues, among other things. These are the types of items explored in this part of the book.

The part called "Archetypes" discusses Jungian archetypes in great detail, giving you a wealth of different archetype examples you can use in your own writing. Don't know what an archetype is? You will after reading this. Understanding archetypes is a big step you can take to improving your craft. And it's actually one that's fun.

I've also included three Appendices: Bibliography, Glossary, and Contact.

The Bibliography has already been mentioned a few times. It contains a list of writing books that I consider to be the best ones written. I have read a *lot* of writing books and these are my favorites.

The Glossary contains a number of terms you may not have encountered before that are used throughout the text.

Finally, Contact simply contains information for contacting me, Michael Hiebert, the author of this book. Please feel free to contact me at any time with your questions, comments, criticisms, or for whatever reason you like. I'll try to answer anything you send my way. I'm here to help. And if you find any glaring mistakes in this book, I'd love to know about them.

Some chapters end with writing exercises you may want to try in order to fully understand the concepts explained. These might be of particular value to writing groups, classroom settings, or for people working together that can critique each other's work once the exercises are completed. By no means are the exercises essential, they are simply there in cases they are wanted.

If you do decide to participate in the exercises, I suggest keeping a notebook specifically for them. They tend to build on one another and it is handy being able to go back and look over your previous work.

One last note on my use of the male pronoun.

First, let me say that the English language puts the writer of a book such as this in a dubious position. Being a language without a gender-neutral pronoun, I have the unenviable task of having to come up with a way to make reference to my mythical "they" throughout this book; my protagonist and Hero that I will be talking about at length. Scholars of late have offered a variety of ideas to make things fair, and I hasten to say that I hate every one. First, my "they" as you see above just doesn't cut it. Then there's the horrible construction of "s/he" which is a sort of transgendered version of two pronouns copulating if you ask me. Far worse, though, is replacing every instance of the single use of a pronoun (such as "he") with the selection of either pronoun ("he or she"). All of these choices are just workarounds to what is, at its core, a failure in the language.

So, since it's a failure in the language and not a failure of mine, I've opted to go the classic route and use the male pronoun throughout this book. Not because I'm sexist. Quite seriously, it came down to a pragmatic judgment in the end. The word "he" is one letter shorter than the word "she."

Allow me to apologize in advance if my overuse of the masculine pronoun offends anyone. It certainly isn't meant to.

And with that apology we come to the end of this introduction and the beginning of our real journey.

Best regards,

Journeys under the Moon
Writing
and the
Hero's Quest

Ill. 0-2: *After a time she heard a little pattering of feet in the distance, and she hastily dried her eyes to see what was coming. It was the White Rabbit returning, splendidly dressed, with a pair of white kid-gloves in one hand and a large fan in the other: he came trotting along in a great hurry, muttering to himself, as he came, "Oh! The Duchess, the Duchess! Oh! Wo'n't she be savage if I've kept her waiting!"*

Part I

The Hero's Journey

> *And where we had thought to find an abomination, we shall find a god; where we had thought to slay another, we shall slay ourselves; where we had thought to travel outward, we shall come to the center of our own existence; where we had thought to be alone, we shall be with all the world.*
>
> —Joseph Campbell[4]

---

[4] *The Hero with a Thousand Faces*, Joseph Campbell, MJF Books, New York, 1949, p. 25

CHAPTER ONE

Structure

> "Every worthwhile accomplishment, big or little, has its stages of drudgery and triumph; a beginning, a struggle and a victory,"
>
> —Mahatma Gandhi[5]

1. THREE ACT STRUCTURE

The three act structure is also known as Mythic Structure and the Hero's Journey. It is a structure for telling stories that has proven itself for thousands of years. The reason it's called a three act structure is because it breaks your story down into three parts, as you shall see—a beginning (Act I), a middle (Act II), and an end (Act III).

Aristotle was the first to write about it, in his book *The Poetics*, but it was around before him. It is actually primal—it's part of our psychic heritage. We're born knowing this structure. That's why nearly every story we write or hear or read follows it.

Pretty much every commercial movie you've ever seen, every New York Times bestselling novel you've ever read, and every top-rated television show (with the exception, maybe, of reality TV shows) uses this structure in one way or another. Learning the basics of it will improve your writing dramatically. Mastering it will make your writing

---

[5] Mohandas Karamchand Gandhi (October 2, 1869 - January 30, 1948) was the preeminent leader of Indian nationalism in British-ruled India. Employing nonviolent civil disobedience, Gandhi led India to independence.

superb. Combining it with the rest of the information I lay out in this book, including the usage of archetypes, archetypal themes as well as the discussions in the part on "Writing Well," will take your writing to a professional level.

The three act structure is so ingrained into our psyche that you are probably already using it and not realizing you are. But, like anything, learning to do it consciously will allow you to control it and make wise decisions with it instead of leaving things up to chance. This structure is the reason you might occasionally get someone to read something you've written and they'll tell you, "There's something wrong with it, but I'm not sure what it is." They are being honest because we all know story deep down inside of us, but we don't know *that* we know it, or *why* it works. But we certainly know when it *doesn't* work.

It is also the reason we can feel plot points before they happen in stories and movies. We just know they should be there. We can also feel if they're missing. Usually this is due to the Hero's Journey being so universal. I say usually because, sometimes, we can watch fifteen minutes of a movie and know how it's going to end. This would be a case of a director or a screenwriter having misused the structure.

I'm *not* even remotely suggesting that this structure will make your writing "formulaic" in any way; although, if you're lazy, it can very well be used as a crutch to allow you to write formulaic plots. Many writers do just that. You see it all the time, more in movies than in books. The same plotlines are rehashed over and over, just substituting a cat for a dog and two twin girls who want to be ballerinas for the boy who longs to be a baseball player. Don't do that. Don't use the power of the structure for evil. That path only leads to hackneyed writing unworthy of your talent.

Use this structure wisely, and apply it the way it's *supposed* to be used and I can promise you your writing will become exponentially better in a very short period of time.

Is it possible to write a story without using this structure? *Yes*. It's been done many times, but the authors always set out to do it on purpose. They did it consciously. And generally at least *some* of the structure is evident in their work.

That's one of the big selling points of what I'm going to show you—you don't need to follow this structure completely. It's infinitely flexible. You can tailor it to your own desires so that it perfectly fits whatever you're writing.

I recommend mastering the structure completely before purposely writing outside of it. Odds are, even if you did try, you'd wind up using it in some fashion anyway. That's how deeply rooted it is in our brains. Our mind has been steeped in it since birth. It seems ageless. Cavemen probably kept the children of their tribes riveted to their rocks with campfire tales about how they almost brought down the wooly mammoth. Most likely they told these stories using some form of three act structure.

It was in use long before we arrived on this planet and will continue to be used long after we're gone. So why not learn to use it properly? It will undoubtedly turn out to be the single most important tool in your writer's toolbox.

2. STRUCTURE IS FORM, NOT FORMULA

A lot of writers are afraid of the word structure. The minute they hear anyone start talking about following a "structure" they immediately think the next step will be that they'll have to follow some sort of "recipe" that makes their writing exactly the same as everyone else's out there.

That's not what structure is.

The best way to think about structure is to consider a house. All houses have a certain structure to them. The structure is beneath the parts we point to when we use the word "house." What I mean is we normally don't see the underlying structure, we see the parts of the house built over top of it.

We all know that the structure is there, though. Beneath that fine siding, nice flooring, decorative paint, beautiful stairways, and bay windows is a foundation of some sort, a bunch of two-by-fours framing the walls, beams for the roof, electrical wiring through the walls, and plumbing pipes under the ground. All of this underlying structure had to be built to specific codes and regulation standards. Yet, we can see none of it when we look at the house.

The weirdest part is: all houses have these same structural elements inside them—you'd see them if you took off the walls and ripped up the floors—and yet, all houses are different. *Completely* different. Some have one level, some have two. Some have three or four. Some have many small rooms. Some have fewer rooms, but bigger ones. Some houses are large and expensive. Some are less expensive and smaller. The variety of house types available on the market is pretty much infinite. Sure, it's *possible* to build two houses the same, but that has nothing to do with the underlying structure and everything to do with the creativity of the architect and the carpenter designing the rest of it.

Let's stick with this house metaphor just a minute longer. I want you to imagine what houses would be like if they didn't have this underlying structure to them. So, no foundation, no framing, no ceiling joists. Could we even call them houses? Some may manage to stand up. For a while, maybe. I doubt many would.

Structure is essential in building a successful house.

Now just imagine if every time an architect drew up plans for a new house, he had to invent a brand new underlying structure for it, too. Every single house had a completely different type of foundation and framing system. No house was allowed to ever use the same structure as another house already built. So the architect would have to be very imaginative with his techniques. I think a number of things would happen. First, quality would decrease very quickly. Second, prices would increase just as fast. The whole scenario sounds like a nightmare.

Why go to all that bother when architects have a structure that has proven itself over hundreds of years of use? It would be absolutely crazy.

And yet, this is exactly what most authors are doing. They're coming up with their own structures when they should be concentrating on storytelling. Structure is just as essential to building a good story as it is to building a proper house so why not use the tried and true method that's been used for literally thousands of years?

The structure allows you to focus all your concentration on what's important: your creativity. It won't make your writing formulaic unless you purposely start writing formulaic stories. If anything, it will cause the opposite to happen. Once you've mastered this structure, you will have freed yourself from having to worry about why certain plot points (or "beats" as they're called in the movie industry and, increasingly, in book plots) of your novel work and why other's don't. Instead, you can just sit back and write the book you want to write. Your imagination can be let loose because, once you get this stuff down, you don't ever forget it. Because here's the secret: *you already know it.*

This is what I've been trying to tell you: this stuff's already in your brain. You were born knowing it. It's something primal and it's in all of us. You just have to learn to control it.

The world around us operates in three act structures. Think about it. The day starts with morning, heads into the afternoon, and ends with night. That's three acts. Stars are born from nebulae, burn for a while, then die out as red dwarfs or go supernova. You, yourself, are born, you live, and you die. The entire world is constantly playing out in three acts right in front of you and you don't even notice it.

Like I said earlier, if anything, following the three act structure opens up your work because it lets you focus on the creative aspect and not have to worry about the nuts and bolts of the process. All the mundane parts of storytelling were long ago perfected. Don't reinvent them. Odds are you won't be able to come up with as good an invention yourself, and think of all the time and energy you could devote to your storytelling instead.

3. STUDYING STRUCTURE (WHY MOVIES ARE YOUR FRIENDS)

Studying structure by reading novels is great and I genuinely think there's a tremendous value in doing so. In fact, you should study the structure of any story you are being exposed to, whether that story is from a book, or a movie, or a television show, a play, or even a dancing finger puppet.

But the problem I find with novels is that they take too much darned time to read. I may be a very fast writer, but for some reason, that doesn't translate into my being a fast reader. I read *extremely* slowly. So I prefer movies to novels when studying my structure because they are quick. I can study a movie in two hours instead of the two weeks it takes for me to get through a novel (actually, for me it's more like a month, but I didn't want to make myself sound that lame).

Movies have other advantages, too.

They tend to wear their structures a little more on their sleeves than novels do. Novels can play a little more fast and loose with the rules and get away with it, whereas a movie can't. This sometimes makes it hard to pinpoint exactly the different structural stages of the story in a novel. With a movie, you can almost do it blindfolded. Actually, sometimes you can do it from the other room of your house if you have a stopwatch, because movies generally always hit the same important beats at the same time.

The other nice thing about movies is that, because they're so quick, you can watch them several times long before you'd ever finish reading a novel. For a twenty-five dollar investment in a DVD, you can buy yourself a piece of study material that you'll actually get a lot out of. Later on, I'll tell you how to go about downloading free scripts off the Internet so that you can follow along as you watch. Scripts for most movies are available. This may sound a bit anal retentive to some of you—and it probably is—but I find it really allows me to nail down the structure of the film.

At the end of Part I, I break out a few movies for you and show you how you can do it yourself. It's a fantastic learning experience. Unfortunately, it will probably ruin any delight you get from watching movies, because your brain quickly becomes trained to start looking for these major plot points. You'll be telling yourself, "Oh, here comes the Inciting Event." Or, "She's headed into the Dark Night before Dawn."

Don't worry, I'll explain all these phrases soon enough.

The structure breaks out a little easier in movies than in novels simply because movies are usually simpler. Since you just can't tell the same story in ninety to a hundred and twenty minutes that you can over four hundred pages, something has to give during the screenwriting processes. Usually, it's some extraneous subplots or something like that. Anything taken out allows you to see the underlying structure more directly, and, once you've seen it, it's easy to assimilate it and use the concepts in your novel writing. You don't have to worry about movies being less complex than novels, the concepts are the same. Once you've developed the tools discussed here, you will automatically adapt them to the complexity of your novel writing.

For all these reasons, most of the examples I use throughout this book come from movies (although some come from mythology, folklore, and fairytales). Rest assured, though, every story fits this exact same structure. The Hero's Journey is a structure for *story*, not for novels or for movies or for any one specific medium of storytelling. There *are* some distinctions between writing for the screen and writing for the page, of course, but they don't fall under three act structure principles. Indeed, a lot of the best novel writing books I own are actually books written for screenwriters. You can check out the Bibliography in the back of this book to find more information on The Hero's Journey and writing in general. You'll see quite a few screenwriting books listed.

So don't be a movie snob just because you like reading Tolstoy and Steinbeck. Remember, movies are your friends. And if you go out to see them, they come with popcorn!

4. FORM FOLLOWS FUNCTION

If you only take one thing away from this book it be this: form follows function. I certainly hope you get more than one thing out of this book, but just in case, now you know what to remember. No matter what, under every circumstance imaginable, form must always follow function. Never the other way around.

This means that you shouldn't create something using a certain technique and then work your writing around that technique. That's a *"no no."* The story drives everything. The story comes first.

Do *not* shoehorn your writing into any form it doesn't naturally want to go into just to make it follow some kind of convention. That even goes for structure I'm presenting here. If you are writing a piece that just doesn't want to work with the Hero's Journey three act structure then let the writing take you the way it wants to go. Don't hold it back. Odds are, as I keep saying, sooner or later it will come back around to the structure on its own, but maybe it won't. Maybe you'll end up writing one of those rare, odd pieces that doesn't follow any conventions yet somehow works.

The story has to be number one. This is one of the single most important things I can tell you. The story controls the method it's written by, never the other way around.

5. THE STRUCTURE IS FLEXIBLE

I've already briefly touched on this. The structure I'm teaching you in this book is infinitely flexible. How flexible? Well, you haven't actually seen it yet, but it divides your story into stages. Under normal circumstances, the stages follow each other exactly as I'll show you, but they don't *have* to. In fact, you are free to alter the stages pretty much to your heart's content.

There is a caveat here. Anyone who's read any of the other great books on three act structure like Christopher Vogler's *The Writer's Journey*, or Blake Snyder's *Save the Cat!*, or anything by Syd Field is going to immediately notice that I have fewer stages than they do.

My structure is paired down to what I consider to be the simplest possible structure that will still build a story effectively. I found the others (especially Vogler's—whose book is fantastic, mind you) to have too much that was unneeded. Vogler based his book on Joseph Campbell's work in *The Hero with a Thousand Faces* so I think that's why his is so complex. Campbell's book reads like rocket science in places.

So, with that in mind, I'll say that the structure doesn't have to be followed too precisely, but it also probably shouldn't be altered a *lot*. But go ahead and try whatever you feel like doing with it. For the most part, stages can be deleted, added to, shuffled around, even changed dramatically, all without losing any of their power.

It's the values of the journey that are important, not the specific stages. The journey as a whole is much, much larger than the sum of its parts.

The structure also isn't tied to any particular genre whatsoever. It can just as easily be used with a romantic comedy novel, or a science fiction novel, or a mystery novel, or a high fantasy novel. Any type of story you can think of will work with the Hero's Journey with no modification. It isn't dependent on content, just like our old house's structure (a metaphor that really is getting old) isn't dependent on its siding or its paint.

The same thing extends to archetypes. Archetype might be a word you had never heard before picking up this book. We'll be going into them in depth in Part III because they are a valuable addition to your writing skill set, but for now I'll just give you the basics.

Archetypes are perfect conceptual symbols representing real-life things we encounter every day. Plato was the first to write about them, although the word "archetype" didn't come into use until later. The philosopher Carl Jung did most of the real work concerning them and found, like Mythic Structure, they are embedded into our psyches. They are actually part of our psychic consciousness. Even stranger, Jung discovered that we are not only born with these archetypes already defined, but that everyone has the same archetypes defined; it's as though there is some sort of connection between our minds. He used the term "collective unconscious."

Most of the major archetypes define people-roles, like Mother or Mentor or Sentinel. An example of a Mentor archetype is the wise old man who teaches the protagonist valuable skills and lessons and often provides him with items, magical or otherwise, to help him on his journey. Sometimes the Mentor will give him a good swift kick in the pants to get him out the door and get the journey started. Some well-known Mentors are Gandalf from *Lord of the Rings*, Yoda from *Star Wars*, and Master Po from the 1970s television series *Kung Fu*.

Archetypes may sound like stereotypes, but they're not. They are a collection of attributes a character can take on that add power to your writing if you learn to use them well. Characters can also shift archetypes, moving from one type to another, almost as though the archetype were a mask.

Ill. 1-1: *Greek soldiers, from a Greek vase about the time of the Battle of Marathon.*

Remember, this isn't an invention of the movies or books or even psychologists. It's a character role we have mapped in our brains, so they strike a chord with us on a primal level when we encounter them. This is why they bring so much power to your work.

If you learn even a few of the major archetypes and their roles and how they commonly act and react in different situations, you'll find you have a much richer supply of material to draw upon while writing.

Archetypes aren't confined to the classic iconic figures we immediately think of, either. Instead of the wizened old man, your Mentor could just as easily be a modern day therapist, a bossy parent, or an over-protective grandparent. Like the three act structure, archetypes are incredibly flexible.

Also in Part III, we talk about defining the theme of your story using animal archetypes. This is an interesting concept that you'll definitely find useful. Many animals display attributes that can be turned into noble quests, and by using the animal archetype you're once again guaranteeing that you're theme will appeal to readers on a primal, visceral level.

All of this is possible within the parameters of the three act structure. It's *that* flexible.

While we're talking about the Hero's Journey in general, I should mention that it's important that the structure doesn't call attention to itself. I mentioned earlier that it's easier to see the underlying structure in movies. This is especially true for bad movies. You want the structure to be invisible to the reader, the same way a house's internal structure is transparent from the outside of the finished house. They should have no idea it's there. If they do; if there's any indication at all that you're following some sort of formula; you're writing lazily and doing what all those really cheesy Hollywood guys do we talked about earlier: you're using the structure to write formulaically. That's not good. What is good, though, is that it's just a matter of practicing to get rid of the habit. And how do you practice? By writing a ton of words, like we also talked about in the last chapter.

See? This is why I never consider any written words wasted. If nothing else, they're practice. It's weird to me that if Michael Jordan goes to the gym and runs up and down the court for an hour practicing shooting hoops and misses more than half he doesn't consider himself a complete failure and go home and crack open a bottle of Jack Daniels and whine to his wife about how miserable his life is and how he'll never make it as a basketball player. Why doesn't he do this? Because it was only one frigging practice and you can't expect every day to be exceptional. That's the entire point of practice.

But writers, as a group, seem to think every time they sit at their keyboard they have to have the words leap from their fingertips as though they were Hemingway or Updike.

Why can't writers just relax and consider those bad days just practice instead of expecting every day to be a Hemingway Day?

This is a huge mystery I don't know if I'll ever understand.

But I do know this: the more you write, the better you get. Even if you write a ton of crappy words, you'll get a lot better really fast. So take my advice and write a lot of really crappy words really fast.

There. That's my pep talk. It'll do you good to remember it.

6. BEGINNINGS, MIDDLES, AND ENDINGS—NOT ALWAYS IN THAT ORDER

All stories have one thing in common—at least all publishable ones do. They have a beginning, middle, and an end, although not necessarily in that order.

Many writers have been very successful shuffling these three parts around in unique ways. Think of movies like *Sliding Doors*, *Run Lola Run*, and *Pulp Fiction* just to name a few.

But even if you put the end at the beginning and the beginning in the middle and the middle at the end, nothing changes in the underlying structure. Everything supporting those pieces just moves along with them. The fact is, mixing up your time like this in a story doesn't make it any harder to write at all. The only complication it adds is having to keep things straight in your own head. But the great part is, if you've used the structure of the Hero's Journey, you know the story's still going to be sound whatever order you tell it in.

The reason the Hero's Journey is built into our primal psyche is because it follows the pattern of our lives. We actually live out the journey ourselves—at least we do if we grow up in a healthy environment—if not, we might get stagnated at certain points along it. Soon I'll discuss the rite of passage, but for now I'll just say that the Hero's Journey is our way of separating ourselves from the mother and bonding with the father, usually through some sort of ritual.

If it reflects our life, it's no wonder that this is the natural way we tell stories.

KEY POINTS

- Nearly every commercial novel and movie that's ever been created has followed the three act structure. There's a reason why it works so well: it's something embedded in our psyches.
- Structure dictates a form, not a formula. If anything it frees you creatively by letting you concentrate on the writing and not worrying about something that's been solved for thousands of years.
- When studying structure, many people prefer movies because they are fast and the same concepts apply.
- Form always follows function. The writing comes first. If the writing is dictating not to follow a certain structure, then don't.
- The three act structure is infinitely flexible.
- You can even mix pieces around (entire acts if you like), delete elements of the structure, add to it. It won't weaken it. What's important is the journey itself.

CHAPTER TWO

A Brief Look at the Path

You yourself must earnestly practice; the enlightened ones only proclaim the path.

—Buddha[6]

This part could've been subtitled "The way our hero finds out what he's really made of," because that's what we're actually talking about when we talk about the Hero's Journey—the quest from the ordinary state in which he starts the book (an archetype Carl Jung referred to as the Initiate) to the almost god-like Hero, and it happens over three "acts" or three separate individual parts of the story that are easily distilled from one another. Notice I capitalized the words Initiate and Hero. I will always capitalize archetypes in this book, even though we won't really discuss them thoroughly until Part III.

1. RITES OF PASSAGE

The separation of the protagonist, who, at the beginning of the story, Carl Jung would refer to as the Initiate archetype, from the mother is a large part of the journey. This is because it's such an important part of

---

[6] Buddha Shakyamuni (563 BCE - 483 BCE) taught over 10,000 sutras (or scriptures) regarding Buddhism throughout his life after supposedly achieving enlightenment beneath the Bodhi tree (this happened when he discovered what he referred to as the "Middle Way"—a path between the extremes of self-indulgence and self-mortification..

growing up. Most cultures have some kind of rite of passage to facilitate it. You can view parts of the Hero's Journey as a rite of passage.

Why do we need rites of passages?

Freud was pretty obsessed with Oedipus complexes, but he had his reasons. Humans are the only animals born unfinished; we need to cling to our mothers after being born in order to survive. We also feed from the breast longer than any other animal on the planet. According to Mr. Freud at least, due to these reasons—and a few others—we become extremely attached to our mothers as symbols of great love and bliss. They are our primary source of protection and comfort without them we would not survive. Being separated from our mother during our early years can cause great anxiety.

It's also because of our attachment to our mothers that our father becomes a source of frustration and sometimes even resentment. We see him as an enemy, trying to come between us and our mother. Freud said the anger we build toward our fathers during this phase of life, like the attachment and longing we have for our mothers, is something subconscious that stays with us as we grow older. That is unless it is somehow expunged from us one way or another.

Again, a child at this stage of development is the Initiate archetype. The Initiate has not been separated from his mother yet and still longs for her. He's still, by all accounts, just a boy, and, as a boy, he seeks acknowledgement, believes himself to be the center of the universe, is ruled by his emotions, and refuses to take any responsibility for his actions. He also believes he will live forever; he has no fear of death.

When the Initiate finally embarks on the Hero's Journey and answers what Joseph Campbell refers to as The Call to Adventure, which, in story terms, sends him from Act I into Act II. The sequence of ordeals that he faces builds in intensity and complexity as he progresses toward the final climax in Act III. This sequence of tests and trials is actually a rite of passage for the Initiate and, somewhere along the way, he stops wearing the mask of the Initiate and replaces it with a different one. Perhaps he slips on the mask of the Warrior or the Shapeshifter.

So the quest can be seen as a journey from boyhood to adulthood with the Initiate breaking free from his attachment to his mother during Act II and integrating into the father tribe. To once again quote Joseph Campbell, the rite of passage is a way "for the individual to die to the past and be reborn to the future."

2. FROM THE WOMB TO THE TOMB (AND BACK AGAIN)

The cycle of life is that you are born from the earth, you live, and then you go back to the earth to be reborn again. It follows the seasons. This is how most early cultures saw it.

The Buddhists and Hindus believe in reincarnation. You die and enter what Buddhists refer to as the Bardo until, forty-eight days later, when you're reborn in either the hells, or as an animal, a human, a demigod, or a god. Christianity believes your soul transcends your body and rises to heaven.

Most myths have some form of afterlife including a resurrection. The Hero's Journey is the same. The protagonist, in fact, must die before he can be reborn as a true hero. That's why, in a way, it's a journey from the womb to the tomb.

But it doesn't end there. The hero must transcend. He must experience an apotheosis. Remember, he is becoming a god, or as close as a God as one can become. It can't be an easy task.

This happens in the third, or final, act usually during the resolution of the Climax.

The reality is that the Hero's Journey is man's quest to the divine, or his quest to find God. In some ways, it actually is a quest to *become* a God. The classic Hero's Journey is also a journey toward the feminine or, as Joseph Campbell sometimes refers to it, toward the "feminine divine."

The theory goes that men are born flawed and must search to correct those flaws. In doing so, they separate themselves from their mothers and, traditionally, bond with the tribal men. Then they quest for a female partner. This is why so many tales abound of knights looking for princesses in high castle towers to save and whisk away on horseback.

Carl Jung pointed out that each of us has two archetypes embedded deeply within us that are so active they often can't be suppressed, the Anima and the Animus. They come out in our dreams. Often, they cause tremendous social problems simply *because* we try to suppress them much of the time. Aspects of them tend to show up when serial killers and those sorts of people are psychoanalyzed. This is a product of trying to hide away a part of the psyche that doesn't want to be hidden. Things that don't want to be hidden generally find their own way out, one way or another.

The Anima archetype is the unconscious female personality existing in both the male and the female and the Animus is the unconscious male personality also existing in both the male and the female. Many people in our society are afraid of their alternate archetypes, so, as I already mentioned, they attempt to keep them suppressed, bringing on all kinds of problems. This suppression can become a major factor in how people act out under times of stress.

In terms of the Hero's Journey, the male Animus quests for his unconscious Anima which is a subconscious representation of his ideal female partner. This quest, according to Carl Jung, proceeds in four distinct phases.

The first phase of discovering the Anima comes in the form of the Eve archetype (as taken from the Biblical Eve); the emergence of the man's object of desire.

From here, it progresses to the Helen archetype (named after Helen of Troy). In this phase, women are viewed as capable of worldly success and of being self-reliant, intelligent, and insightful, even if not so virtuous. This phase shows a lack of respect for women's virtues and a general view of them lacking faith and imagination.

The third phase is the Mary archetype (named after the mother of Jesus). At this stage, women now seem to possess virtue, although it may be in an esoteric and dogmatic way.

The final stage of discovering the Anima arrives in the form of Sophia (named after the Greek word for wisdom). With this phase comes complete integration, and women are now seen as particular individuals who possess both positive and negative qualities.

But the quest of the hero is also a quest to find his own inner self so, by the time he's reached the end, the protagonist has faced his Anima and acknowledged its existence. He's become comfortable with his femininity. He's also usually sought out a mate, not as a replacement for his mother—who he no longer feels a boy's attachment for—but for himself.

So the journey starts out as a venture departing from the mother figure and heading towards a death and a rebirth and ends with a search towards a new feminine. Thus, Joseph Campbell referred to it as a quest from the womb to the tomb and back again.

3. BECOMING A HERO

In Act I, the Initiate always begins the story as part of the status quo. Then something happens to make him question his ability to remain where he in his life. This event, known as the Inciting Event, is generally an external one. It's what pushes the story into action and launches the Initiate over the threshold into Act II where the protagonist will take on a series of tests and trials of ascending difficulty; each one with the dramatic purpose of revealing character growth and new strength.

Once the Initiate moves beyond his initial stage of development, he begins to change, and, by the end of the journey (in Act III), he is unrecognizable from who and what he was when he first set out. he has become a man. He no longer thinks he will live forever. In fact, he has stared straight into the eyes of death and knows just how mortal he is. His insecure longing for his mother is gone. He's independent, but seeks out feminine relationships other than from his mother—he now looks for proper partners.

This last point is why Campbell called the Hero's Journey the journey toward the feminine divine. But why the divine? Because Campbell equated all women as symbols of the goddess—they were by their very nature all divine. He was once asked why it was always the *Hero's* Journey he talked about and never the *Heroine's* Journey and what was the Heroine's Journey, anyway?

Campbell's response: "The heroine has no journey. She's already perfect."

4. MYTHOLOGICAL JOURNEYS

Nearly all mythological stories have archetypal themes. What I mean by archetypal themes is that most of them, like the archetype concept, have basic story tropes that ring true for nearly everyone on a very visceral and psychic level. These stories are made up of elements your mind expects to hear in them. These elements were set down in your psyche before you were even born. We'll talk about archetypal story themes and how to find them for your books in detail when we get to Part III. Another thing nearly all mythological stories have in common and, for that matter, nearly all stories in general, is that they follow the Hero's Journey because, by its very nature, the Hero's Journey is an archetypal path.

For instance, in the Roman myth of Cupid and Psyche, Venus—the goddess of love—grows extremely jealous of the princess Psyche's beauty. So much so, she orders her son, Cupid, to shoot Psyche with a magical arrow that will cause her to fall for the ugliest man in the kingdom. Venus helps equip Cupid with the special arrows needed to achieve this task. Cupid then sets out to obey his mother, but, fortunately for Psyche, when he lays eyes upon Psyche, Cupid accidentally pricks himself with one of his own arrows and falls instantly in love with her.

After that, Cupid continues coming to see her, but only at night, always telling her she mustn't ever lay eyes upon his face. But one night while he sleeps, Psyche takes a lamp and does look upon Cupid's sleeping face. Because she has disobeyed his request, Cupid is forced to abandon her, leaving Psyche wandering the world in search of him.

She goes through many trials before the two are reunited again. Once they are, Psyche is made immortal by Jupiter, the king of the gods.

This "Reader's Digest" version of the myth that I just told you shows the Hero's Journey at work. We have a protagonist (in this case, Psyche), driven by an Inciting Event (Cupid, being asked by his mother, Venus to go and shoot Psyche with a magical arrow that will make her fall in love with the ugliest man in the kingdom). That's all in Act I. It's not until Cupid leaves on his quest to do his mother's bidding that we enter the world of Act II and the trials and tests begin. Even though, ultimately, it will turn out that Psyche is the Hero—or, in this case, I suppose Heroine is a better word—of this story, the first test is for Cupid: Can he follow through with his mother's wishes? When he lays eyes upon Psyche, he accidentally pricks himself with his own arrow and falls desperately in love with her and knows that he cannot. So he fails his first test. Now

Ill. 1-2: *Cupid being equipped by Venus with magical arrows that will make Psyche fall in love with the ugliest man in the kingdom. Venus's jealousy sets up a Hero's Journey that ultimately leads to Psyche becoming a Hero with immortality being handed down to her by Jupiter, the king of the gods.*

not only must he return home a failure, he must keep his and Psyche's love a secret.

So Cupid comes to Psyche only at night and gives Psyche her first test, telling her she must never look upon him while he sleeps. However, it's Psyche's lack of willpower that is her downfall. She gives in to her urge to view his face, and Cupid discovers she's disobeyed him. Because she fails her test, he abandons her, leaving her to walk the kingdom alone, facing a slew of new tests and challenges throughout the remainder of Act II, each one tougher than the last, ratcheting up the stakes and heightening the tension, until she finally crosses the threshold into Act III where things come to a Climax.

But Psyche comes out victorious and becomes the Hero, returning with the prize, or the "Elixir" as we'll be calling it in this book. In the case of this myth, the Elixir is immortality, handed down to Psyche by Jupiter.

The Climax is always the biggest part of Act III. It is followed by a very short part known as the denouement that sort of "wraps everything up." In the case of a lot of myths and fairytales, it's simply the " . . . and they lived happily ever after . . . " line.

This short mythological story is a perfect example showing that you don't need a long narrative to use the principles of the three act structure. They can all be applied with any story of any type at any time.

An even briefer example comes from Norse mythology, where we encounter the story of Siegfried slaying the dragon. He sets out to do so in revenge, after the dragon Fafnir kills Siegfried's friend's father, Hreidmar, and steals all his gold. Siegfried is successful in his quest. He destroys the dragon Fafnir and returns a Hero.

In Act I, containing the Setup and Inciting Event, the dragon Fafnir kills Hreidmar and steals his gold. This prompts Siegfried into action. Act II sees Siegfried setting out for revenge and encountering adventures along his way to meet the dragon before battling it. Act III is the actual fight between Siegfried and the dragon where Siegfried ulti-

Ill. 1-3: *In Norse mythology, Siegfried goes out and slays the dragon Fafnir after the Fafnir kills Siegfried's friend's father, Hreidmar, for his gold. The slaying of the dragon motif is one that recurs often in myths from many cultures and different countries.*

mately slays the beast and, presumably, returns with the Elixir of Hreidmar's gold.

The slaying of the dragon is a common theme that is seen over and over across many cultures and myths and in many fairytales. Often, the prize is the hand of a fair maiden the dragon has captured and is holding hostage. Sometimes it is a portion of the dragon's gold. It can also be the keys to an entire kingdom.

Knights generally set out valiantly toward the unknown upon hearing news of such beasts or are given commands to go and attack. Then, after a series of tests along the way, they face the dragon in their final Climax before claiming victory over whatever Elixir is at stake.

5. FAIRYTALE JOURNEYS

The three act structure is everywhere, including fairytales.

A favorite from English folklore is *Jack and the Beanstalk.* In the story, Jack lives with his mother and they have no income other than the family cow, which, unfortunately, has stopped giving milk. So Jack's mom asks Jack to take it to market one morning and sell it so they can buy food. Along the way, Jack encounters an old man who offers to take the cow off his hands in exchange for some "magic beans." You will find the "old man" motif used again and again in literature. It's an archetype called The Mentor, although in this case, it's a Mentor disguised as a Shapeshifter. All of this archetype business is explained in Part III.

His mother's anger and frustration isn't unreasonable when Jack returns home with no money or anything else except a handful of beans that he says are magical. His mother throws a fit and tosses the beans out the window. Then she sends Jack to bed without dinner.

When Jack wakes up, he finds the beans have grown into a huge, gigantic beanstalk that's twisting up into the clouds from his backyard. Being the adventurous lad that Jack is, Jack climbs the stalk and, at the top, discovers a strange city floating in the sky. Eventually, by following a path, he comes to a humongous house that turns out to be the home of a giant. The giant is away, but when Jack enters the house he meets the giant's wife. She is very pleasant and makes Jack something to eat. Soon, however, the giant comes home and the wife quickly hides Jack before he can be spotted. Even still, the giant seems to sense a human is nearby:

JOURNEYS UNDER THE MOON

Ill. 1-4: *A scene from* Jack and the Beanstalk.

Fee-fi-fo-fum!
I smell the blood of an Englishman
Be he alive, of be he dead
I'll have his bones to grind my bread

The giant doesn't find Jack, though, since his wife has hidden Jack so well. So, he goes about his business and soon Jack overhears him counting his treasure. Jack decides to leave, but before he does, he steals a bag of gold coins and then quickly climbs back down the beanstalk to safety.

Twice more Jack makes the trip up the beanstalk and visits the giant's home, and each time he is helped by the giant's wife. But she becomes more and more suspicious of Jack's motives. It gets harder for Jack to steal away with any treasure.

But he does manage.

On his first return trip, Jack steals the hen that laid the golden eggs. On his second return, Jack nabs a golden, magical harp that has the ability to play all by itself.

But it is this last time that Jack comes by far the closest to getting caught. The giant even ends up chasing him down the beanstalk.

As Jack reaches the bottom, he leaps to the ground and shouts to his mother to bring him an axe. She does and with a few swift swings, Jack chops the beanstalk down. In doing so, he kills the giant.

After that, Jack and his mother live happily ever after, enjoying their newly-found riches.

Now, other than being a bit unfair to the wife—I mean, why did she have to die? She did nothing wrong. And actually, neither did the giant. Jack was the one doing all the stealing—the story has a very basic structure.

Act I: The Setup is that the cow has stopped giving milk and Jack must sell it. The Inciting Event is that Jack trades the cow for magic beans that his mother throws out the window. We don't actually enter act II until Jack wakes up the next morning and sees the beanstalk in his backyard.

Then the trials, troubles and tribulations all begin. All the fun stuff happens in act II. Notice how things get progressively tougher for Jack? This is important. Things grow harder and harder until, finally, we enter Act III when we hit the Climax: the giant chasing Jack down the beanstalk. The Climax is resolved with Jack the swinging an axe and chopping the beanstalk down.

And then the small denouement: They lived happily ever after having murdered some nice innocent big people.

The second story I'm using here is *Little Red Riding Hood*. *Little Red Riding Hood* was originally a French fairytale, but, like a lot of folklore, adopted and adapted over the years.

A little girl in a red cloak walks through the woods to deliver some food to her sick grandmother.

What Little Red Riding Hood doesn't know is that there is a wolf in the woods who would like very much to eat her. As she meanders along, he stalks her from behind trees and bushes, ducking in and out of shadows. Red whistles merrily as she goes, completely oblivious to the danger she is in.

Eventually the wolf approaches her and is very pleasant. He asks where she's headed and she innocently tells him. He feigns sympathy for her grandmother and suggests she picks wild flowers to give her when she gets there. Little Red Riding Hood decides that's a great idea and does just that.

Meanwhile, the wolf rushes ahead to the girl's grandmother's house and, knocking at the door, pretends to be Little Red Riding Hood. The grandmother invites him inside.

Now, in the classic version of the story, he swallows the grandmother whole at this point. In other, usually newer, tamed down versions, he simply locks her in a closet. Either way, once the grandmother is out of the picture, the wolf disguises himself as her, jumps into her bed, and waits for Little Red Riding Hood to arrive.

When the girl gets there and comes into the bedroom, she immediately notices her grandmother looks different than usual. "What a deep voice you have," Red says to the disguised wolf.

"The better to greet you with," he replies in a high pitched voice.

"Goodness, what big eyes you have," the girl says.

"The better to see you with."

"And what big hands you have!"

"The better to hug you with," the wolf responds.

And, finally, the girl says, "What a big mouth you have!"

To which the wolf leaps out of bed straight at her, bellowing, "The better to eat you with!" With a swoop of his claws, he snatches up Little Red Riding Hood, and, just like he did with the grandmother, swallows her in one great gulp. Then he falls into a deep sleep in the bed.

Now enters the huntsman into our story. In the newer, tamer versions of the tale where nobody is swallowed, the huntsman shows up a few minutes earlier, just in time to save Red from being eaten. But in the classic tale, both she and the grandmother are consumed by the wolf. Also, traditionally, it isn't a huntsman but a lumberjack who comes to the rescue at this point.

Using his axe, the huntsman splits open the wolf while he sleeps and pulls out Little Red Riding Hood and her grandmother, both of whom are unharmed. Then the three of them fill the wolf's body with heavy stones so that when he awakens and tries to run away, he won't be able to. In fact, the stones cause him to stumble to the floor and die, leaving everyone else living happily ever after.

Can you see the three acts? The first act is Little Red Riding Hood leaving the safety of her village for the danger of the woods. The woods themselves represent the trials of Act II. Everything that goes on up until the lead in to the attack on the girl ("What a deep voice you have.") is in Act II.

The lead in to the attack is the threshold of Act III, where we have our Climax (Little Red Riding Hood being swallowed, resolving in the huntsman saving her and, ultimately, the death of the wolf) and the Denouement, "They all lived happily ever after."

EXERCISES

1. Go through some of your favorite fairytales. Perhaps break out the old Brothers' Grimm books or Hans Christian Anderson. A particularly good one is Hans Christian Anderson's version of *The Little Mermaid*. It's very interesting to compare it to the original. *Alice's Adventures in Wonderland* is another great book to look at for structure. As you read, try and break the stories out into their three act structural components. Try to see where the setup and starting stage ends, launching the protagonist on some sort of "quest" and breaks the story into the stage full of trials and tests for the protagonist which is Act II. Finally, see if you can spot where Act II leads into Act III where the protagonist has his final showdown with the antagonist. Here's a hint: generally, right at the end of Act II, times are darkest for your protagonist.

2. Now see if you can encapsulate the Climax to these stories and find where they begin and resolve. If you can find the resolution, you should be able to pinpoint the Denouement quite easily.

3. Try outlining a fairytale of your own at just a basic level; briefly describe three acts the protagonist could go through with a Climax and a Denouement. Don't write the actual story. If you have the time, do a few of these, they are great learning tools, not just for learning how about three act structure, but also about outlining.

KEY POINTS

- The three act structure, or Hero's Journey, or Mythic Journey as it's often called, describes a rite of passage. The Initiate breaks from the mother figure, goes through an array of trials and tribulations until finally facing his ultimate struggle. It's at the peak of this struggle that he experiences a resurrection and becomes a Hero.
- The journey of the Hero is actually a journey to seek out God, however God is always found by going full circle and coming back to yourself.
- The three act structure is all around us. We dream in it, we even live in it. Our days have a morning, noon, and night. We are born, we live, and we die, The seasons (although there are four) act like three. There's the death of winter, the rebirth of spring, and the living of summer and autumn.
- All ancient mythologies were based on the three act structure.
- Most fairytales are based on the three act structure.

CHAPTER THREE

The Basics

You have to monitor your fundamentals constantly because the only thing that changes will be your attention to them. The fundamentals will never change.

—Michael Jordan[7]

The three act structure looks like this:

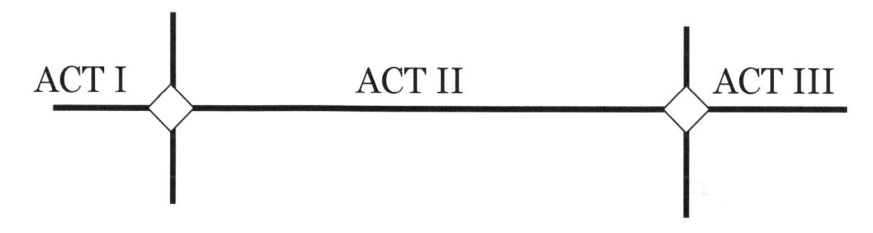

```
ACT I    |    ACT II    |    ACT III
```

This is a line graph of your story, with your book beginning at the left and ending at the right. It is broken into three parts, or acts. Notice that Act I is the shortest of the three. Act III is about 25% longer than Act I, and the remainder of the whole thing is taken up by Act II. This means that the majority of the book, by far, falls into Act II.

Act I is where your story begins. You set everything up in the first act, showing how the protagonist exists at the beginning of the story in his Normal World. Then you have some "big event" take place that

---

[7] *I Can't Accept Not Trying: Michael Jordan on the Pursuit of Excellence,* Michael Jordan, Harper, San Francisco, 1994

shakes up his whole life. Maybe it's an earthquake, or a telegram. Maybe it's some old friend he's never really liked showing up on his doorstep. *Something* happens. This something appears in the form of the Herald archetype. The event itself is called the Inciting Event. At this point, the protagonist has a decision to make. The event has opened a doorway for him to step through *if he wants to*. But he knows, if he does, it's a one-way trip. There's no coming back. But it's the path to adventure.

If the protagonist decides to pass through the door (and of course, eventually he always *does* or you wouldn't have a story), he enters the new and secret world of Act II.

Act II is an act full of danger where the protagonist has to figure out and adjust to this New World. He meets people and things and has to decide if they are enemies or allies. He finds out who his main adversary is if he doesn't already know. He may find a Mentor if he hasn't already encountered one and be taught new skills or given special items. Or he may learn things on his own. Each struggle he makes it through brings yet another one right on its tail, every ordeal a harder and more extreme test of his abilities than the last. By the end of Act II, the protagonist has endured so much that he's exhausted and beaten down. He no longer just wishes he'd stayed home, now he just hopes death comes quickly and isn't too painful. Everything is hopeless.

But Act III is yet another New World, one where the protagonist knows he still must face his final standoff against the antagonist. Before that happens, though, the protagonist comes up with a plan to use against his adversary. Then we head into the Climax where things don't always work out the way the protagonist planned, but they do usually work out one way or another.

In most stories, the protagonist eventually winds up victorious. But victory doesn't come without its costs. The protagonist must suffer a death and a resurrection ("of sorts") before he can become the true Hero he really is. In other words, he has to give up everything he has in order to become his true self. It's like Dorothy in the Wizard of Oz. She had always had the power to get home, but she needed to see the mighty Oz and understand his desperate secret before gaining the knowledge to utilize her power. Only then was the knowledge disclosed to her that allowed her a true way back home to Kansas.

Some things are just meant to happen in certain ways.

Once he's won the Elixir, which may be the hand of a princess, or wealth and treasure, or simply the knowledge that the New World exists, the Hero returns home. At the end of Act III, after the Climax, during the stage called the Denouement, you show the Hero back in the old world and the way that world is now. It can't be the same as it was during the Setup of your book in Act I. Things must be different now because the protagonist is different. He's no longer flawed or is flawed differently and so the world is no longer flawed or is flawed differently. The world has become a different and better place because of his existence and because of his ordeal.

I want to make one more point about the length of Act II being 70% of your entire book.

This is why pretty much every novel that lies unfinished in a drawer somewhere is stuck someplace along that dark tunnel known as Act II—usually in an area authors have come to refer to as the "muddle in the middle." This is a point, sort of halfway through Act II (which means it's halfway through the book) where everything tends to stall. You either find yourself just writing the same scenes over and over again, or you've painted your characters into a corner with nowhere to go. Or you're just completely lost and can't find your way out.

Or maybe it could be you've gotten bored of writing the thing. The middle of the book's a good place for that to happen too, if you have "Muddle in the Middle Syndrome" at work.

Well, I have good news. The structure I'm about to show you has no "muddle in the middle." It simply doesn't exist. There's no way to paint yourself into any corners because you always have a direction to go. And you shouldn't get bored, because your characters will always be doing something new. And it all happens automatically. Sound too good to be true?

Let's put it this way. Writing isn't supposed to be like working on a chain gang, yet for a lot of authors it seems to be just that. It's supposed to be fun. Remember when you first started doing it? You can get that sense of wonder and fun back. Trust me. It's still there. Like the Christmas snow that Frosty's made from, it never really goes away.

But we'll get to all that in a moment, I promise. For now, I need to explain more about the little diagram sitting at the top of the chapter.

There are four points that anchor your story, and, for me at least, I have to know those four story elements before I can start writing. I don't need to know anything else, but I do need to know these four. They each form a cornerstone for the story as a whole and are vitally important so I think, even if you end up writing a different direction before you hit, say, the last two, you have to start out aiming for the four of them. So when I write, I go through my initial brainstorming session and that's what I aim for, to come up with these four things.

They are: the beginning, the ending, the first Pivot Point, and the second Pivot Point.

That's it, just four.

Beginning and ending are probably pretty straightforward (although they may not turn out to be once I clarify them further), but you're probably thinking: What the heck is a Pivot Point?

Well, see the two white diamonds on the graph? Those are Pivot Points. They're places where one act meets another. By nature, as you will see, they are places in your story that are very dramatic and can contain huge emotional turnarounds. In fact, more than anything, Pivot Points are points of emotion.

Because they are probably unusual and new to you, let's talk about them first.

JOURNEYS UNDER THE MOON

FIRST PIVOT POINT

The first Pivot Point anchors Act I to Act II. At this point in your story, something has caused your protagonist to willingly accept the idea of leaving his normal life behind and accept the call to adventure. He's decided to take the Hero's Journey. This is a decision not made lightly. Most protagonists are hesitant to leave the warm comfort of their normal world for the unknown and, at first, refuse the call to adventure. So many do, in fact, we even have a name for them. We call them Reluctant Heroes.

For your character to have taken this step—this gigantic leap of faith—and have been motivated to such a degree as to change his life completely, something drastic and life-transforming will have taken place.

Perhaps a loved one died, like Luke's aunt and uncle in *Star Wars*. Perhaps someone acting as a Mentor archetype came into the story and gave him the motivation to move on, like Gandalf did with Bilbo in *The Hobbit*. Whatever the reason, the protagonist's life will already have started to change. Maybe the characters around him haven't seen it yet, but we, as readers, will have. We'll have felt it, instinctively.

The Pivot Point also gives you a chance to perhaps show another side of your protagonist than the readers have seen so far. You might be able to flesh him out with additional characterization. If he's acted a certain way through the opening Setup and the Inciting Event and even through the Debate stage where he hummed and hawed about whether or not to take the plunge to adventure, now you might be able to reverse things a bit and show that he's an even more complex character. This is your chance to use all the emotion you want.

It's on the emotional turnaround of this first Pivot Point that the protagonist enters the New World of Act II.

SECOND PIVOT POINT

Similarly, at the second Pivot Point between Act II and Act III the protagonist once again experiences an emotional point, only this time it is far greater than the first one. You can't even compare the emotional level of Pivot Point 2 with Pivot Point 1. The protagonist will have just finished completing a long series of dark trials and tests and have gone through utter hell.

It is at the Pivot Point that the protagonist experiences a glimpse of renewed hope. It happens right before the subplots are re-established with the main plotline, and things almost seem on an upswing, especially compared to how bleak they had been during Act II's final scenes.

There's a reversal of energy as the protagonist ventures into yet another world—Act III: the domain of the antagonist.

Ill. 1-5: *The myth of Pandora shares some similarities to the fall of man in the Garden of Eden in the Book of Genesis. Zeus gave Pandora a beautiful box with orders not to open it, much like God told man and woman not to eat from the tree of knowledge. But Pandora disobeyed Zeus and she opened the box and let out a host of evil that instantly spread across the world.*

KEY POINTS

- Act I is the shortest of the three Acts. Act III is a little longer than Act I, and Act II is seventy percent of your story.
- The protagonist starts out comfortable in the normal world. He is flawed, but may not realize it. The world itself is also flawed, but the protagonist is fine with the flaws. Until an Inciting Event occurs to shake up that world. At that point, the decision to make a move is given to the protagonist. He enters a Debate stage where he decides whether or not to act. If he does decide to go forth, the precipice between Act I and Act II is called a Pivot Point. There is also one between Act II and Act III. Pivot points are one way doors, and normally very emotionally charged scenes.
- Act II is full of struggles and ordeals of ascending difficulty. In the middle of Act II the protagonist goes through a Pseudo Climax that then flings him through the rest of Act II which nearly destroys him. By the time he reaches the Act II/Act III Pivot Point, the protagonist feels he has nothing left in the world. He knows his showdown with the antagonist is coming, but he is not confident in his ability to be victorious at all.
- Act III is the final standoff against the antagonist. In most stories, the protagonist wins and, in doing so, goes through an apotheosis out of which he becomes the Hero. He returns home with the Elixir, whatever it happens to be. It may be the hand of a maiden, the keys to the kingdom, or simply the knowledge that this new world outside of his village actually exists.

CHAPTER FOUR

Act I: The Beginning

> *Beginnings are usually scary and endings are usually sad, but it's the middle that counts. You have to remember this when you find yourself at the beginning.*
>
> —Sandra Bullock[8]

Beginnings and endings are vitally important to books, but she's right; middles are of utmost importance, too. And middles are by far the hardest part to write. Beginnings generally aren't so tough because we're all hyped up on starting a new project. We generally sail through them. We may not write them well the first time out, but at least they usually go down on the page fast.

Act I is the first part of the structure we have to discuss.

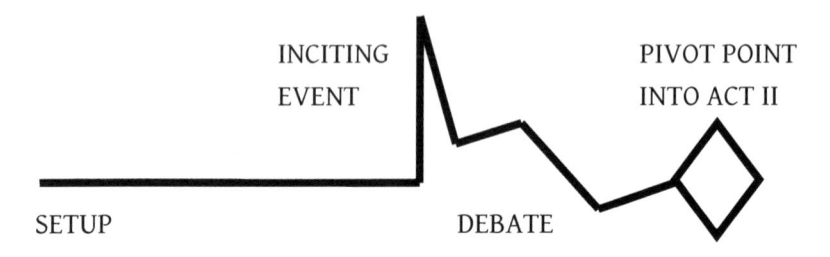

```
                INCITING              PIVOT POINT
                EVENT                 INTO ACT II

     SETUP                  DEBATE
```

If you were to look at a graph of the first act, it would resemble something like this. The graph shows the Setup as a long, flat line followed by a spike where the Inciting Event happens and then we move

---

[8] Sandra Annette Bullock (July 26, 1964 -) is an American actress, comedian and producer. She won an academy award for her role in the 2009 film, *The Blind Side*.

onto the Debate stage which is shown as a rocky slope that heads toward the Pivot Point into Act II. In reality, the Debate stage might not be as long as it's depicted here. It can be quite short. In my graph, I've drawn it nearly as long as the Setup, but there are often times that it will be this long. Just remember you want to make your Setup as short as possible because your story doesn't actually begin until the Inciting Event.

Now let's dig into this act a little deeper.

YOUR PROTAGONIST IN THE PRESENT WORLD

1. SETUP

The Setup really exists for one reason and one reason only: to show the protagonist living the way he currently does and to show the current state of the world. You want to give readers a good indication of the status quo at the beginning of your story so they will have something to directly compare with when the protagonist returns as the Hero to the world after having gone through his journey.

There are two things that are crucial at this point. One, your protagonist must be flawed in some way. Throughout the story (probably during the Climax), this flaw will either be fixed or changed into some different sort of flaw. And, this one's a bit more subtle, the *world* must be flawed in some way, too. And when the protagonist returns as Hero, the world is either no longer flawed or it is flawed in a different way than it was before.

It's also important to remember that antagonists should be flawed as well. The more you can humanize your antagonists the better. Always remember, most people don't think they're evil. They just have different internal ideas and rationalizations than the good guys do. History writes the rules of who's considered good and who's labeled as evil.

You may use some of the time during the setup to drop tidbits of backstory if you absolutely must, but remember the golden rule: don't show or tell the reader anything they don't absolutely need to know. And if you can hold off doing it until later, hold off until the last possible minute. If the reader never needs to know something, leave it out of the book. This not only builds suspense, it also keeps your story from getting bogged down.

You can also use the Setup time for bits of characterization if you want, but I wouldn't go too overboard. Your story *hasn't started yet*. Your story doesn't officially start until the Inciting Event happens, so be careful. A slow Setup is the death of a lot of novels. Everything is just pabulum until you reach that next plot point, so get there as quickly as you can. We don't need to know everything there is to know about the protagonist's life before the story even begins.

2. THE INCITING EVENT

This is the call to adventure. It's where your story actually *starts*. It's the Herald archetype, even though it might not be, and usually isn't, a person. It's the big chunk of meteorite coming toward the Earth in *Armageddon*. It's the realization that the polar ice caps are melting at an astronomical rate in *The Day After Tomorrow*. It's knowing that if he doesn't stay in Bedford Falls, the board will vote with Potter and everything George Bailey's father stood for will have been for nothing.

The call to adventure also sets up a goal for the protagonist, if he chooses to make the quest. It may be the main goal, or it may be a temporary goal with more goals to come in the future. But this goal will be the first driving force that sets the protagonist off through the beginning of your story.

Sometimes the goal changes multiple times. Other times it stays the same throughout the whole story. In *The Lord of the Rings*, there was a single goal—throw the Ring of Power into the fiery pits of Mount Doom beyond the black gate of Mordor. In *The Hobbit*, along with Bilbo's main goal, which was to act as burglar for the attack on the Smaug's lair in the Lonely Mountains, Tolkien had a number of smaller goals for him and his thirteen companions that kept changing as they went along on their adventure.

When I mentioned in the last chapter that one of the main cornerstones for me when I'm writing a story is the beginning, I was talking about the Inciting Event, not the Setup. The Setup isn't the beginning of your story, the Inciting Event is.

3. DEBATE

Once the Inciting Event has happened, there's still a chance for your protagonist to back out. He can still change his mind and decide he's not that interested in going on a grand adventure and would really rather stay at home and have a cup of tea. This is exactly what Bilbo tried to do in *The Hobbit*.

Joseph Campbell calls this point Refusal of the Call. Generally, the would-be hero is reluctant to leave his ordinary, cozy world no matter how flawed it might be. He's used to the flaws, he's comfortable with them. Like most people, he fears the unfamiliar.

What he needs is a bit of nudging to get him out the door. This is where a Mentor archetype usually steps into the picture. Think again of *The Hobbit* and Gandalf or *Star Wars* and Obi-Wan Kenobi.

I should point out, in case it's not obvious, that the Hero's Journey is for all types of stories, not just stories where characters go on real, actual quests and fight dragons for gold. The journey doesn't have to be a "literal" journey. We could be, and probably in most cases are, talking about a metaphorical, internal journey. Your protagonist may not actually have to go anywhere to embark upon his quest. It's just a matter of taking matters into his own hands.

Eventually, something *does* get the protagonist on his way, and there are an infinite variety of methods to go about doing this. If you start studying stories you'll build up a subconscious repertoire of them and your mind will begin conjuring up ideas of its own.

What's important, though, is that the protagonist sets off on the journey in a way he knows he can't turn back from. The doorway to Act

II only goes one way. There's no returning except by going all the way through. And even then, the protagonist won't come back because nobody ever returns the same way they set out. They change so much that they return as someone else completely different.

4. PIVOT POINT I: ENTERING ACT II

Okay, I'll admit it. I stole the term Pivot Point from Syd Field.

These are two places in your story full of emotional upheaval for your protagonist. Anytime there is an emotional change, especially a really dramatic one, it is a form of conflict, and when you're writing fiction conflict is good. Conflict is what we want. So these very dramatic, life changing moments should be celebrated. They can make your book incredibly powerful.

The first Pivot Point doesn't have near the drama as the one at the end of Act II, but it does show that the protagonist is capable of change. It might be a place to show some aspect of your protagonist you haven't had a chance to display yet. Perhaps

Ill. 1-6: Originally a Hans Christian Anderson tale, this scene shows the Little Mermaid just after she's visited the sea witch and bought the potion that gives her legs instead of a mermaid tale which is the Inciting Event that takes her into Act II.

he has some hidden sensitivity, or some inner strength you can showcase in this scene. Or maybe there's something else, something that happens to play opposite to whatever behavior he's been exhibiting so far throughout the Setup, Inciting Event and Debate sequences. Showing these other facets of your main character will add depth and a sense of realism to him, and the first Pivot Point is a perfect place to do that.

This first Pivot Point can also be an emotionally charged farewell scene if your book really is a "let's go on an adventure" book. Of course, the adventure doesn't have to involve a bunch of elves and dwarves. It could be a kid travelling across the states to bury his dead father because he just received a telegram, or an old woman going to visit her daughter overseas for what may be the last time because she's just been diagnosed with terminal cancer.

This scene could also be a moment of quiet inner reflection where the protagonist faces his own doubts and tries unsuccessfully to muster the courage he knows he'll need to succeed.

EXERCISES

1. Come up with a story idea, or, even better, use one you already have in the works, where you know at least two of the cornerstones for your story: the Inciting Event and the resolution to the Climax. Knowing these, you know how the protagonist is going to change when he returns as the hero, so it allows you to define who he is at the beginning of the story—he's the opposite of who he'll be at the end of the story. Write a character description of this person at the beginning of the story and the world he exists in. Make sure both the protagonist and the world are flawed in some way.

2. Come up with an Inciting Event that will rock the world that the protagonist lives and change it in ways that make it less tolerable than it was before. Just come up with an event and leave it beneath your character description in note form. If you are using a story idea you already had lying around or perhaps are actively working on, ask yourself if your inciting event could be bigger and splashier? The Inciting Event is such an important part of the story that it should be very memorable and it should hammer the very heart of the protagonist's world so much, it almost pushes him into the adventure. Colossal Inciting Events are what sell books and movies. They're the stuff that gets written on the back covers of novels.

3. Now have your protagonist decide he must make changes to his life in order to fix the problems brought on by this event. These changes could be internal or external. He may be forced to leave on an actual journey (setting out to find his roots, maybe, or joining the army), or he may go on a metaphorical one (and quit

his job, or leave his girlfriend). Have him decide a course of action and write it in your notebook beneath the event.

4. How has your protagonist already between the description you made of him in the first step and coming to the decision to take action? Make some notes regarding this change. Congratulations, you have just outlined the first act of a story. And you already know your ending, so you know where you're writing toward.

KEY POINTS

- Act I consists of the Setup stage, the Inciting Event, the Debate stage, and the Act I/Act II Pivot Point.
- The Setup is where you show your protagonist in his normal world. You don't want to spend too much time in it because it's boring. Your story doesn't actually start until the Inciting Event occurs.
- Your protagonist must start the story flawed in some way. The world must also be flawed some way.
- The more flawed and farther back you can set your protagonist at the beginning of the book, the more powerful your ending will be when he overcomes those flaws.
- Your antagonist, to properly humanize him, should also start the story flawed some way. Also, remember, nobody thinks they're evil. People have their own points of view. They have complete rationalizations for their actions despite how they may look externally.
- The Inciting Event should set up certain goals for the protagonist if he decides to accept the call to respond.
- There is no specific length for the Debate stage. It can be a fairly quick decision, or it can be something the protagonist agonizes over for a long time.
- Pivot Points are emotionally charged story points of change for your protagonist. Don't be afraid to write them that way. They can be very dramatic. Something in your protagonist has changed to make him leave his home or, if it's not a physical journey, to leave the stability of his normal life behind.

CHAPTER FIVE

Act II: The Barren Wasteland

> *The most beautiful people I've known are those who have known trials, have known struggles, have known loss, and have found their way out of the depths.*
>
> —Elisabeth Kübler-Ross[9]

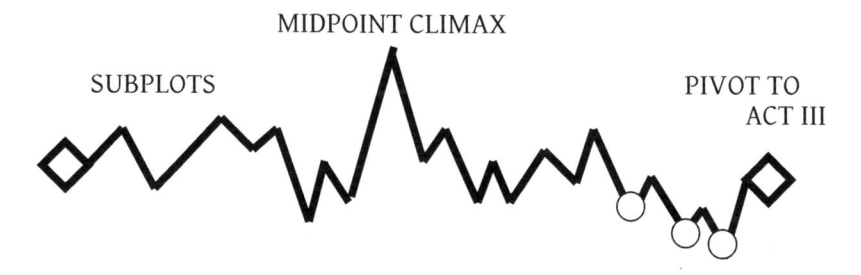

The above graph is a rough indication of what you can expect to encounter throughout the long stretch of time while inside of Act II. It start and ends with a pivot point connecting it to Acts I and III, there's an indication of where subplots should (but don't have to) spin off, there's a big spike in the middle which we'll talk about soon, called the Act II Midpoint, then there's three important spots of interest at the end that for now I've just designated by circles.

The erratic spikes along the graph symbolize your protagonist battling his way through a series of ordeals.

---

[9] Elisabeth Kübler-Ross (July 8, 1926 - August 24, 2004) was a Swiss American psychiatrist. She was a pioneer in near-death studies and discovered the five stages of grief.

TRIALS & TESTS, ALLIES & ENEMIES, AND CONFLICT, CONFLICT, CONFLICT . . .

1. YOUR PROTAGONIST AGAINST OPPOSING FORCES

Act II is a New World for the protagonist. He has left Act I with some sort of goal, whether it is to put an end to the war against the Empire, or destroy the Ring of Power, or to rid Gotham of the Joker, or to divulge the secrets of the black housemaids to the world in the story of *The Help*, there's a goal. But Act II isn't like the world the protagonist left behind. This one is full of challenges and tests where he learns what works and what doesn't. He meets strangers and must sort out which are his allies and which are his enemies. He must fight adversaries, and each encounter grows more and more laborious.

Often there is a scene with a bar or a saloon early in the act. Think about Rick's place in *Casablanca*, or the Cantina scene in *Star Wars*.

It's important that throughout this act the tension continues rising and the stakes keep increasing. If the protagonist manages to make it through one ordeal, the next one he faces must be tougher and require greater insight into a solution. With each accomplishment, the reader should see the protagonist grow. The protagonist is a surrogate for the reader and readers want to feel as though they're becoming true heroes right alongside your character.

2. SUBPLOTS

Your first subplot often starts shortly after entering Act II. Some books don't have subplots. Some only have one. Some have four or five. Starting a new plotline gives you a chance to introduce a brand new cast of characters. Plotlines are generally referred to by letter, your main one being your "A" Plot, your first subplot then becomes your "B" Plot. If you have a second subplot, it's your "C" plot, and so on.

JOURNEYS UNDER THE MOON 53

Subplots, if your story has them, can start at any time during the second act, but quite often they will all just start one after the other right at the beginning of Act II.

There's not even a hard and fast rule saying that subplots *have* to start in Act II. You can start them anywhere you like if you choose to. You could even start one or more in Act I. Remember, form follows function. It's just common for them to begin right after the opening of Act II.

Often the "B", "C", and "D" Plots weave in and out of the "A" Plot and sometimes will tie into the central theme of the book. Each subplot is

Ill. 1-7: *"B Plots" often involve romantic interests for the protagonist. The story of King Arthur and Guinevere and Guinevere's indiscretion with Sir Lancelot could be considered a "B" Plot. This is tale shows up in Chrétien de Troyes's* Lancelot, The Knight of the Cart *and is a common motif in Arthurian legend.*

just like a mini-plot line, with its own beginning, middle, and end. Each one has its own Setup, its own Inciting Event, its own Debate stage, its own period of conflict, its own Climax, and its own resolution. It probably all happens a bit quicker in the subplots, of course, just because they are shorter than the main plotline, but everything's present and accounted for.

Sometimes you can write very powerful subplots by having them tie back to your "A" Plot and Climax at the same time. It's not an easy thing to pull off, but the results can be well worth the thought energy and effort you put into it.

Traditionally, your "B" Plot involves a romantic interest with your protagonist that will pay off when the "B" Plot intertwines back with the "A" plot at the beginning of Act III. When this happens, usually the protagonist wins back the heart of the girl and also discovers a potential solution to be applied in the Climax where he'll have his final showdown against the antagonist. This happens just before he's about to enter the Climax. But you don't have to be traditional by any means.

There's no rule stating you absolutely need a subplot, either. Indeed, many successful books have been written without them. Some of the simplest mythologies have no subplots. The story of Calypso holding Odysseus hostage on her island so she can make him her immortal husband comes to mind. For seven years, Calypso enchants Odysseus with her singing as she strolls across her weaving loom, with a golden shuttle. During this time they sleep together, although Odysseus soon comes to wish for different circumstances.

Wanting to return to his wife, Penelope, Odysseus gets his patron goddess Athena to ask Zeus to help release him from his island prison. Zeus issues Hermes to order Calypso to free Odysseus. He tells her it was not Odysseus's fate to be with her forever. She argues that the gods condemn goddesses for having relationships with mortals.

But, eventually, Calypso concedes and sends Odysseus on his way, giving him wine, bread, and a boat.

3. ACT II MIDPOINT CLIMAX

Now we come to the secret of why there's no "muddle in the middle" with this method of writing. It's because you've got something to write toward as you come to the middle of the book and something to write away from as you leave it.

Let me explain.

Near the middle of Act II, which should be very close to the middle of your book, a natural phenomenon occurs. The protagonist goes through a Pseudo Climax.

The Pseudo Climax is very much like the Climax you have at the end of your book, only it can't be as big and loud as your final Climax or it will take away from the overall reading experience of your story—it will overshadow it, and this often happens, especially in movies.

Just like in the real Climax, your protagonist will experience one of two things at the resolution of this Pseudo Climax. He will either seemingly peak (experiencing an "up")—and it seems like things can't possibly get any better than they are, or he experiences a "down" (and the world collapses around him)—and it seems like things can only get better from here on in.

If he peaks, it is a false peak.

If the world collapses around him, it is a false collapse.

Either way, after the Act II Midpoint, the stakes are all raised. All of the dangers of the world are reset to a higher value. It's a whole new ball of wax. Not only that, often you will come out of the Act II Midpoint with some sort of ticking clock, giving the protagonist only a certain amount of time left to finish off the antagonist or solve the problem of the imminent disaster that is looming.

Many times the Pseudo Climax at the Act II Midpoint will change the rules of the game and cause one or two things to happen. Sometimes even both may result. There could be a shift in the protagonist's goals, and/or something may be revealed that completely changes the story as the readers know it so far.

For an example of the first one—shifting the protagonist's goals—think about *Star Wars, The Phantom Menace*. Obi-Wan and Qui-Gon are trying to stop the Trade Federation's invasion of the planet Naboo when they are forced to land on Tatooine due to ship trouble and meet young Anikan. Qui=Gon discovers the boy's medicilorian count is off the charts and decides he must be the Chosen One meant to lead the Jedi out of the darkness of the Sith. Now, suddenly, Qui-Gon's goal is to get young Anikan to the Jedi Council on Corascant, but the only way to do that is to buy him out of slavery. They decide the best way to get the money is to let Anikan enter the pod race.

The pod race is the Act II Midpoint Climax, which, in my opinion, overshadowed the Jedi battle Climax at the end of that movie.

Two examples come to mind of movies where the Midpoint Climax completely changed everything the audience thought they knew about the story up to that point. The quintessential perfect example is *Chinatown* where Evelyn Mulray reveals that Katherine is both her sister and her daughter.

Quite the surprise.

Suddenly your mind zooms back through the last forty-five minutes of film you watched and reorganizes everything accordingly.

Another excellent example is finding out Bruce Willis is dead in the *Sixth Sense*. Everything changes on that beat.

And in case two weren't enough, check out *A Brilliant Mind* where you finally realize Russell Crowe is schizophrenic and his "friend" doesn't actually exist.

Next time you read a book or watch a movie, start getting ready for the Pseudo Climax around the halfway point. Without fail, you'll find it. And it's something a lot of writers don't know about.

I think this is the cause of author ennui that appears around the middle of the book while you're writing it. You get stuck in the middle of Act II and suddenly it seems like nothing's going anywhere and you start second guessing everything. What you need is to have your protagonist experience a dramatic emotional change, something to write toward, like a semi-climax. It gives you a direction to go. It's a turn around. And it gives you something to write away from once you've got there.

4. THE REST OF ACT II: RAISING THE STAKES

Act II continues onward as a collection of scenes pitting the protagonist against forces opposing him from his ultimate goal—whatever that goal is now, whether it's the same goal it was before the Midpoint Climax, or some brand new goal now that he's gone through the Midpoint ordeal. Each conflict he enters continues to be a greater test than the last, ratcheting up the stakes as he moves through Act II toward the story's Climax in Act III.

At this point, though, the protagonist almost seems to have things more or less under control.

You still want to keep the suspense growing as the story builds throughout the remainder of the second act and there are various ways of doing this, such as withholding important information until it is absolutely needed—by holding things back, you naturally make the reader want to read on.

There's also the much used, but still very effective method of having the built-in "ticking clock" I mentioned earlier. Some kind of mechanism that you started after the Midpoint Climax. It doesn't have to literally be a time bomb that will go off in three quarters of an hour if the protagonist doesn't manage to take out the antagonist (although that works), it can be something as simple as the girl he thinks he's fallen in love with is leaving town forever on the five o'clock train unless he manages to stop her. He doesn't have her phone number and he's trying to get to the station but downtown New York is grid-locked. To make matters worse, someone just stuck a gun in his ribs and asked him for his wallet.

All of these scenes serve a purpose, which is to drive the story forward. If they aren't serving that purpose, they must be rewritten or cut out of the book. Act II is a series of scenes that gets us from point A to point B or, in this case, from Act I to Act III. These particular scenes are very important because, by far, Act II is the longest section of your story. You want to keep the momentum of the story going forward at all costs, despite how tempting it will be to stop and meander and go off on tangents. Don't. Write to a target. Well, not on your first draft, but on your second one. On your first draft, do anything you want. But on subsequent redrafts, Act II has to take off like a thoroughbred and keep kicking up dust like it's Secretariat.

As a rule of thumb, Act I generally takes up the first fifth of the book, Act III probably a little less than two fifths and all the rest is given to Act II, other than a tiny amount that's used for the Denouement at the very end.

Now let's discuss those three circles at the end of the Act II graph I presented you with at the beginning of this chapter. These are special points, called Darkness Closes In, All is Lost, and Dark Night before Dawn. I will admit, I stole the name "All is Lost" from Blake Snyder, writer of the wonderful *Save the Cat!* books.

5. DARKNESS CLOSES IN

It's right in this stage where you throw a monkey wrench into the protagonist's way. He's been doing too well for the last little while. We all know it. The readers know it. It's time to make him see things aren't so simple.

Now the bad guys regroup. The bomb starts ticking down faster. The girl your protagonist met at the pizza joint dumps him for his friend Chuck who farts while he sings karaoke.

It's just enough to cause the protagonist to stumble. But soon, he'll do a lot more than stumble. Because all of this naturally leads us to the next part of Act II, where things naturally just get worse.

6. ALL IS LOST

The All Is Lost point is a "false defeat." It's where the hero knows the journey's over and he can't possibly go on any further. He's doomed.

It's in every movie you've ever watched. It's where Luke knows he can't win the battle against Vader because he's exhausted. It's where the Joker in *The Dark Knight* has the bombs on the boat and Batman can't possibly save everyone with only ten seconds left. It's just when they thought Christmas couldn't get any worse, a S.W.A.T. team comes through the window and arrests the Griswolds.

All aspects of the hero's life are in shambles. Everything he's worked toward was for nothing. All hope is lost.

At this point, Joseph Campbell says the character must experience a death. Now it doesn't have to be a "real" death, although that works. In *Star Wars*, Obi Wan gives up his life so that Luke and his buddies can make it to the Millennium Falcon in time to take off before the tractor beam grabs them. But it can also be a metaphorical death. Something inside the hero dies. A piece of their soul. The Grinch's tiny heart.

In *Save the Cat!* Blake Snyder calls this scene, "the whiff of death."

The reason we need this death to happen is because the All Is Lost stage is our Christ on the Cross moment. It's where the old world dies for the protagonist. His old way of thinking dies, and everything about what used to be him goes with it. This death clears the way for what he is to become.

This death is an archetypal symbol that is rooted deep inside all of us. It holds great meaning. Without it, your story would lose a lot power.

7. DARK NIGHT BEFORE DAWN

We have one more part right at the end of Act II that may only be a few seconds for your protagonist, or it could last five minutes. It's the point right before he musters every last ounce of energy he has and reaches way down deep and pulls out that last, best idea that will save the day only to come up completely empty. He's got nothing. Right now, he's just looking for the strength to go on.

This is a primal story point. We've all been there—hopeless, clueless, drunk, stupid, sitting on the side of the road with a flat tire and no car jack. Then, and only then, are we able to admit our humility and our humanity and give up our control and let fate handle the rest.

This plot point is all about humility. You want to show that your protagonist was beaten and knows it; show us that he'll learn from this lesson.

This scene is important because without it, your protagonist could potentially come off as unlikeable even after all he's gone through and even though he will still wind up saving the day.

However, be careful. You want him to exhibit humility in a way that doesn't knock your readers over the head with it. In other words, do it

Ill. 1-8: *This illustration of* Sleeping Beauty *shows the prince just about to kiss her and wake her from eternal sleep. This is a perfect Act III plot point in the story, as Sleeping Beauty has already gone through the Setup and Inciting Event of Act I and the trials and tests of Act II. This illustration was drawn by English artist Walter Crane in 1882.* Sleeping Beauty *is part of the* Household Stories *by the Grimm's Fairytales. Sleeping beauty is the perfect example of the Damsel in Distress archetype which is a sub-archetype of the Damsel.*

subtly. It's way too easy to go overboard here.

8. PIVOT POINT II: ENTERING ACT III

Your protagonist has made it through the stage of challenges and trials and he's been beaten almost to the point of death (and actually, in one way or another, *has* experienced death). And you've managed to write your way through the hardest act of the novel. Congratulate yourself. The rest of this is, comparatively, a cakewalk.

The Pivot Point at the entrance to Act III is a highly charged emotional place for your protagonist. It can't even be compared to the Pivot Point between Act I and Act II. Your protagonist has just gone through hell and back. The ordeal should have changed him almost beyond recognition. The final transformation will occur in the Climax.

But the journey hasn't been for nothing. All the struggles have brought new strength and wisdom he's probably not even presently aware he possesses. He may have found or been given items, magical or otherwise, that will help him in his final ordeal against the antagonist that he knows he still must face.

Once again, he's entering a brand new world. This one is the domain of the antagonist. The world of Act III.

EXERCISES

1. Draw a line representing Act II on your page. Make a mark at the center where your Act Midpoint Climax is going to occur. Now make a series of dots along the left side of the of the line where you want to have your protagonist encounter obstacles in his path. These obstacles will be connected by narrative, of course, so they won't be a continuum, they will be discrete encounters. Looking back at the outline you made for your first act, try to think of some obstacles your protagonist might face in Act II while he proceeds on his "journey." Think about your antagonist in your story? Is it a person? A thing? An idea? How is it rebelling against the character? Remember to make each obstacle the protagonist faces slightly harder than the last. Jot down as many ideas as you can in point form.

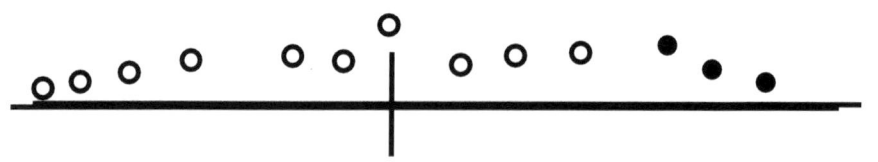

Sample encounter graph for Act II. Notice how the white circles move farther up with each conflict on the left side of the midpoint climax? That represents the growing complexity of the struggle. Also note that they don't have to be evenly spaced. The three black dots at the end represent the Darkness Closes In, All is Lost, and Dark Night before Dawn points. Notice also that the intensity of the encounters drops after the midpoint Climax but then continues to grow past what it had been in the first half of the second act. It's okay to give your audience a reprieve sometimes.

2. Come up with and insert an Act II Midpoint Climax. Your story should grow to it just like it would a regular Climax. Remember that:

    1.) It should be a turning point in your story.

2.) Things should change
3.) New information should be unveiled.
4.) Possibly, the goals of the character will change.
5.) Everything as we know about the story until now might be different once the Pseudo-Climax is over.
6.) This Climax should be the hardest encounter your protagonist has yet to face. He can either be successful or fail, but either way the Climax should resolve with all the stakes of Act II being raised.
7.) Try to start some sort of "ticking clock" that will make him have to race against time for the remainder of the act. Is the girl he's in love with going to move away in a week to Europe? Is there a nuclear bomb set to go off in five hours? Does Ben Affleck have to get a bunch of American reporters out of a Canadian embassy before they are found and killed? These sorts of things keep the intensity up.

Remember, you are just sketching out ideas, not writing. This is simply an outlining exercise and don't worry, you're not going to use the outline anyway, so don't get overwhelmed by it.

3. The next major stage of Act II is Darkness Closes In. Here is where the antagonist or his forces regroup and rally against the protagonist. Think of a way to do this that is original and surprising. Just write down a few sentences. If your antagonist is a thing or an idea, your protagonist may suffer a loss of faith. Remember, you are only making notes, not writing full paragraphs or anything. This should all be done very quickly.

4. The next stage is All is Lost, where the protagonist knows he's defeated. He gives up. It's where he realizes he's come all this

way for nothing. Again, write a few lines of how you would handle this scene if you were actually writing this book. The protagonist should experience some sort of "death." It doesn't necessarily have to be his own death, or a real death. It can be a metaphorical one. But some kind of death must happen in order for the old to die away and make room for the new.

5. The last stage in Act II is the Dark Night before Dawn where the protagonist shows his humility. He knows he's been defeated and he's learned his lesson. How can you how this without telling? Remember to make it subtle. It doesn't have to be a long story beat. It can be very short. Jot down an idea or two.

6. Finally, how much has your protagonist now changed since entering Act II? He has gone through a host of ordeals and even experienced a sort of death. He fought through a climactic midpoint and somehow survived. He should be almost unrecognizable. Who is he now? Does he even know? This is your second Pivot Point. Write some notes about your protagonist's emotional state. If it helps, write it from his actual point of view, using "I" statements.

KEY POINTS

- Act II encompasses most of your story and is a long string of challenges and tests your protagonist must go through before he is able to have his final showdown with his foe.
- Every struggle in Act II should be harder than the last. Tension should considerably rise, as should the stakes. The protagonist meets people and must decide who his allies are and who his enemies are. He may meet the antagonist throughout this act, or henchmen of the antagonist.
- At the beginning of Act II is traditionally where subplots spin off. You can have as many subplots as you like. Traditionally, however, the "B" Plot (the first subplot) is the romantic interest plotline.
- There is also more often than not bar or saloon scene near the beginning of Act II where the protagonist can meet new people, some of whom will be friends, some of whom won't. It is up to the protagonist to figure that out.
- If the protagonist did not discover a Mentor in Act I, he may find one sometime in Act II. Mentors are there to help show the way in this new world and help prepare the protagonist for the dangers they must face.
- In the middle of Act II is a point called the Midpoint Climax. It is actually a Pseudo Climax. It is exactly like the real Climax at the end of your book, only it can't be as big or as loud or as flashy or it will dwarf your real ending. The protagonist may win or lose the Climax. If he wins, it is a false achievement and if he loses, it's a false loss.
- At the point of the Pseudo Climax, things change. The story as the readers know it may get turned on its head. The protagonist's goals may suddenly shift. Often, the false

Climax ends with some sort of ticking clock, accelerating the protagonist through the rest of Act II.
- Near the end of Act II are three important points, each one bleaker than the last for the protagonist. The first is Darkness Closes In. This is where the bad guys regroup and let the protagonist know he's been doing too well up until now and that's about to change.
- The second "dark point" is called All is Lost. It is here that the protagonist loses all hope and wishes he could return home. He sees no way out of the mess he's in. Sometime during this stage, he experiences some sort of "death," either real or metaphorical. This is important.
- The final point may last a minute or it may last ten minutes and is called Dark Night before Dawn. It's here that the protagonist absolutely feels he's come all this way in vain and sees no point in continuing. This is a point of humility and is important to include so your protagonist doesn't come off as unlikeable.
- The final step in Act II is to reach the Pivot Point that is the one-way door into Act III. There, the protagonist no longer resembles the person he was during the Setup of Act I.

CHAPTER SIX

Act III: The End of the Story

"The story must build to a final action beyond which the audience cannot imagine another."

−Robert McKee[10]

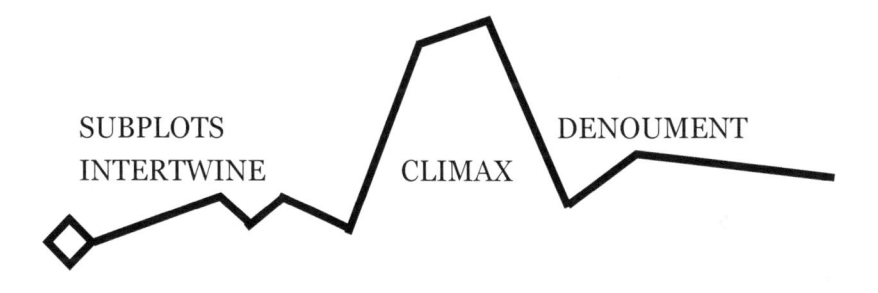

SUBPLOTS INTERTWINE   CLIMAX   DENOUMENT

1. SUBPLOTS INTERTWINE

Traditionally now, the first thing that happens upon entering the new world of Act III is that the "A" Plot and the "B" Plot will intertwine, converging back on each other into one plot again. And they will do so in a way that the protagonist not only succeeds in getting the girl back (if it's a romantic subplot—which traditionally it usually is), but also that he's provided with a hint as to how to proceed in the upcoming showdown against his adversary. If you have multiple subplots, they may all combine back into the main plotline at this point, often in a scene featuring some sort of gathering such as a party or a wedding.

---

[10] *Story: Substance, Structure, Style, and the Principles of Screenwriting*, Robert McKee, Harper Collins, New York, 1997

The classic fusion of "A" and "B" is the hero getting the clue from "the girl" that makes him realize how to solve both—beating the bad guy and winning the heart of his beloved.

However it happens, the protagonist must come up with an initial plan to use against his adversary in the upcoming Climax. If he has a team that he wishes to use against him, he may have to repair relationships that have been broken within that team. The team may need to be trained, or outfitted with weapons and armor.

2. CHASE SCENES

If your book features a chase scene of some sort, it is very common for it to fall at the beginning of Act III. I am uncertain as to why this is true, but it seems to happen more often than not. When it does, the idea for the initial plan of attack on the antagonist or even the lead-in to the climactic battle against the antagonist can come out of the chase scene. If you have subplots and a chase scene, the reintegration of the subplots and the chase scene are often combined. This was especially true of old movies where the gallant hero would be on the run from the bad guys and have to save the heroine while fighting off the foes until he reached the real battle awaiting him.

3. THE CLIMAX

CLIMAX STRUCTURE

The Climax can be a bit daunting, but I will break it down so it's simple. Nearly every Climax follows the same basic structure, even though on the surface it might appear not to. The reason it appears different is because the parts might be stretched out or slightly modified, but that's all.

The protagonist goes into the Climax knowing he must battle against the antagonist. Remember the antagonist doesn't have to be a person. It can be a thing, an idea, or even just a concept. But the protagonist needs to know what he's up against.

He also knows that the odds are not in his favor. Even if he's got a team of superheroes behind him, he's terribly outnumbered and outgunned. He's got the plan he came up with in the last scene, but it's far from being a perfect plan. It's important that the plan has two attributes: it has to have at least a shred of rationality to it so there's a chance it will realistically work in the reader's mind and, at the same time, it has to have the sense that it's completely insane. These two things are generally best conveyed to the reader in the form of dialogue.

Let's take two examples, the movie *The Avengers* and *Star Wars: A New Hope*. In *The Avengers*, the plan is simply to have our heroes go into Manhattan and take out Loki and his army of alien soldiers. Before the rest of the heroes get there, Loki and Robert Downey Jr. (Iron Man) meet in Stark Tower and Loki tells Iron Man that it's hopeless. He has an *army* on its way (so the plan is completely insane). To which, Iron Man replies: "Yeah? Well we've got a Hulk." (Which gives the plan a shred of rationality.)

Same thing with *Star Wars*. When told they have to shoot a two meter target on the Death Star to start a chain reaction that will cause it to explode, Wedge says, "That's impossible, even for a computer." (The plan's completely insane.) To which, Luke answers, "It's not impossible, I used to bull's-eye womp rats in my T-sixteen back home. They're not much bigger than two meters." (The plan has a shred of rationality.)

Once the plan is decided on, it's put into action and, at first, the protagonist—or team if there's a bunch of characters working together—start out doing quite well. It actually looks like they might pull this one out of the proverbial hat. Things are going a little too well, actually, and, like things normally do in such situations, they slowly begin to unravel.

Soon the bad guy is winning. The heroes lose ground. Even worse, it looks like a trap! The antagonist was expecting them all along. Your protagonist is now in a losing situation with no backup plan.

At this point, a ticking clock is started in one form or another against them. In *The Avengers*, it's the nuclear missile launched from the S.H.I.E.L.D. carrier toward Manhattan. In *Star Wars*, it's the Death Star beginning to target the Rebel base on Yavin V. The audience hears a countdown start and knows the heroes are doomed.

It is only now, with absolutely no other choice and nowhere to go but down, that your protagonist (and if you have a team, it is time that only your would-be Hero steps forward) reaches deep down inside of himself; he searches far into his own soul and pulls out his last best idea, the one he didn't know he had. That bright spark that somehow comes from the divine.

Blake Snyder calls this the "God Moment."

Whatever solution your hero comes up with, it has to be something he wouldn't have *considered* before going through the ordeal he faced to get to where he is now in Act III. And it *does* need to have a sense of the divine in some way.

In *The Avengers*, it's Robert Downey Jr. sacrificing his life to save humanity by using all of his suit's power to save Manhattan. He does this by taking the nuclear missile heading toward it off its present course and lifts it up and out of the atmosphere through the window that the tesseract has made into another dimension; the dimension that the alien army warring in New York streets is coming down from. Tony Stark (Robert Downey) knows it's a one-way mission. That's what makes this the God moment—nothing is more divine than self-sacrifice.

In *Star Wars*, Luke's solution is absolutely divine as he speaks to Obi-Wan from beyond the grave and Obi-Wan tells him to "Use the force." Then, disabling his computer and taking off his scanning system, he flies in blind and takes his shot, blowing up the Death Star with just a half second to spare.

This is the recipe for a great Climax. You can modify the components; you can stretch them out, you can add to them, you can make them more complex, but at their most basic, they all have to be there. And they almost always are. Think of the book *The Hobbit*. It definitely stretched it out, but it has this climactic structure, exactly.

ROMANTIC COMEDY CLIMAX

Just in case you think this Climax only works for action stories or adventure stories or fantasy stories, let's consider a non-existent romantic comedy and I'll show you how it works perfectly there, too. I'm just going to make one up, not only to show you how the climax works, but also how easy it is to come up with stories when you have archetypal constructs to call upon.

Meet our protagonist: Computer web designer Jason Cobb who likes watching old horror flicks, has a thing for old radio shows, dresses nice for a computer geek and has an intense fear of commitment. But, otherwise, Jason is quite attractive in a cute-funny way. Maybe Zac Efron plays him in the movie.

Jason works for a place called Interweb Communicardz in New York City.

Now meet our romantic interest: the very lovely, not so geeky, Elizabeth. She's also a web designer, but more on the graphic side of things, whereas Jason's more a coder. Elizabeth gets a new job with Interweb. She's probably played by Jennifer Lawrence.

Jason likes to tell goofy jokes. In fact, the first thing he does upon meeting Elizabeth in the lunchroom the day she starts is tell her a goofy joke. She likes it. She likes him. She decides she likes goofy geeky guys who dig old horror flicks. They wind up having a few lunches together. Eventually he invites her over to watch *Dawn of the Dead*.

Soon, they're spending all they're time together, eating pizza, listening to old radio shows and watching horror movies full of blood and gore. Problem is: Elizabeth doesn't know where she stands. The relationship doesn't seem to be going anywhere. Jason doesn't give her any feedback on *them*.

One day she outright asks him, "What exactly are we doing?"

"What do you mean?" Jason asks back.

"What do we have? What would you call our relationship?"

Jason thinks this over. "I think you make a great pizza and movie friend."

This isn't really the answer Elizabeth wanted. She tells her friends what he said and they tell her to dump him to the curb and move on. He's a waste of time. He's never going to give her what she wants.

Meanwhile, Jason's agonizing over his response. It's not what he really wanted to say. He wanted to tell her how much he digs her. But something won't let him say that. He's just somehow . . . scared.

He tries to muster the courage to tell her how he really feels about her, but before he can get out the words, Elizabeth dumps him.

We're at the Darkness Closes In point in the story and Jason's life goes in the toilet. He starts showing up late for work. Then he starts not showing up at all. He can't bear to see her. Soon he loses his job. He asks his friends about her; how's she's doing? They tell him she's dating some guy, but it's not serious.

Then Jason finds out (near the end of the second Act, around the All is Lost point) that Elizabeth has given her notice at Interweb and is moving out of New York and back to Kansas where she grew up. She's going to move in with her mom until she gets her own place. She flies out in three days.

Now we've hit the All is Lost point.

Jason freaks out. He doesn't know what to do.

Two days go by. He decides to call her. When he does, he discovers, her phone's already been disconnected.

We've just hit the Dark Night before Dawn.

And we enter Act III.

There is a subplot we haven't talked about involving a mutual friend. This is how Jason gets his information about what Elizabeth is up to even though they've split up. From this friend, Jason finds out Elizabeth's flight time and airline information. He decides he has to head her off at the pass and win her back before it's too late.

He has a plan. It's crazy, but it's a plan. He's going to dress up in his nicest clothes, get in his car, buy her a dozen roses, stop her at the airport, and tell her the same joke he won her over with the day they met in the lunchroom at work.

So he gets in his car, races to the florist, and buys the flowers.

Then he gets gridlocked.

Time is ticking. Elizabeth's flight leaves in less than an hour. Jason has over fifteen miles to drive.

He gets frustrated. He hasn't moved in ten minutes.

In an act of defiance, he pulls up on the sidewalk and starts bouncing off the curb, flying down the side of the road, dodging mailboxes and telephone poles, weaving in and out of pedestrians. He skids around corners almost on two wheels. He goes the wrong way down one way streets. The flowers lying in the backseat of his car tumble around and the box flies open. But he doesn't notice. He is hell bent on reaching that airport before Elizabeth's flight leaves.

Finally he sees the airport. According to his watch, Elizabeth's flight leaves in twenty-five minutes, but Jason knows she always shows up late or just in the nick of time for everything. So he thinks she'll still be in the ticket lineup. He guns the accelerator and whizzes down the empty tarmac toward the parking lot, screeching to a sideways halt beside the doors leading to the ticket counter. He grabs the flowers that are scattered and broken around his backseat and does his best to arrange them back into a bouquet. They look like the sort of bouquet a two year old gives to his mother after picking flowers from a field. It doesn't matter. Jason just needs to see Elizabeth.

He goes running through the doors, unaware of his disheveled hair and clothes all unkempt now from his tumultuous drive in. just as he makes it inside the main building he spots Elizabeth walking toward the ticket counter. She's halfway there, maybe twenty feet away. He jogs up and gets in front of her, startling her.

"What are you doing here?" she asks, wide-eyed.

"Here," he says, handing her the broken flowers. "These are for you."

"Um, thanks?" she says.

Then he tells her the joke and the corners of his mouth lift in that cute little grin she fell in love with.

And for just a minute there's that twinkle in her eyes and he sees it and so does the audience and he knows he *has* her. It's worked! It wasn't all for nothing. He's got her back. His smile widens. Her blue eyes grow bigger. He can almost hear music in his head.

Then an announcement comes over the PA system announcing her flight starting to board. It shakes her back to reality, reminding her of why she's leaving. Reminding her of what her friends said. Reminding her of what *Jason* had told her. *They made good pizza and movie friends.* She pushes the flowers back into his chest. "Here," she says. "I don't want your flowers. I don't need anything from you. I'm leaving. I've already decided I'm leaving."

He stands there, his head hung, the broken flowers drooping from his hands, watching her walk the rest of the way to the ticket counter to finish arranging her flight. And while she does, Jason reaches deep down inside for that one last solution. And it has to be something special. Something from the divine. Something he would never have done before going through the ordeal of meeting her and living out their relationship.

And when it comes to him and it happens, nobody's as surprised as Jim is.

"But—" he calls out, across the room. "But I love you!"

Without turning her head, Elizabeth says back, "What did you say?"

Jim steps forward halfway toward the counter. "I said 'I love you'" The woman on the other side of the ticket counter just smiles at Elizabeth.

Now Elizabeth does turn around and the two of them embrace. Somehow, in the "God Moment", Jason got over his fear of commitment.

The story ends with them back together again, both deciding to fly to Kansas together and live off of Elizabeth's poor mother.

See? It works for any story, equally well.

4. CHARACTER ARCS

It's not enough for the hero to just win, he must change. Your hero starts the story as an average guy with a flaw in a flawed world and ends the story as a Hero who is either no longer flawed or flawed in a different way. And, in becoming unflawed, somehow the world has also become unflawed or is now flawed in a different way. Whichever it is, the world is a better place for the hero having experienced everything he has gone through.

This change in your protagonist is called his character arc. Character arcs are vitally important to your story. All principal characters should arc, but your main character absolutely *has* to. Even in serials, where you have one book continuing on to the next, there has to be some sort of progression and growth and it can get tricky. This is why a lot of series will lose their audience around the fourth book or so. The characters are no longer growing. They aren't arcing. They have become stagnant.

The character arc of a character starts from the moment of the Inciting Event and continues throughout the trials and tests of Act II, but it's not until the Climax that the arc becomes final and complete (it actually becomes final and complete at the point of the Resurrection). And it's important that it becomes final and complete in an emotionally charged and satisfying way.

Although I just said all principal characters should arc, there is a caveat to watch out for. Readers will automatically feel that whichever character arcs the most—that is, experiences the greatest change—is the Hero of the story, despite what you might think as the writer. You may have a character slay the dragon and win the princess's hand in marriage, but if a side character shows more growth than the warrior doing the slaying, that side character is going to subconsciously be considered the Hero.

George Lucas almost had a problem with this in the original *Star Wars* movie. In a lot of ways, Harrison Ford's character arcs more than Luke Skywalker. He almost feels like the Hero in the end. You don't want two

Heroes, unless it's a special kind of story, called a "buddy story". *Toy Story* is a "buddy story". Both Woody and Buzz are Heroes. Although, even in "buddy stories," generally one character can be pegged as the *main* protagonist. With *Toy Story*, it's Woody. The reason is because of the types of changes the characters go through. Woody's changes are more *primal* than Buzz's.

5. THE RESURRECTION

As I just mentioned, it's during the resurrection that your protagonist finishes his character arc and thus it is in the resurrection that he truly becomes the Hero. The death or near-death or metaphorical death he experienced in the All is Lost stage during the end of Act II cleared the way by killing off his old way of thinking and his old way of interacting with the world, making room for the new Hero to take its place. Now, the only way to do that is to have him be brought to life as that Hero.

So, no matter what, your hero must experience a resurrection of some sort and virtually everything in the story beforehand should purposely grow to this moment in the story. It generally falls right at the resolution of the Climax. You could also call this the Apotheosis or Transcendence moment of the story.

Once this happens, the character's transformation into his new form is complete. He is now the Hero he set out to become in the beginning, rising up like a phoenix from the ashes of his old self.

This is the final part of the Climax and, like the character arc, it's important that it's done in a way that is as emotionally charged as possible.

For an example of a resurrection scene, let's go back to *The Avengers*.

After Iron Man gets rid of the nuclear missile and saves mankind, he falls—apparently dead—back to Earth, where his body lies lifeless in the street. Then, standing over top of him, the Hulk lets out a ground-shaking roar and Iron Man's eyes snap open. The roar brought him back to life, so to speak, causing his "resurrection." This is his "return from death" scene where he becomes a true Hero.

This is as good a place as any to point out that the Climax isn't any specific length. It can be as long or as short as needed. Again it's a case of form following function.

In *Catcher in the Rye*, The Climax was simply Holden Caulfield watching his sister on the carousel and barely took a paragraph. In the movie *Juno*, it was simply a minute of screen time with *Juno* dropping off the note saying she's still in for the adoption with just Vanessa despite the fact that Vanessa and Mark are breaking up. In *The Avengers*, The Climax runs probably twenty minutes while the heroes battle Loki and his army from outer space and destroy most of downtown Manhattan.

6. ENDINGS

When I spoke earlier of the fourth anchor point of your story being the ending, I was talking about the resolution of the Climax, not the very end of the book.

Stories can end in different ways. Your Climax can either end positively charged (which is an "up" ending, or an idealistic ending where the hero gets what he's after) or negatively charged (which is a "down" ending, where your hero doesn't succeed, and may possibly even die). Or it can end ironically, which is sort of a positive and a negative charge simultaneously. That's what makes it tricky to pull off. Sometimes in ironic endings, characters don't get what they want, but realize the world is a better place for it. Examples of movies with ironic endings are:

- *The Deer Hunter* (with Christopher Walken singing God Bless America over all the slain soldiers)
- *The Others* (because all along, they thought the house was being haunted when it was *them* haunting the house *and* because all along the mother enforces strict Christian rules when, in the end, it was she who had sinned)

- *Terms of Endearment* (when Emma begins to die, her mother begins to live)
- *Rain Man* (in the end, Charlie is taught life's lessons from Raymond who, ironically, is incapable of understanding them).
- *Jerry Maguire* (after struggling to change his value system from egotistical, greedy sports agent, who's "good at friendship, bad at intimacy," Jerry almost loses everything. In fact, even after his commitment to change, he does lose his girl, Dorothy, and then his star player, Rod Tidwell, is critically injured. But, in the end, Rod comes back and winds up with a huge contract. Ironically, it's the money that pushes Jerry back into Dorothy's arms, so it was all for nothing).

7. THE DENOUEMENT: THE NEW OLD WORLD

The Denouement exists almost as an epilogue in a story. It's a chance for the reader to catch their breath after the Climax. Denouements should not be long. Once your Climax is over, your story is done, so you should get out as quickly as possible. The last *Lord of the Rings* movie, *The Return of the King*, is a perfect example of what *not* to do. I thought that thing was never going to end. The ring had already been destroyed, so the movie was over. It didn't have the same ending as the book where Sauron comes back and levels the Shire, so it went straight from there to an extremely extended Denouement. Halfway through it I was thinking I should already be home eating Cheetos and watching *Criminal Minds*.

You don't want your readers impatiently waiting for the end of your book. It's much better to end the book sooner rather than later and leave them wanting more.

The Denouement exists primarily for two reasons; the first is to give you a chance to wrap up any loose ends you might still have hanging around from any of your plot lines, and the second is more important.

If the Hero was successful, it's a chance to show him back in the real world, having completed his journey, with the "Elixir" he brought back with him. The Elixir may be treasure, new found love, freedom, or even just the knowledge that the special world he encountered exists. Anything, really. It is usually reflective of the goal the Hero was trying to attain throughout his quest.

Whatever it is, the Hero is not the same as he was before the journey. The Elixir he returned with, combined with the changes in himself, have caused a change in the world, and it is here that we see it. The world is a better place for the ordeal the Hero faced because somehow he endured.

If the hero wasn't successful, it's a chance to see how his ordeal and lack of success ultimately affected him and the world around him.

This is a very important scene to include as, without it, your story loses much of its power and meaning. In a lot of ways, the Denouement is the flip side of the coin you showed the readers during the Setup stage of Act I.

It's also very important to start your story before the protagonist ventures on his journey with his attributes "set" as far away from how he'll wind up after his journey as possible. The difference between the two is your character arc as we've just discussed, and you want to make the arc as great as possible. Just make sure you have a dynamic dichotomy going between who your protagonist is at the beginning of your story when he is simply the Initiate—the archetype of the character just starting out, and who he will become as the Hero—the archetype of the character returning from the journey. The larger your difference, the more emotional impact your story will have, and the greater power it will bring to your readers.

We can take a classic example of a Denouement from Shakespeare's *Hamlet*.

During the Climax of *Hamlet*, Hamlet fences with Laertes. After several rounds, the Queen Gertrude inadvertently drinks wine that has been poisoned by Hamlet's uncle Claudius. Between bouts, Laertes pierces Hamlet with his poisoned sword.

This begins a new melee, during which Hamlet uses Laertes's own sword against him. Gertrude then stumbles and falls to the floor, telling Hamlet she's been poisoned in her last dying breath.

In the Denouement, the dying Laertes reconciles with the dying Hamlet and reveals Claudius's evil plot against him. Hamlet uses the poisoned sword against Claudius and forces him to drink his own poisoned wine, just to make sure he dies, too.

In his final moments, Hamlet names a new heir to the throne. Horatio, Hamlet's best friend, attempts to kill himself in his despair, but Hamlet stops him, explaining that someone must live in order to give a full account of everything that took place.

In the end, Hamlet's body is ordered to be borne off in honor.

Ill. 1-9: The death of Hamlet. The Denouement to one of Shakespeare's greatest tragedies.

JOURNEYS UNDER THE MOON

8. RETURNING WITH THE ELIXIR

Superficially, the journey is all about obtaining the goal the protagonist set out for in the beginning (or the one it turned out to be once his goals all changed halfway through the quest). That goal can be anything. It can be a princess's hand in marriage, it might be gold and treasure, it might be the keys to the kingdom, it might be learning how to live again, it might be finding true love, it might be to save the world.

Achieving this goal will change your protagonist. He will become a Hero and the goal he achieved or obtained is the Elixir.

The Elixir is what the Hero returns to the old world with and because of the Elixir, and the changes in the Hero, the old world is now different. It is a better place than it was before the Hero set out on his journey when he was just a simple man without his heroic skills, knowledge, and power.

The traditional story of the Hero returning with the Elixir is the tale of Jason and the Argonauts and their quest for the Golden Fleece.

The story goes like this:

Athaman the Minyan was king of the city of Orchomenus in Boeotia. He took Nephele as his first wife and bore two children, a boy named Phrixus and a girl named Helle. Later, Athamus became enamored with Ino and left Nephele to marry her. Nephelle departed Athamus in anger, bringing drought upon the land.

But Ino was jealous of her stepchildren and, so, she plotted their deaths.

Knowing this, Nephelle's spirit appeared to the children one night with a winged ram with fleece of gold.

Ill. 1-10: Jason from Jason and the Argonauts, in search of the Golden Fleece.

The ram had been created by Poseidon. She told the children they must get away before Ino kills them and so, climbing upon the ram's back, they flew far out over the sea, but, in the process, Helle unfortunately fell and drowned.

The place she drowned at is now known as Hellspont.

The ram continued onward, taking Phrixus safely to Colchis.

Once there, Phrixus sacrificed the ram back to Poseidon, and it became the constellation Aries. However he kept its Golden Fleece on an oak grove sacred to Ares where it was guarded by a dragon.

The Golden Fleece remained there until Pinder employed Jason and his Argonauts to set out on their voyage to retrieve it.

Now, this story doesn't tell you the journey of Jason and his Argonauts, it only explains the origins of their end goal: the Golden Fleece. It is this Elixir that they risked life and limb to obtain. It was the "Holy Grail" of their expedition. It is important that, in your stories, your Heroes have goals. Even if the goal is just to find themselves, the goal should be made prominent and evident. The goal provides motivation for your characters and gives them the will to go on, even when the outlook is at its bleakest.

EXERCISES

1. Come up with a Climax

    Outline a Climax to your story using mythic journey structure. Ask yourself these questions and write the answers in your notebook:

    1) What is my initial plan? It needs to be both crazy and still have an element of rationality.
    2) The plan has to start out looking like it might work, despite the odds, but things turn bad. Soon it is obvious that the plan will not work.
    3) To make matters worse, the antagonist has created some kind of ticking clock. Think of the sort of things that could be used as ticking clocks. Someone old and dying that the protagonist needs to say goodbye to. The oxygen in a scuba suit. Money. For Cinderella it was until the stroke of midnight when she once again became a simple house maiden. Think about your story and come up with a ticking clock that the antagonist can use against the protagonist in the Climax.
    4) The protagonist has no Plan B. It's over. Everything looks bleak. He's in way over his head. It is now that he must reach deep inside himself and pull out that last good idea and has to be something he would never have considered before starting his journey. It has to be connected to the divine in some way. If you have a group or a team, it is the protagonist alone who comes up with this second solution. It's usually just in the nick of time, too. This is where brainstorming (or mind mapping) comes in. Think of all the different ideas your almost-hero could

come up with. The cleverer the idea, the better your story.

5) The protagonist implements the new plan and succeeds. The day has been saved. He may die in his effort, but he will have died a success. It is after this success that he goes through a resurrection contrasting to the death he experienced in the All is Lost stage at the end of Act II. Your protagonist is resurrected as the Hero. He is no longer the person he was when he started his journey, nor will he ever be again. Think of how you can work the resurrection into your Climax and write down a few sentences.

Remember; just make quick notes through all this. This shouldn't be more than a paragraph or three long. Then sit back and feel good about yourself. You just wrote your first blockbuster Climax.

2. Write a Denouement
Outline a denouement to your story. This should be very simple now that you have the rest outlined. Look back at the setup of your book first. The key to the denouement lies there. The denouement is the antithesis of the Setup. You want to show how much your Hero has changed due to his struggles and how much the world has changed for having the new version of him in it.

3. Try to write an ironic Ending
This one's for those of you who like challenges.
See if you can come up some ideas to give the story you've been outlining an ironic resolution to the plot. Remember, ironic endings are endings where things are left ambiguous or the protagonist manages to acquire the goal he has been after all

along only to find it isn't what he'd hoped for. The world was actually better without it. Look at the examples I gave earlier in this part of the book.

KEY POINTS

- Traditionally, right at the beginning of Act III, all the subplots remerge. It is the romantic subplot where the important things happen. The protagonist generally gets the girl back and, in doing so, also come s up with an initial plan to use against the bad guys at the Climax.
- If the story has a lot of subplots, they will often remerge at a party or a wedding of some sort.
- If there's a chase scene in the story, it will often appear here too.
- Climaxes follow a basic structure. The would-be hero (or team) goes in with a half-witted plan that sounds crazy but has the semblance of rationale to it. Just enough that it *might* work, and since that's all they've got, they go with it. Initially, the plan starts working all right but soon the tide changes and the antagonist gets the upper hand. Now the good guys are in trouble. To make matters worse, the antagonist unleashes some sort of ticking clock. Now the protagonist reaches deep down in his soul for that one idea that he never would've even considered before going through his ordeal and what he pulls out comes from the divine. It's what Blake Snyder, author of *Save the Cat!* calls the God Moment. The protagonist puts this new plan into action and successfully wins the day.
- It's important that, after or during the final showdown with the antagonist, the protagonist experiences a resurrection of sorts to correspond to the death he experienced in the All is Lost scene at the end of Act II. It's not until he is "resurrected" that he becomes the true Hero and is able to achieve the Elixir.

- Returning home with the Elixir, we enter the final stage of Act III, the denouement. In this stage, it's important to show how much the protagonist has changed and how much the world has changed for him being in it. They should either no longer be flawed or flawed in a different manner than before.

CHAPTER SEVEN

Studying Structure

> *Fraud and falsehood only dread examination. Truth invites it.*
>
> —Samuel Johnson[11]

1. PICKING UP THAT PEN

Whether you are reading a book, watching a movie, or just lying around on the sofa watching television, you should take the time to study what you are taking in, because it's all story and, at its basic level, story is story. It doesn't matter if it's a novel, a movie, or even a puppet show, you can learn something from it. Even bad stories have something to teach us. In fact, sometimes you learn more from bad writing then you do from good writing.

The best way to examine structure is to do it formally, with paper and pen in hand and break out each part of the three act structure as it comes up. Sometimes that's not feasible, though, or sometimes you're just too lazy to go to all that trouble. During those times, just do it in your head. Say to yourself, "Okay, that was the Inciting Event." Then: "All right, there's the first Pivot Point. Now we're in Act II."

You can get really anal retentive about examining structure (and I do this a lot) and download free movie scripts off the Internet and follow along with DVDs you have at home. Usually, I like to break out movies

---

[11] Samuel Johnson (1709 - 1784) was an English poet, critic, and writer.

after I've watched them for enjoyment purposes at least once. With the script in hand, you're almost certain not to miss anything.

Reading movie scripts is fun and an education in itself. And they're easy to find online. A good site is *Drew's Script-O'Rama*, but there are many others out there. Just Google "download free movie scripts" and you will find a whole slew of them. What's important, though, is that you aren't too picky about which scripts you want. Many are unavailable, but at the same time, lots are out there waiting to be downloaded. I spent weeks looking for the script for Pixar's *The Lorax* and never did find it. Not for free, anyway.

Also, if possible, you want to grab the "shooting script." This is usually the final or close-to-final script that made it onto the screen. Quite often, especially with classic or popular movies, there will be many different versions available of scripts in progress. *Star Wars*, for instance, has at least ten scripts that are easily found, ranging from early drafts right through to the one they shot for the big screen.

However you do it, practice breaking down stories. The more you do it, the better you'll get at it, and soon it will just come naturally for you. In fact, soon you'll just feel the different parts of the three act structure before they even come into play. That's what you want. Because at that point, it's like playing piano. Your subconscious has absorbed it enough that, when you're writing, you'll be putting these parts into your own work automatically. They will just spin out of the right side of your brain the way they should and suddenly your writing will take a giant leap forward. You'll be creating very sellable, professional, and commercial fiction.

2. MOTION PICTURE BREAK OUTS

Now I'll go over some major motion pictures and break them out according to the three act structure I presented in Part I of this book. I've only listed a very small handful of movies for a number of reasons. Mainly because there are so many books available that break out movies. But also because, with all the information I've given you in this book, you can do it yourself. And you'll learn a lot more from doing it yourself than you will from reading my breakouts.

Casablanca

Robert McKee, the writer of *Story*, calls *Casablanca* the best picture ever made. Trust me, I know. I went to a three day seminar of Mr. McKee's and the last day was spent watching *Casablanca*. The entire day. Eight hours of it. We would watch the movie for five minutes and then discuss what happened on the screen for twenty minutes. Then watch five minutes more, then discuss for another twenty. It almost hurts to talk about the movie anymore to this date. I can practically recite it from memory.

Having had this experience, though, I must say that I do think he's onto something. *Casablanca* has a lot going for it. I'm not sure if it's a perfect film—or at least as perfect as McKee thinks it is—but it's pretty close.

Let's see if I can break it out. I'll try to do it considerably faster than he did.

ACT I
Setup

We see refugees being rounded up by policemen and are told the scum of Europe has gravitated to Casablanca. We are showed that we are in the time of occupied France. A plane lands, a swastika clearly visible on its tail. From the plane exits Major Strasser, a hardened German. He is greeted by the Prefect of Police in Casablanca, Captain Louis Renault, among others.

Strasser asks what has been done about the murders of the couriers. Renault tells him his men are rounding up twice the usual suspects. The German Consul, Heinze, says they already know who the murderer is. Strauss says, "Good, is he in custody?"

Renault tells him there's no hurry. He'll be at Rick's tonight. Everybody comes to Rick's. Strasser says he's already heard about this café and about Mr. Rick himself.

At Rick's that night, we see a refugee and another man arrange a deal for fifteen thousand francs in cash.

Meanwhile, we see Rick deal with an angry customer who wants to gamble, but Rick won't let him. When asked about the couriers, Rick says they caught a lucky break. Yesterday they were just couriers—now they're the honored dead. Ugarte tells him he is a very cynical person. Ugarte provides exit visas to refugees. But after tonight, he says, he'll be done and he'll be through with Casablanca. He shows Rick an envelope and tells him it contains letters of transit. He says he can sell them for more money than even Rick can ever imagine.

Inciting Event

Since Rick is the only man Ugarte trusts, he asks him to hang onto the letters of transit for him.

Debate

Rick considers Ugarte's request, finally saying he will, but not overnight. Then Rick stops Ugarte and says he heard a rumor that those couriers were carrying letters of transit. Ugarte says he heard that rumor too.

o ACT I/ACT II Pivot Point

Rick has just stuck his neck out for someone for the first time in the movie when all along he's kept saying, "I don't stick my neck out for nobody." He's already not sticking to his own rules. Inevitably, it's what's going to turn his world upside-down.

ACT II
Raising the Stakes / Building the Suspense

Strasser tells Rick they're going to make an arrest in his club tonight. Rick realizes it's Ugarte. Strasser says he can't warn him. There's no way out. Rick tells him not to worry, he doesn't stick his neck out for nobody.

This is the movie's common theme: "Rick sticks his neck out for nobody." He says it several times through the story. He also doesn't like politics.

After the arrest, Strasser questions Rick, especially in regards to one Victor Laszlo, a resistance leader who has come to Casablanca. When he is done questioning, Laszlo comes through the door with Ilsa Lund on his arm. She is beautiful and used to be Rick's beloved. Strasser questions Laszlo before Rick has a chance to see Ilsa, but Sam, the piano player, notices her right away. He pretends he doesn't though.

When Laszlo leaves Ilsa alone, she asks the waitress to have the piano player wheel his piano to her table. Ilsa asks Sam about Rick. He tells her to leave him alone and that she's bad luck. Then she asks Sam to play the song "As Time Goes By" for her.

Act II Midpoint

Sam starts playing the song and Rick immediately comes out yelling at him that he had told him to never play that song again. But he sees Ilsa sitting there and stops short.

Rick now spends the rest of Act II torn over the reappearance of Ilsa. He makes Sam play *him* the song one night when the two of them are alone in the bar after curfew. He gets all maudlin and melancholy.

We are given a flashback to Paris where Ilsa and Rick parted ways. They were supposed to meet up later at the train station but Ilsa didn't show. This is why Rick's been bitter ever since.

It turns out she never came to meet Rick because she was married to Victor Laszlo and while dating Rick, she thought Laszlo was dead. Then she had found out he wasn't.

It turns out Rick has quite a record, according to Laszlo. He ran guns to Ethiopia. He fought against the fascists in Spain. Laszlo finds it strange that Rick always seemed to be fighting for the underdog.

Darkness Closes In

Laszlo tries to buy the letters of transit for him and Ilsa. Rick isn't selling. Laszlo doesn't understand. Rick tells him to ask his wife.

Rick's Place is closed on shady political grounds he's caught in the middle of.

All Is Lost

Ilsa comes to Rick asking for the letters of transit. She tells him he can ask his price. When he says no, she calls him a coward. When he still won't sell them, she pulls out a gun. He gives her the letters. They kiss passionately.

Dark Night before Dawn

Ilsa tells Rick that she was married to Victor and found out he was alive and that's why she hadn't met up with him at the train station. She tells Rick she's always loved him and that she'll stay with him this time.

- **ACT II/ACT III Pivot Point**

Rick is back to the way he was in Paris. He realizes he's spent years being a bitter man for the wrong reasons.

ACT III
Subplots Intertwine

Rick and Laszlo have a discussion the next day, and Rick sees how passionate Laszlo is about his cause.

Climax

Rick tells Renault he's concocted a plan to set up Laszlo with the letters of transit so the Germans will get him on a silver platter. In return, he wants Ilsa's safety assured. He will leave with Ilsa on the flight and hand Victor Laszlo over to the Germans at the airport. It's all a lie to save Laszlo and get him safely out of Casablanca. Rick even lies to Ilsa to get her to go on the plane with Laszlo because he knows it's best for her.

They barely make the flight. Victor Laszlo shakes Rick's hand before boarding the plane.

Denouement

Rick's stuck his neck out for somebody. Again.

The Germans get there just a moment too late to do anything about the plane taking off. Strasser starts to call the tower, but Rick shoots him right in front of Renault. Strasser expects Renault to arrest Rick, but instead Renault's reaction is to, "Round up the usual suspects."

Juno

Plot Summary

The movie is best summarized by its tagline: A comedy about growing up . . . and the bumps along the way. In fact, this is an important view of the movie when it comes to deciphering what the actual Climax is, as we shall see.

ACT I
Setup

We meet Juno MacGuff, a witty teenager probably too smart for her own good. The story opens with a Juno voice-over with the prophetic words: "It started with a chair." Then we flash back and see what happened in that chair. Juno and her friend Bleeker, who is a friend with benefits, had "benefits" in it. It's a chair that is now in a front yard with Juno seated upon it drinking Sunny D.

Inciting Event

Juno soon finds out what she expected: that she's expecting. She's preggers.

Debate

Being pregnant leaves Juno trying to decide what to do about it. She tells her friend, Leah, that she's pregnant. Leah just assumes Juno's going to get an abortion. She asks Juno if she wants her to call the clinic for her. Juno says no, she'll call herself.

Juno tells Bleeker, the baby's father, about her condition. He asks what she's going to do. She eludes, in a very Junoesque way, that she'll be "taking care of it"—if it's okay with him, that is.

He says he guesses that it is.

On Juno's way out the door to the abortion clinic, we meet Juno's dad and stepmom, Bren, who's obsessed with dogs.

At the clinic, there's a single protester outside. Juno knows her. They strike up casual conversation before Juno goes inside. As Juno walks away, the protester (Su-Chin) yells, "Your baby probably has a beating heart, you know. It can feel pain. And it has fingernails."

Inside the clinic, Juno finds the clinic very "clinicky" (which is a word I just made up). Juno looks at all the other women, sitting there, waiting to see a doctor. Suddenly, all Juno can see is their fingernails. Su-Chin has got to her. The scene cuts away to Juno entering her friend Leah's house, out of breath and sighing.

She couldn't follow through with it.

- ○ **ACT I/ACT II Pivot Point**

Juno decides to put the baby up for adoption. She's made a decision that she knows will change her immediate and possibly her far ranging future.

ACT II

Unlike a lot of stories, the subplot doesn't start right away. Instead we have Juno and Leah going through the Penny Saver ads looking for adoptive parents for her baby. They find a couple that sounds promising.

We cut away to Bleeker in his bedroom. His mom calls from downstairs, telling him that Juno phoned for him earlier. We discover that she doesn't like Juno very much.

Meanwhile, Juno and Leah break the news of Juno's pregnancy to Juno's dad and her stepmom. They tell them about Juno wanting to put the baby up for adoption. Surprisingly, her parents take the news quite well. Her dad says he's coming with her to meet these prospective new parents. Juno agrees that's a good idea.

We meet the couple—Mark and Vanessa. They are perfect. They have it all: a good relationship; a nice house; they live in a nice neighbourhood; the whole shebang.

There's a lawyer present for the meeting. Everyone decides on a closed adoption. So far, things seem to be going swimmingly. In fact, the only reason we're not bored as an audience from lack of conflict is due to the witty writing which is extremely good.

Subplots

The one and only subplot in the movie takes off now. It will become a very important plot line throughout the remainder of the story.

Juno finds out she has common interests in music with Mark. The two of them end up in Mark's bedroom discussing music for a short while with Juno checking out Mark's musical instruments. This Juno/Mark relationship is our "B" Plot.

Raising the Stakes / Building the Tension

At school, word starts to get out that Juno's pregnant. However, nobody realizes Bleeker is the father of the baby.

ACT II Midpoint

A Plot: Time moves ahead pretty quickly. We get to Juno's five month ultrasound. Juno sees her baby for the first time. Bren, her stepmom, is with her. We see that their relationship is far from the stereotypical daughter/stepmom relationship when Bren sticks up for Juno after the ultrasound technician says something insulting to her. It's an emotionally high point in the movie. This is an example of taking a classic archetype, the Wicked Stepmother, and turning it on its head to make it fresh and unexpected. Diablo Cody, the writer of *Juno* actually does this quite a bit through the movie.

Continue Raising the Stakes / Building Tension

Both plot lines continue to rise in tension as they weave back and forth.

B Plot: Juno goes to visit Mark and Vanessa on her own so she can show them the pictures from the ultrasound. Vanessa isn't home. Juno and Mark wind up watching a horror movie together. They have a lot in common. The audience gets the feeling there might be something happening between them.

Vanessa comes home and finds the two of them together. By her reaction, we get the feeling <u>she</u> thinks there is something between them, too.

Mark and Vanessa walk Juno back to her car and Vanessa mentions she's worried Juno might back out of the deal once she has the baby. Juno says she won't.

When she gets home, Bren gives Juno crap for going to Mark and Vanessa's. She says it was inappropriate.

A Plot: Juno goes to Bleeker's and finally tells him about the private adoption situation she's hooked up. She says nobody's going to tell his folks it's his baby. Bleeker says he's relieved by that.

B Plot: We cut to Mark and Vanessa's house. Vanessa's painting the baby's room. Mark tells her she should wait. It turns into a fight.

A Plot: Juno and Leah go to the mall and spot Vanessa there. Juno tells her the baby is kicking and let's Vanessa feel it. Vanessa says it's magical.

B Plot: Juno's on the phone, talking to Mark about a weird CD he made her that she's been listening to. We're really getting the feeling that something's going on between them.

A Plot: Juno finds out Bleeker is going to the prom with another girl, Katrina De Voort. This pisses Juno off, even though she and Bleeker are supposed to be just "friends with benefits". She winds up taking a side off of him in the hallway at school.

B Plot: Juno drives in anger to Mark and Vanessa's house. When Mark answers the door, the first thing she asks is: "Is Vanessa here?" Mark's answer: "Nope. We're safe." Juno: "Cool." All this dialogue completely points to a covert love affair in the works.

Darkness Closes In

Mark tells Juno he has something for her. He gives her a comic with a pregnant Japanese girl on the front, kicking ass and taking names. The comic is called *Most Fruitful Yuki*. Mark puts on some music. A slow song comes on that he says he danced to at his prom. Juno says she can just picture him slow dancing like a dork. She mockingly places her hands on Mark's waist and begins to move back and forth. Soon they are dancing.

All is Lost

Juno's belly bumps up against Mark. Mark says, "I feel like there's something between us," and they both laugh. Juno puts her head on Mark's chest and he pulls her close and says, "I'm leaving Vanessa."

Juno freaks out about this. We find out, as Juno is yelling and Mark is defending, that Mark did indeed have feelings for Juno, but those feelings were not reciprocal. Mark suddenly realizes Juno is just a teenage girl and calls himself an idiot. Juno begs him not to get a divorce. She wants him and Vanessa to adopt her baby.

On her way out the door, Juno passes Vanessa who asks her what's wrong. Then Vanessa asks Mark why Juno's crying. Then, right in front of Juno, Mark proceeds to tell Vanessa that he doesn't think he's ready to be a father. Juno runs to her vehicle and drives off.

Dark Night before Dawn

Juno pulls over to the side of the rode and buckles over the steering wheel, crying—unwinding for the first time since she became pregnant.

Everything has changed now. All hope she had about having a normal life again after all this is now lost.

- **ACT II/ACT III Pivot Point**

Once again, Juno's life has been turned upside down. She had spent Act II becoming used to the idea of being pregnant and that she would be giving up the baby at the end of her pregnancy. Now she's forced to re-evaluate everything she's gone through up until now. She's re-evaluating her relationship with Mark and Vanessa (especially Mark). And she's re-evaluating her decision to not have an abortion in the first place.

Act III

The scene cuts to Bleeker in his room with his guitar and then back to Juno. When we're back to Juno, she's lying on the hood of her car, contemplating her future. The camera pushes in as she gets an idea.

Subplots Intertwine

Hopping off the hood, she rummages through her vehicle and finds a crumpled up Jiffy Lube receipt. She unfolds it and pulls out a pen, ready to write something...

The Climax

We go back to Mark and Vanessa's and watch as their relationship begins wrapping up. They're being coldly civil to each other.

There's a loud knock on the front door.

Mark opens the door and sees Juno pulling away in her van. There's a folded piece of paper on the doormat. He unfolds it and holds it up the wrong way. "It looks like a bill from Jiffy Lube," he says.

Vanessa takes the note, turns it over, and reads it. "It's for me," she says.

That's the Climax. It's a pretty passive Climax and actually ends without resolution until later in the Denouement, but we know something wonderful was written on that piece of paper. It's enough of a Climax for a small movie like this. In fact, it's perfect.

Now, let me pause here and say that some of you might be tempted to say that the Climax of the movie is when Juno has the baby. After all, that's a pretty intense part, right? Sure, but it's not the Climax of the *story*. The story is about Juno growing up. It's been all about her getting pregnant and figuring out what to *do* with the baby, not *having* the baby.

For this reason, the actual birth belongs in the Denouement and not here.

The Denouement

Juno meets with Bleeker and divulges that she is actually in love with him. He tells her he feels the same.

We move ahead to Juno lying in her room, staring at the celling. Suddenly, she sits up, thoroughly freaked out. She finds her father and tells him her water just broke.

Juno has a baby boy. Vanessa is at the hospital. She gets to see her son. Juno and Bleeker decide they don't want to see him. He never felt like theirs.

Juno shares a special moment with her dad.

The scene cuts to the nursery in Vanessa's house, focusing on an antique rocker. There's another Juno voice-over, bookending the one that opened the film: "It ended with a chair." The camera pans past a framed note on the wall (it's the handwritten note Juno left on the doorstep on the back of the Jiffy Lube receipt). It says: *Vanessa—if you're still in, I'm still in. Juno.*

The final image of the film is Juno and Bleeker sitting on the street curb with Bleeker playing guitar and the two of them singing.

Star Wars: A New Hope

You can only have one Hero in your story. This is an airtight, case is closed, no messing with rule. Even in *the Lord of the Rings* where there's an entire movie devoted to the *Return of the King*, the King isn't the Hero. The Hero was established in the first book (or movie). It's Frodo. The rule of thumb is that your Hero is whichever character experiences the greatest emotional change throughout your story and has the biggest character arc. Frodo literally goes to hell and back to rid Middle-earth of the Ring of Power and the journey changes him in ways he could never have imagined before leaving. The King—Aragorn—isn't much different in the third book (or movie) than he was in the first. He might get a title credit, but he's not the Hero.

I point this out because when Lucas filmed *Star Wars*, he almost messed up. It wasn't his fault. It was actually Harrison Ford's fault. Ford played such a strong role as Han Solo, he managed to make the audience see a change in his character that was never really in the script. Han Solo came full circle from a dastardly space pirate to someone trustworthy who returned in the end to help the Rebellion right when they needed him most. The audience fell in love with Han Solo and, because of this, his change nearly trumped the change in Luke Skywalker—the real Hero of the story. If it had it would have caused a conflict of Heroes and made the ending of the movie much less satisfactory. Luckily, Luke's journey to find himself was strong enough to hold up to Han's unforeseen development and, in the end, everything worked out fine.

ACT I
Setup

Star Wars opens on action. We see the Imperial Cruiser, larger than anything we've ever seen in theatres before, engulfing the small Rebel ship and then we cut to the evil Darth Vader invading the ship and capturing Princess Leia, but not before Leia inserts a message into a small droid. The droids manage to get into an escape pod and leave the battle scene. They are left unharmed because "no life is detected" on their vessel. They crash land on Tatooine, a dust planet. The droids are found by Jawas—basically nomadic tradespeople—and are purchased by Luke Skywalker and his Uncle Owen. Luke is a moisture farmer who works for his uncle and aunt. He dreams of joining the Rebellion, but his uncle tells him he can't because he still needs him for at least one more season on the farm.

Inciting Event

While trying to fix one of the droids, Luke accidentally retrieves part of the message Princess Leia recorded into R2D2. It seems to be for someone named "Obi-Wan Kenobi" and Luke wonders if the girl in the message means old Ben Kenobi. He takes the droid to Ben and discovers Ben and Obi-Wan are the same person and that Ben knew Luke's father. Luke also learns his father was a great Jedi master and Ben tells him he should join the Rebellion and learn the ways of the Force. Obi-Wan is the classic Mentor archetype. Not only does he wind up teaching Luke the ways of the Force, right in this opening scene where we meet him, he gives Luke his father's light saber. Giving useful gifts is a primary action of Mentors.

Debate

Luke is torn. He wants to do what Ben says but he knows his uncle will never permit it. He has no choice in the matter. Ben gives him a ride home in his sand speeder.

- **ACT I/ACT II Pivot Point**

Luke arrives home to find Imperial storm troopers have burnt his home and killed his aunt and uncle while looking for the droids. Now, not only is there nothing stopping Luke from joining the Rebellion, his determination to do something about the war is more fixed than ever. He is driven.

ACT II
Subplots

Luke and Obi-Wan head to the cantina. The beginning of Act II is the traditional place to have a bar scene, even if this bar scene is a little out of the ordinary. It's a chance for the protagonist to encounter a bunch of new people in the new world and have to sort out very quickly which ones are friends and which are foes. This is what happens with Luke here in the Cantina where we meet Han Solo and Chewbacca. This is also the start of another plotline, which really gives us three plots going at this point, although we haven't really been privy to the "C" Plot yet.

"A" Plot: Luke must save the princess who left the message on the R2 droid.

"B" Plot: Han will give Luke and Ben passage on the Millennium Falcon. In return, he gets part of the reward for rescuing the princess and will use it to pay the bounty Jabba the Hut put on his head. Luke's not quite sure he can trust Han yet. Luke and company get chased off Tatooine by a couple of Star Destroyers.

"C" Plot: Princess Leia is captive onboard the Death Star. Vader's men ask her for the location of the Rebel base. She lies and gives them the name of a deserted planet. They destroy her home planet of Alderaan instead, both as a warning and as a display of the Death Star's capability to destroy planets.

Raising the Stakes / Building the Suspense

Onboard the Falcon, Ben teaches Luke in the ways of the Force. The Falcon runs into the Death Star and gets caught in a tractor beam. The team is able to hide while the ship is searched. They find out the princess is onboard the battle station. Han emphasizes that he's only in this for the money. After that, he's gone.

Dressing up as storm troopers, temporarily slipping on the mask of the Shapeshifter archetype, Han and Luke take Chewie to the detention area where Princess Leia is being held.

Act II Midpoint

Luke manages to free Leia in a shootout, but Vader senses the presence of Obi-Wan Kenobi. Now everything's been reset to a whole new level of danger.

Darkness Closes In

The team is trapped in the garbage room with the walls closing in and no way out. R2D2 barely manages to get them out in time and save their lives.

All Is Lost

Obi-Wan Kenobi is struck down dead by Darth Vader in a light saber fight as Luke and the rest of the gang race for the Millennium Falcon. For a moment, just before he dies, Ben slips on the mask of the Martyr archetype. Note that Mentor archetypes are probably the most versatile of all archetypes. The death beat here in the story makes the All Is Lost point particularly dark and tragic.

Ben managed to get the tractor beam taken out, but Vader's men have a homing beacon on Han's ship. Han makes the jump to lightspeed and heads for the Rebel base on Yavin V. Once again, we are reminded by a point made by Leia how Han is only in it for the money.

Dark Night before Dawn

They've seen the power of the Death Star. Aldaraan has been destroyed. It looks like everyone is doomed.

- **ACT II/ACT III Pivot Point**

Luke gathers all his strength to engage in a battle plan designed by the Rebels to be launched from their secret base on Yavin V. It will try to take advantage of a vulnerability the Rebels think they've found in the Death Stars design.

ACT III
Subplots Intertwine
A Potential Solution

Everyone reunites at the Rebel base on Yavin V. The Rebels have found one potential weak point in the Death Star's design, and to exploit it will require some very accurate shooting. They have a plan, but it has to go off without a hitch. They go over the plan and, through dialogue, we discover that the plan is both crazy but, at the same time, has a shred of rationality to it.

Climax

The rebels start their attack runs, but take on heavy casualties. Their number one shooter ends up being blown to bits. Now it's up to Luke. Luke comes in low, takes aim . . . and misses. It's over. He knows it. He's ready to give up. Furthermore, Han just took his reward money and left like he said he was going to. Luke actually thought he was better than that.

Luke comes in for his final run. It's the only chance he has left before the Death Star blows the Rebel base to smithereens. Then he hears Ben's voice in his head: "Use the Force, Luke."

But Luke's taking heavy fire from behind and R2D2's been injured. He can't shake the tie fighters behind him. Until . . . something starts blowing up the ships on his tail. He looks back and it's Han. He's returned! Now it's clear sailing right to the target area!

Once again, Ben's voice echoes in Luke's head. "Use the Force, Luke."

Unhooking his targeting gear and his nav computer, Luke goes in blind to make his final shot just in time.

His hit is successful! The shot goes straight down the blast hole and into the Death Star's reactor, exploding it from the inside. The Rebels win!

Darth Vader, however, manages to escape the exploding Death Star at the last minute, spinning away in his custom tie-fighter.

Denouement

The end of the story shows Luke and Han receiving medals for their work in helping the Rebellion. We also see a finely polished C3P0 and R2D2. There's a celebration and fireworks and everyone not wearing a black helmet goes home happy.

The Help

ACT I
Setup

When the movie starts, we are very quickly given a firm setting in Jackson, Mississippi in the early 1960's. We meet Aibileen, a black maid for a white southern woman, Miss Leefolt, who mistreats her. We also meet Skeeter, a young woman who wants desperately to make it as a writer. She gets a job with a magazine writing "Miss Myrna" letters. We are also introduced to most of the other characters in the story, but just in passing.

Inciting Event

Aibileen helps Skeeter with her Miss Myrna column. However, what Skeeter really wants to do is publish a book written from the point of view of the black help and what it's like working for white folk. She asks Aibileen if she can interview her and says she will be paid for the work. Aibileen dismisses the idea out of hand, saying she couldn't begin to imagine the trouble she'd get into if someone caught her talking about Miss Leefolt.

Debate

Aibileen slowly begins to hate the treatment she receives from Miss Leefolt. When a tornado is about to hit the city, Aibileen is sent outside for something, being told that she shouldn't be so worried about a little rain. Instead, Aibileen goes into the bathroom she's forbidden to enter, making sure that Miss Leefolt sees her. Then she stands there with the door locked for a few minutes before flushing the toilet.

She is fired.

Now she could use the money from helping out Skeeter, but she tells Skeeter she's still hesitant because she doesn't want her house burned down.

Meanwhile, because of what Miss Lefolt did to Aibileen, one of Aibileen's friends, Minny, bakes Miss Lefolt a "special" chocolate cake and brings it over to her. The cake has her feces in it, and she tells Miss Lefolt this after she's ate her second piece.

Now Minny will never work in Jackson again. She's been blacklisted.

She tells Aibileen it was worth it, but Aibileen feels responsible and so she decides to take Skeeter up on her offer so she can give some of the money she'll make to Minny.

Skeeter wants more maids willing to be interviewed, but Aibileen thinks there's no way anybody else will ever agree.

- **ACT I/ACT II Pivot Point**

The biggest change in character has occurred in Aibileen, who has gone from a demure maid to finding her inner strength. She's stood up for herself, despite knowing she'd lose her job. She's now mustered the courage to talk openly about Miss Lefolt's mistreatment of her to Skeeter .

ACT II
Subplots

No fewer than four new subplots spin off almost immediately from the main "A" plot.

"B" Plot

Yule May, another maid, needs money for tuition to send her twin boys to college. She asks her employer, Hilly, for a seventy-five dollar advance, but is turned down.

"C" Plot

Minny does find a job after all. She takes work as Ceilia's maid. Celia can't cook or keep house, but she doesn't want her new husband to know this, so the fact that Minny's been brought on must be kept secret.

"D" Plot

Hilly Leefolt heads up the Junior League. They take on projects like the African's Children's Hunger and the Home Health Sanitation Initiative. During their meeting, there is some dispute about an initiative not being posted in the newsletter.

"E" Plot

A guy named Stuart is coming to town and being set up as a date for Skeeter. Her hopes are not very high.

Act II Midpoint

"A" Plot   Skeeter continues interviewing Aibileen. Minny comes in and gives Skeeter crap for taking advantage of Aibileen. Skeeter tries explaining that she's on their side and is hoping that maybe her work might change things. But the tension ramps up as the scene progresses until, finally, Minny leaves, slamming the door behind her. A few seconds later she comes back in and says, "Okay, I'll do it."

Now Skeeter has two maids willing to talk.

Raising the Stakes / Building the Suspense

"E" Plot   Skeeter goes on her date with Stuart and hates him. They have an argument at dinner and she storms off.

"C" Plot   Minny teaches Celia how to cook. Celia, in stark contrast to the other employers, tells Minny how grateful she is to have her coming by.

"A" Plot   This scene starts positive; Skeeter's editor, Miss Stein, calls and says she loves what Skeeter's done so far. It will sell, if they can release it soon. But they need to interview more maids. Skeeter gets off the phone and tells Minny and Aibileen they need to find a dozen more.

The scene quickly goes negative as they agree a dozen maids will be impossible to get. Then it goes even deeper into the black as Aibileen tells a story about her son dying.

"B" Plot   Skeeter asks Yule May to be interviewed, bringing up her boys going to college. She declines.

"E" Plot   Skeeter's date, Stuart, comes and apologies. He invites her for dinner again. They go.

Throughout the movie, the reminder of racism is constantly reinforced through the use of television and radio broadcasts. These grow more and more intense as the story continues; increasing the tension in what is otherwise a rather slow paced movie.

Darkness Closes In

"A" Plot   Colored people are asked to leave a bus because of a shooting, and a television news broadcast plays somberly in the background. Back at Aibileen's, Aibileen and Minny begin to worry about what they've done. What will happen if they're caught? Their worry ratchets up the suspense.

"C" Plot   Celia won't come out of the bathroom. Minny finally kicks in the door to find her lying in a pool of blood having just had a miscarriage. She tells Minny this is the third baby she's lost and she hasn't told her husband about any of them. This news hits Minny hard. It's scenes like these that keep the movie edgy.

"B" Plot   Yule May is arrested for stealing a ring from her employer, Hilly. It was a complete set up. Everyone knows it. This acts like a second Inciting Event three quarters of the way through the film.

"A" Plot   Skeeter goes back to Aibileen's to find twenty maids ready to talk now. The Yule May incident pushed them to action. One by one they begin to tell their stories, despite the danger.

"C" Plot   Celia shows up at Miss Leeloft's bridge party with a pie she made herself, but nobody will let her in because she got pregnant by Leeloft's ex-boyfriend. She leaves, grief stricken. Back at her place,

JOURNEYS UNDER THE MOON

Minny tells her not to take any more pies over there. She says they hate her because they think she's white trash. This scene turns the tables on the racism and shows it from a white perspective.

All Is Lost

"A" Plot   The news broadcasts hit a crescendo. John F. Kennedy is killed. Aibileen freaks out and thinks they're all in grave danger.

Minny says maybe they need some insurance of some kind. She finally tells them all the story of the feces pie and wants it included in the book. She says if that story is in the book, Hilly will go to her grave insisting the book isn't about Jackson, no matter what.

Dark Night Before Dawn

"A" Plot   Skeeter tells them they can't put it in the book. It's far too dangerous. Minny says fine, if that story's not in the book, she can pull the rest of her stories out, too. With great hesitation, Skeeter includes the pie story.

○ **ACT II/ACT III Pivot Point**

Stakes have been raised to a maximum. Tension is high. Skeeter is second guessing some of the things in the book, worried about a lawsuit. Aibileen thinks they might be in grave danger. If you look at Aibileen at the first Pivot Point and compare her with how she is here, it's almost a complete turnaround. Even our subsidiary plots have all gone dark.

ACT III
Subplots Intertwine

"ACDE" Plots Everyone attends the African Children's Benefit Ball put on by the Junior League. Stuart and Skeeter have really hit it off now. We see them kiss. Ceilia comes out drunk and confronts Miss Leeloft about what happened at her house and makes a scene.

A Potential Solution

"A" Plot   Skeeter finishes her book, but knows she must tell one more story, and for that, she needs information from her mother. She wants to know what happened to their old maid, the one she looked up to as a mother figure when she was a child because her own mother wasn't there for her.

Climax

"A" Plot   Skeeter asks her mother about the maid, Constantine. Constantine taught Skeeter everything she knows. Her mother tells the story in a flashback. We see that the maid was fired because the mother didn't want to look silly in front of her friends, not because the maid did anything wrong.

"I'm going to go find her," Skeeter says.

"Your father went up to Chicago and looked for Constantine the next day," her mother says. "She's dead."

"A" Plot   Skeeter and Hilly have a faceoff about the book that crescendos almost to a fist fight. Right at the top of the tension, Skeeter's mother comes outside and breaks it up, ridiculing Hilly and taking Skeeter's side.

Denouement

"A" Plot   Skeeter's book, *The Help*, is printed. She breaks the advance out between all the people who participated in writing it. The women around the neighborhood begin reading the book.

"E" Plot   Stuart, Skeeter's new boyfriend, is mad as hell about the book. He thinks she shouldn't have stirred up trouble and calls her selfish. They break up.

"A" Plot   Skeeter has a heart to heart with her mother where Skeeter's mother says she thinks courage must miss a generation and thanks her for bringing it back to the family. There's a bit of reconciliation about what happened to their old maid, Constantine.

"C" Plot   Celia's hubby, Johnny, comes up the drive just as Minny's walking into their house. Thinking she's been caught, she starts yelling. He tells her he's not going to hurt her. That he really wants to thank her. He's known all along that she's been here. They invite her in, where Celia's cooked an entire dinner by herself. Minny gets to keep her job and it no longer has to be a secret.

"A" Plot   Aibileen and Minny go to church where everyone claps for Aibileen. The preacher gives her a copy of *The Help* and says he knows she couldn't put her name on it, so they all put there's on it instead. Churches over two counties signed the book.

"A" Plot   Hilly fires Aibileen for apparently stealing some silver, even though it's a complete setup. She says she's calling the police. Aibileen tells the child to leave the room then says to Hilly, "I know something about you. Don't forget that."

She leaves the house and the movie ends with AIbileen doing a voice over, saying, "Once I told the truth about what it felt like to be me, I felt free." And her tears give way to a smile.

Toy Story

Toy story is what's called a "buddy movie" or a "buddy story". Like Thelma and Louise, it's tough to pick a main character. Note, however, that there *has to be a main character.* Even in buddy stories. It doesn't matter which one you pick, or if you like them both so much you simply can't choose which one you like the best, you *have* to. One of your characters has to lead. And if you don't know which it is when you start writing, you will by the time you're finished, because it's always the one in the story who changes the most emotionally. Or, to put it another way, the one who experiences the biggest character arc.

In the case of Toy Story, the main character is Woody. Buzz changes a lot, too. He learns to accept that he's just a toy which is a huge change on his part, but Woody learns to accept Buzz for who he is and that's a primal change. Primal changes are what you're looking for. These are the things Carl Jung said naturally attract us to storytelling. We want to see redemption in our fellow man or, in this case, our fellow toy. So really, Toy Story is all about acceptance.

Another thing you'll notice about Toy Story is how basic the storyline is. There's just one central plotline with absolutely no subplots, other than incidental "events" such as Andy moving, and so on. Even the villain is only fleshed out through the eyes of the principal characters. You only see him onscreen for seconds by himself. It makes for very clean story telling.

ACT I
Setup

During the setup we find out the toys come alive when no humans are around. We also learn that Andy is moving. We see Andy and Woody happy and that Woody is Andy's favorite toy. Then we hear the birthday party going on downstairs. The green army men are dispatched.

Inciting Event

Andy gets a Buzz Lightyear for his birthday. By the way he treats it, it feels suspiciously like Woody's been replaced by Buzz as the favorite toy.

Debate

Woody argues with Buzz about him not being a real Space Ranger and that he can't really fly. Buzz says he can and does some pretty impressive moves. Woody gets more and more frustrated until finally Woody drives a remote control car at him which, through a number of odd collisions, causes Buzz to fall out of Andy's bedroom window into the night.

- **ACT I/ACT II Pivot Point**

The remote control car tells the other toys this was no accident. The other toys all think Woody is a murderer and that Buzz is dead.

ACT II
Raising the Stakes / Building the Suspense

Unable to find Buzz, Andy grabs Woody to take him to Pizza Planet. Meanwhile, Buzz makes it into the minivan. He's not happy, but Woody and Buzz are once again joined up.

Believing it to be a rocket ship, Buzz jumps on a Pizza Planet delivery truck at the gas station. Woody is forced to follow him. Now they're separated from Andy. Separation is always good. It always causes tension.

Once they reach Pizza Planet, still separated from Andy, Buzz and Woody end up in the crane game. This is where the Sid element enters and the stakes and tension really begin to rise. Sid is the Shadow archetype of the story. He destroys toys and they fear him. Playing the crane game, Sid pulls Woody and Buzz from sea of alien toys they're in the game with.

ACT II Midpoint

At Sid's house, we see toy monstrosities: baby dolls with one eyes and spider legs, a toy fishing pole with fashion doll legs, a skateboard with a combat soldier's torso. All sorts of horrible mutations built by Sid. And Woody and Buzz are trapped with them all and the whole time, Andy's house is right next door. Yet there's nothing they can do to get there.

Instead of a high ACT II Midpoint Climax, this story has an emotionally low one—something you don't run into that often, but you do see occasionally. Remember, though, just like the Pseudo Climax being a false peak, this low point is a false low.

Buzz and Woody get a chance to escape from Sid's bedroom while Sid's eating dinner. While they do, Buzz sees a TV commercial for Buzz Lightyear toys and realizes he's not really a Space Ranger after all. Woody was right. He is just a toy. Buzz is crestfallen.

Back in Sid's room, the mutant toys reveal that they're actually just as scared of Woody and Buzz as Woody and Buzz are of them. They turn out to be quite friendly, despite the way they look.

Darkness Closes In

Sid comes in and pulls out a rocket. He decides he's going to blow Buzz into space. But right then, a storm hits. Sid decides to delay his launch until tomorrow.

All is Lost

Buzz is ready to give up, but Woody gives him a talk and tells him that right over there at that house next door is a kid who loves him. It takes some doing, but Buzz digs in his heels and regains his composure.

Dark Night before Dawn

Outside the door, Sid's dog Scud is waiting to eat Woody and Buzz if they leave Sid's room. Woody has no idea how to save Buzz.

- **ACT II/ACT III Pivot Point**

Buzz no longer thinks he's a Space Ranger, but he is happy just being Andy's toy. Woody is now ready to throw in the towel because he does not see any way out. Things have almost reversed for them from before.

ACT III
A Potential Solution

The mutant toys all gather around. Woody asks for their help, telling them he has a plan.

Climax

The next day, Sid takes Buzz outside to launch him with the rocket and all the toys come to life scaring the heck out of him. "From now on you must take good care of your toys, Sid," Woody says in a sickly voice. "Because if you don't, we'll find out . . . " Sid runs off, screaming.

Denouement

It's moving day and Andy's unhappy because he can't find Woody anywhere. Buzz and Woody see the moving van heading off and know they can't make it unless they do something drastic. So they do. They use the rocket that Sid was going to use on Buzz. They don't make it into the back of the van, though. Instead, they drop into the sun roof of the car and land right beside Andy in a box.

Part II

Writing Well

*don't be dull and boring and
pretentious, don't be consumed with self-love.
the libraries of the world have
yawned themselves to
sleep
over your kind.*

–Charles Bukowski[12]

---

[12] *Sifting through the Madness for the Word the Line the Way*, Charles Bukowski, *So you want to be a writer?* HarperCollins, New York, 2003

CHAPTER ONE

Some Notes on Style & Etiquette

Excellence is doing ordinary things extraordinarily well.

–John W. Gardner[13]

1. GETTING OUT THE WORDS

The act of writing well and consistently, especially if you wish to be at all prolific, really consists of staying in your chair in front of your computer and typing out words. The trick, I believe, is to not care so much what those words are.

Of course, I'm talking about first drafts.

First drafts don't matter—they're throwaways. Just get as many words as you can onto the page. The words should run together and form sentences linking their way from thought point A to thought point B to thought point C. Keep it up and, eventually you should reach a point where you can type "The End."

Of course things don't always go well, especially if you're writing fast and just slopping down the words. You'll often find yourself going off on tangents that wind their way through little streets and avenues you hadn't planned on taking; we call these side trips. It's kind of like going on a drive to Disneyland with your Uncle Bob—you know you're going to

---

[13] John W. Gardner, American Writer and Secretary of Health, Education and Welffare, 1912-2002.

get there eventually, but you also know you'll probably see every World's Largest Chicken Egg along the way.

But sometimes these side trips can turn out surprisingly beneficial and bring up plot ideas you hadn't thought about before. Sometimes your entire book will shift and become something new. It's surprising how often this new thing is better than the old thing you originally envisioned.

I write a lot of words and I write them very quickly when I'm putting down first drafts. I've been known to hammer out twelve thousand words in one day (that's a very good day, mind you). And, of course, I'm taken on a lot of little side trips I probably wouldn't go on if I wrote more slowly and methodically and stuck to a tighter outline. But I find working the way I do benefits my writing because it adds character to it.

I over-write, so when I go back and finally edit my lousy first draft, I get to cherry pick the good stuff. By doing it this way, I have a lot more flexibility.

I don't believe in wasted words. Every word you write is useful in one way or another. If I pull a lot of words out of a book, I don't delete them, I save them in a morgue file because I never know when they might come in handy.

Don't get me wrong; I'm not against working from outlines. I actually *do* write from one. It's just a very loose outline and I tend to veer off of it a lot. Occasionally, though, I'll pick the outline up, study it, and say to myself, "Hmm. I guess I should make the next turn back onto the interstate." Then I slowly get myself back on track. The main thing is, I start my book where the outline starts, and I try to resolve my book where the outline resolves. For the rest of it I just try my best to hit the high points of what I've sketched out.

Remember, usually I'm writing this way and using an outline that someone's already *paid* me to write to. Therefore, I'm taking a big chance that my editor might come back and say, "We hate this book. It's not the book you told us you were going to write."

But I think, as long as you hit the big story points and your beginning and ending are intact, nobody's going to notice that you forged a few new paths along the way. Besides, if you can throw down words at the rate I'm talking about, you'll have the benefit of finishing your book so far ahead of schedule that if they do have a problem with it, you can go back and make changes. Also, you'll have already completed your rewrite before you present your manuscript to your publisher or anyone else and the rewrite phase gives you a chance to tighten up how well your story follows the outline.

So I'm a big fan of writing fast and writing lots and not caring what words spew out of me during the first draft. My only concern is that they keep coming.

It's during the second draft when you want to take your time and start to look at things differently. After fixing all the structural components, second drafts are for adding those little bits of setting that you whizzed past the first time around and maybe dropping in some symbolism. Perhaps that sword you put into your story could represent your protagonists "warrior heart" and maybe he could break it in a fit of anger right before the climax of your book, symbolically showing that he's lost his will to fight.

I call it Second Draft Thinking. You sweat the small stuff on second drafts, forget about it all on the first ones.

Second drafts are where you make all your writing come alive and shine. But you need all those mucky words from the first draft—all those extra words you spilled onto the page in a big mess—to build the diamond from. Like a sculptor with a big chunk of clay, you need something to carve away so you can create a masterpiece.

Once you finish your first draft don't immediately start your second one unless your deadline requires it. Put your first draft aside and ignore it; wait anywhere from a couple of days to a couple of weeks before starting your rewrite. Everyone's gestation period is different, but everyone has one. One of the worst things you can do is finish a novel and then immediately start redrafting it. I usually wait a week or so before even looking at it again. If you return too soon, you will not be able to rewrite it properly.

Even then, before even thinking about rewriting it, *read* it first. You might think you know what you wrote, but, chances are, if you were putting words out as fast as I'm talking about, you probably didn't write the exact book you think you did. Go ahead and make notes as you read if you like, but give it one good read without redrafting before you start your second round.

The point of waiting before picking it back up again is that you need time to become objective enough to see your work through fresh eyes. If you don't wait long enough, you will either automatically love it, or universally hate it. More likely, you'll find yourself skimming most of it because you can't stand to look at it anymore.

What you'll probably discover is that there are problems with your plot in some places. Usually they are time related. Events take place before other events that they depend upon so you have to jostle chapters around. This isn't a tough thing to fix, and if that's all the major issues you find, congratulate yourself and breathe a big sigh of relief.

Commonly, you'll reach the end and realize it just doesn't work, but you can't pinpoint why. Here's a hint: almost always, if the end of the book doesn't work, it has something to do with the beginning of the book. Your resolution at the end of your novel relies heavily on your setup at the beginning. It's almost like they're tied together with an invisible umbilical cord. So, the solution usually involves either making a change to your opening or your ending or, quite possibly, both. I discussed this in further detail during my discussion of the Hero's Journey three act structure in Part I.

2. AUTHOR/READER TRUST

Beginnings are particularly important in stories because they set up something called Author/Reader Trust. It's sort of like a contract between you and your reader and it happens in your first thirty pages or so. It is during this opening span that you basically show your reader:

a) That you're a good writer and he can be confident that you're capable of sustaining his interest for three to four hundred or more pages, and

b) What "kind" of story he can expect, and the types of things he can expect to happen in it.

You see, people want their stories to behave in "expected" ways. By this, I don't mean they want to see the same things happen that they've seen a million times before. Far from it. Readers like to be surprised. What I'm saying is that they don't want the writer to exercise his power and make things behave inappropriately to the genre or type of story that's being told. The story shouldn't suddenly make a slamming left turn into Crazy Land.

What is "Crazy Land"? Well that depends on the story. Some stories, like zombie novels, are basically no-holds-barred. You can pretty much get away with anything, and the reader expects you to try to. In fact, he probably expects to see a lot of gore and blood and death and he wants it mixed up in unique ways, different from the usual macabre fanfare of headshots and chainsaws. So, instead, maybe he'll enjoy a scene with a zombie getting his head microwaved or mix mastered. Maybe something with a weed whacker would be a welcomed change.

Now consider what would happen if you put any of these scenes into the middle of a movie like *Steel Magnolias*. You'd probably have a lot of people walk out of the theater demanding their money back. Even if they were the same people who came to see the zombie movie a week earlier.

The reason they'd be so upset is because the scene is inappropriate to the story *Steel Magnolias* set up at the beginning of the movie and so the audience trust would be broken. If the screenwriter and director somehow hinted that there would be zombies and lots of gore somewhere in the middle of *Steel Magnolias* during the movie's opening, then it might be fair game. But I doubt the movie would've done as well at the box office.

Let me give you a real example that actually happened to me.

I love Quentin Tarantino movies. Ever since *Pulp Fiction*, I've been a diehard fan. I also really like Robert Rodriguez films. So, when I found out they were working together on a project, it was with great anticipation that I waited to see *From Dusk Till Dawn*.

Now there's something strange about me you have to know for this story to make any sense at all, and that is, when it comes to movies, I try desperately to avoid seeing or reading or hearing anything about them before I go to the theater. I avoid trailers like the plague. I just feel they give too much of the film away. Usually all the good stuff is in the trailer. All the "sound bites." In a perfect world, I manage to pull this off, and go into the theater basically blind. If I had it my way, I wouldn't even know the title if it's something I know I'm going to like. You know, such as a new Tarantino and Rodriguez flick.

Considering this, in hindsight, I got what I deserved. But let me continue.

There's another thing about me you have to know: I absolutely *detest* vampire movies. Unless it's got Buffy in it, I can't stand them. They just grate on me like someone running a nail down a plate. An ex-girlfriend dragged me to Anne Rice's *Interview with a Vampire* and I think I managed to stay in the theater twenty minutes before I had to flee. It was *that* bad. I'm glad there are no vampires in real life, because I have a feeling they wouldn't like me much, either.

Anyway, do you see where I'm going with this yet?

So I take my seat with my super-sized bucket of popcorn and giant Diet Coke that cost, like, the same amount as my car payment and the cinema lights begin to dim. The movie previews come up and I try my best to avert my eyes like I always do, concentrating on my popcorn instead of the screen, all the while anxiously awaiting the beginning of this new Tarantino masterpiece.

Then the movie starts. And if you haven't seen it, it's worth seeing just for the opening ten minutes. It fades in to the gas station scene out in the desert, and I'm watching, eyes glued to the screen, waiting for the cool Tarantino spin that's going to happen right at the beginning of the plotline because that's what he always does. He's a master at it.

The guy comes into the gas station and makes a purchase. Then he leaves. Everything's cool.

Then *boom!* Some other guy comes flying out of the washroom with a gun set on the temple of someone he has hostage and I'm on the edge of my seat. This movie rocks! This popcorn and pop was *worth* half my mortgage payment. I've never *seen* a better movie than this. It's one of the best movies *ever.*

Let me tell you, From Dusk Till Dawn stayed the best movie ever for at least another ten minutes. Maybe even fifteen. Tarantino had me. In my mind, in those fifteen minutes, he and I had forged a contract about what I was going to get from this film. He had promised me a movie full of twists and surprises with guns, hot women, fast cars, and over-the-top violence, and none of it was going to slow down until the reel hit the hundred and five minute mark.

Well, I'll say one thing. The movie turned out to be full of surprises. Only they weren't the good kind. Not for me, at least. I'm sure everyone else in that theater had seen at least one trailer or read a review or had some knowledge of what the movie was about. They were all *normal* people. I was undoubtedly the only one who sat there stunned during the bar scene when, for no discernable reason at all, the girl jumps on the table, opens her jaws and shows a mouthful of fangs. Then she proceeds to tear open a guy's neck. My own jaw dropped. I was like, "What . . . what just happened? *That* can't happen. We had a *deal.* You *promised.* Vampires weren't part of our deal."

I felt gypped.

This is how your readers will feel if you break Author/Reader Trust in your books. You have to tell the story you set up to tell. You can't have Bilbo Baggins up a tree with wargs trying to get him down and then, out of the blue, have Arnold Schwarzenegger show up in a UH-60 Blackhawk helicopter and shoot all the wolf-things for him and then say, "I'll be back," before flying off over the Misty Mountains. Not unless Gandalf mentioned something about UH-60 Blackhawks and Arnie back at the Shire, possibly before the dwarves showed up. Maybe he told Bilbo about some psycho with a piece of shrapnel lodged in his head that had been spotted flying some strange device around Middle-earth. "But be not alarmed. He might yet be of some use, my little hobbit."

Author/Reader Trust means you've agreed to give your reader a fair shake. If you're going to have some fanged temptress tear out the throat of some guy's neck at the top of Act II, you better, at the very least, have a vamp on the cover of your book. Better yet, make some indication in your first act that vampires exist and tend to tear out throats and that certain bars are particularly unsafe.

Like most things, Author/Reader Trust isn't something you have to worry so much about on your first draft. It's during your revision that you make sure you've kept to the tropes set down at the opening of the story. If you find you haven't, then you have to fix it, either by taking out the parts that don't fit the story's promise or by rewriting the beginning and updating the contract.

Ill. 2-1: Sir Galahad is a knight of King Arthur's Round Table and one of the three achievers of the Holy Grail. He is renowned for his gallantry and purity, and some believe he is perhaps meant to be the knightly embodiment of Jesus.

Either way works. Which one you do really depends on how much you've veered away from your opening statement of what your story is agreeing to tell to your readers.

3. START WITH SOMETHING INTERESTING

You should always open your story (and your chapters and your scenes, for that matter) with something interesting. This seems like common sense to me, but it's amazing how many manuscripts I critique that open with two or three paragraphs of beautifully rendered setting. I mean, it's well written and it's nice, but it's boring as cheese. People want characters, they want them doing stuff, and they want them doing stuff in cool settings. Of these three, the first two are the most important.

You should definitely mention a character in your first paragraph, and that character should be doing something. This was the reason J.D. Salinger used to say you should always open a story with dialogue—it guarantees you start it with someone doing something. I'm not sure I agree with old J.D., but I do think you need to show character, action and setting right up front. Preferably in the first paragraph.

Even better, do all three in the first sentence.

Sound impossible? It's actually quite easy.

Let's try an example:

Martha sat with her back to the wall, the way she always did in the old Victorian mansion when she was sewing buttons over the eyes of dead cats.

How's that? Grab your attention? You may not like the contract this story's laying out for the reader, but you can't deny that it has an interesting character, doing something interesting—and ominous—in an interesting setting.

It fits all three requirements.

EXERCISES

1. Try writing stream of consciousness for thirty minutes. Just write as fast as you can, not caring what goes down on the page. Shut off your left brain as much as possible and let your right brain take over. If what you're writing seems to be making no sense, don't worry about it, just keep going until the thirty minute mark is up. When you're done, reread what you've written. I think you'll be surprised at what you find. This is a great exercise to do every morning—or whenever you start your writing sessions—to get your warmed up and ready to write.

2. Write some opening sentences. Make sure they contain an interesting character, in an interesting setting, doing something interesting. See if you can get that all to happen on the first line. Do four or five of these.

KEY POINTS

- There is no such thing as "wasted words." Every word you write is a form of practice, whether you wind up using it or not.
- First drafts should be written very fast, using right-brain thinking as much as possible. Try not to think too hard about the process, or your Internal Editor will get in the way.
- Don't worry too much about sticking to your outline during the first draft. Try to hit your major story points, but if you meander away from them, that's okay. First drafts are supposed to be messy; they're like looking at partially finished carvings.
- The second draft is where you go back and make things shine.
- Don't start second drafting immediately after finishing the first. Give the original draft some time to settle.
- Authors set up a contract of expectations between themselves and the reader during the beginning of the book. This contract should never be broken, or the reader will feel cheated.
- Always start each chapter (and especially your book) with an interesting character doing something interesting in an interesting setting. Do this in as little time as possible. Try to get it down to a single sentence if you can.

CHAPTER TWO

Building Scenes

> *A James Cagney love scene is one where he lets the other guy live.*
>
> —Bob Hope[14]

All the structure in the world isn't going to help you if you can't put a scene together. And, just like everything else to do with writing, building scenes is a craft that can be learned. So if you aren't very good at it at first, don't fret, you will be. It's not rocket science. It's actually pretty simple.

I do a lot of novel critiques and, apart from structural problems, I see scene construction as the second biggest fault. I think this is where the "telling and not showing" thing comes in, which is always a bit of bugaboo, because what does that really mean, anyway? And the truth is, sometimes it's okay to tell and not show. It really depends on the situation. Like most things in writing, the rules can be broken, just make sure you *know* you're breaking them when you do. If you're doing it on purpose, it's one thing. If you're doing it out of ignorance, it's another thing entirely.

---

[14] Bob Hope (May 29, 1903 - July 27, 2003). Bob Hope was an English-born American comedian, actor, singer, and dancer who appeared on Broadway, in vaudeville, movies, television and on the radio. He was best known for his numerous USO shows entertaining U.S. military personnel.

In his book *Story*, Robert McKee says that a novel can have up to sixty or more scenes in it. In her book *Write Away*, Elizabeth George says a novel should have around forty scenes. So . . . which is it? Sixty or forty?

I guess that depends on whether you're Robert McKee or Elizabeth George. Since Mr. McKee hasn't written too many books that I know about and Ms. George has, I'm more apt to go with her number. Plus, it lines up a lot closer to my personal experience and I've got quite a few novels under my belt.

But the truth is, unlike movies, there are no hard and fast rules with novels about how many scenes you should have and how long things should take. Movies time things down to the minute. Each page of script should take about a minute to shoot and generally your scripts are confined to a strict length of around a hundred to a hundred and twenty pages long, unless you are somebody well known in Hollywood—then you can do what you want.

Novels, on the other hand, can vary from three hundred to four hundred pages and your publisher probably won't even blink. He doesn't mind if you submit seventy-five thousand words or a hundred and fifteen thousand. That's quite a large tolerance in comparison to Hollywood standards.

Yet, although there may not be hard and fast rules about the length of your book, there *are* some rules that should be followed about your scenes. Just like with the *structure* of the novel, there is a *structure* your scenes should be following too. And if you do, it will go a long way toward making them pop off the page.

In fact, scenes are built a lot like miniature three act structures. They have beginnings, middles, and ends. The beginning generally sets up the scene, the middle builds in tension and raises the stakes, and the ending hits a Climax. Only it happens a lot more quickly than the big overall structure going on in your book. So, the whole time you're going through this long drawn out process in your story, you're actually going through a whole bunch of mini-ones at the same time. How cool is that?

But there's more to it.

1. POINT OF VIEW

Generally each scene of your book is told from a singular point of view. If you change points of view in your book, you usually start a new scene. Sometimes you can put a section break and start a new point of view that way, but it's a little clunky and really should be reserved for those special occasions when you really need to use it because you just can't get around it.

So, whose point of view do you want to tell a particular scene from?

Well, that depends.

If you're writing a murder mystery, you probably don't want to ever tell a scene from the point of view of the murderer because the minute you put the reader in his head, unless he's got some mental illness that makes him forget he murders people, your readers are going to know who did it. Because the big rule of thumb in writing is this: you can't hide information from the reader. That's a big *"no no."*

"So what do I do then?" you might ask.

Easy. Never make the murderer a point of view character.

"Well, aren't I still hiding information, though?"

No, you just aren't making it accessible. I know, it kind of sounds like a sneaky way of saying the same thing but it's not. It's different. Sometimes you can determine whodunit in a mystery novel simply by figuring out whose point of view the writer hasn't used. If there's only one left, it's probably the killer.

So there's one person you don't want to make the point of view character, but who *do* you want to make the point of view character?

The general rule of thumb is this: when possible, scenes should be told from whatever point of view gives them the most emotional strength. That usually means from whichever point of view has the highest emotional stake in the conflict going on in the scene. If it's a scene of Mom and Dad having an all-out screaming match, it might actually be best to tell the scene from the point of view of the four-year-

Ill. 2-2: *The banquet of Damocles depicts two morals: whoever wears the crown is bound to have threats sent their way, and the threats are always much greater than the act itself. Notice how this single image displays so much conflict.*

old daughter who's lying in her bed down the hall with her pillow over her head.

She may have the most emotionally at stake.

As for which point of view and which tense to use for your story (first person, present tense; first person, past tense; third person, present tense; second person, present tense (if you want to be weird), etc.) Gardner Dozois, long time editor of *Asimov's Science Fiction,* once told me all stories should be written in close third-person, past tense, unless you have a reason to write it in a different manner.

2. CONFLICT

Every scene must absolutely be full of conflict. You want your entire book full of conflict and the only way to guarantee that is to shove your scenes full of it. To quote Robert McKee:

> *When the protagonist steps out of the Inciting Incident and into Act II, she enters a world governed by the laws of conflict. To Wit: Nothing moves forward in a story except through conflict.*

Every single scene in your novel must have some sort of conflict or it's not only wasting space on the paper, it's also wasting your reader's time having to read through it. Conflict is what good writing is all about. Show me a story without conflict, and I'll show you a story that desperately wants to be put out of its own misery. Not only do scenes need conflict, the conflict has to ratchet up as the scene progresses.

There is one exception to this rule: if you have one scene (and *just* one, *maybe* two in a long novel—*absolutely* no more) that shows great characterization or is truly funny, then you might be able to include it. But being funny is tricky and can backfire on you easily. I'd make sure it not only shows characterization and is, in your eyes, funny, but also has some conflict in there, too. In other words, cover yourself. And if you are writing funny stuff? Just be sure that everyone thinks you're funny. Not just you and your mom.

3. USING INDEX CARDS

Many writers use index cards for writing out their scenes. These are useful for a number of reasons, the main one being that they are small. They force you to not write a lot of information on them. All you can fit is a very concise version of your scene. And the great thing is, once you have a few key scenes written on a stack of 4" x 6" index cards, you can stuff them in your pocket and then take them out and examine them whenever you get the urge, wherever you happen to be. They're great for coffee shops and pubs.

Index cards are fun. You can play with them. They're tangible. You can change their order and see how the scenes work in different ways, playing them off each other in variations you wouldn't normally try. You can literally shuffle them up and just deal them out and see what you get.

Index cards can even replace an outline. They can *become* your outline, if you're that opposed to outlines. And you don't need to put *every* scene down on a card, just the key scenes of the three act structure. Another nice thing about them is that if you happen to think up a new scene while you're out at dinner or at the movies, you can just pull out a blank card and jot the idea down before you forget it.

4. SCENE ENERGY

There's a certain dramatic energy in a scene that changes as the scene progresses. Let's say for example, Jim wants to start a business making jellybeans and he needs a loan. So we need a scene where Jim walks into the bank and has his appointment with the loan manager.

Because Jim has the highest emotional stake in this scene, we're going to tell it from his point of view.

Jim's dressed up in his best suit. He's got new business cards made up. He's well-prepared. He's even had a good breakfast. He's ready for anything. He's determined to get that loan and start his own company. Visions of a worldwide jellybean enterprise flood Jim's mind as he sits in an uncomfortable plastic chair in the bank waiting area while the loan manager does whatever she's doing that's made her ten minutes late so far.

So Jim starts the scene with positive energy (+), or on an up note.

Finally, Jim sees the loan manager coming across the bank. But on her way over to him, she stops and talks to someone at a desk. He overhears her tell the other employee how her boyfriend dumped her last night and her cat threw up all over her new afghan sweater and she just wished the whole world would go to hell.

She says she almost didn't come in and can't believe it's not lunch time yet. Then she says she hates men. Eventually she makes it the rest of the way across the room to shake Jim's hand and gives him a false, shark-toothed smile before leading him into her office.

Jim's positive energy starts to wane.

As the scene progresses, Jim tells the loan manager all about how he plans to take on the world of jelly bean domination, but she seems disinterested. She looks out her window. She clicks some things on her computer. *Is she checking her email?* Jim wonders. He pulls out the business plan he spent the entire weekend working on to show to her, but she barely gives it a glance, only flipping through the first two or three pages in a patronizing way. When he offers her one of his new business cards, she tells him that won't be necessary.

Jim begins to complain that she hasn't taken anything he's said seriously. He even accuses her of checking her email, When he does, she literally flips out on him. She tells him she doesn't have any more time for him today and asks him what does he know about anything anyway? She tells him nobody's interested in buying jellybeans from someone who looks like a pervert, and that if he doesn't get out of the bank in the next two minutes, she'll be calling security.

Jim slinks from the bank, ending the scene full of negative energy (-), or on a down note.

Notice that this scene started with one emotional charge (in this case a positive one), built to a crescendo until it reached a Climax, then ended on an opposite emotional charge (in this case a negative one) from what it started on.

According to Robert McKee, all your scenes should do this. You want to go into the scene charged one way and come out charged the other. If you use the index card method of scene writing, make sure you put the energy of your scene, the energy coming in and the energy going out, right on the card. I've included an example card for the above the scene. You'll see an arrow pointing through the action of the scene going from positive to negative.

Robert McKee goes on to say you should then line up your scenes so that the emotional charges butt up against each other. So, for example, if scene A is a +/- then scene B should be a -/+ and scene C a +/-, and so on, but that seems like overkill to me. Then again, everyone who's anyone in Hollywood has attended McKee's three-day movie seminar, so he must know something. I went to his class a few years ago while he was in Vancouver and got a lot out of it.

I just question what you'd do if you did follow his instructions and lined your scenes up so carefully the way he suggests and then had to move a single scene or delete one or add one. It would throw all the rest of them out of whack.

5. HERO'S JOURNEY: MAIN PLOT POINTS

When I'm writing, I find it invaluable to pin down the four cornerstones of my three act structure as quickly as possible. I know I can't start the actual writing until I have those in place. Once I do, I can truck ahead and know that I will be somewhat okay, even without anything else even closely resembling an outline.

I know everyone writes differently; some people outline; some don't; some use a variation of the two. I know one woman who actually gets angry if you try and talk to her about outlines. Like *really* angry—I'm serious. I try to keep an open mind.

My outline is what I like to call an Evolution Outline. It evolves after I've started the writing process. I keep coming up with new ideas even after I have finished outlining and started to write the actual book and I go back and modify the outline to reflect those changes as I go.

But when I first create my outline, it wouldn't matter what type of outline I'm making, there are four things I need to have in place after brainstorming my initial ideal. Those are the four cornerstones to the story's three act structure. In other words, the Inciting Event, the Act I/Act II Pivot Point, the Act II/Act III Pivot Point, and the Climax (or at least the resolution of the Climax—the resolution is usually enough).

Scene: Jim asks bank manager for loan

Setup: Jim has arrived at bank confident. He is ready to take on the world and build a jelly bean empire!

Rising Tension: The bank maanger had a rough night. She doesn't even pay attention to Jim's proposal. He gets more and more frustrated with her as he proceeds.

Climax: Jim finally blows up at the bank manager. He explodes in anger. He's disgusted in her.

Denouement: With no hope left for his loan, Jim is escorted off the presmises by security guards.

Ill. 2-3: *A 4" x 6" index card showing the scene described of Jim going into the bank and asking the manager for a loan to start his jellybean company. Index cards are a great way to keep track of scenes, and they're fun, too! Notice how it shows the energy of the scene on the right side of the card fall from positive to negative as the scene progresses.*

Of these, you really need to know the resolution first. This is because you need a target before you launch your arrow. A story is a linear roadmap—this is true even if your story is told out of time—from point A to point B, and if you don't know where you're headed, you can't possibly know what to write next. If you start with the resolution firmly fixed in your mind and then work back from there and pluck out the other three cornerstones, you will have a firm foundation to build on.

Actually, coming up with the resolution and the Inciting Event together is usually a good way to start working on any story.

Knowing your resolution will tell you how you should write the beginning of your book. In fact, once the resolution is in place, the beginning should just fall out automatically. It's almost guaranteed that if there's a problem with your beginning, you'll find it in your ending and vice versa. That's how integral these two components are to each other.

As Syd Field says in his book Screenplay:

> The ending comes out of the beginning. Someone, or something, initiates an action, and how that action is resolved becomes the story line.

After I set down my four key points, I slowly start filling in the rest of the main stages of the three act structure. Once all those scenes are roughly sketched, I still have all the freedom in the world to write my in-between scenes any way I see fit. I usually don't outline these; I leave them to come out organically in the process. Even the key scenes from the three act structure are so roughly sketched in that there is still lots of room for my creativity to shine through while I'm writing. My outline for each of these scenes is generally a half page or so, double spaced. No more than a page at most.

Quite often during my first draft the in-between scenes I hadn't outlined will lead me places I didn't see coming, so I may end up changing the previous scenes I wrote to accommodate this, but that's okay. At least I had some sort of roadmap before I started.

What's important is that I don't just start out blind.

That's the key. Too many writers just start writing and then wonder why they never finish their books or why their books don't turn out very good. At least if you have a minimal outline, you have somewhere to go, especially if you get lost somewhere in the dark recesses of Act II. Having the Midpoint Climax to write toward gives you something to aim for, no matter where you may happen to be at the time, even if it's way off your outline.

6. GIVING CREATIVITY BLOCK A SWIFT KICK

We've all been there; it's one o'clock in the morning and we've been staring at the computer screen now for three hours and the view hasn't changed. Just that big white rectangle with your name and address in the top left corner and the words Untitled centered about a third of the way down the page. You want to start writing, but you have no idea where to go.

Or maybe it's even worse. Maybe you're halfway through your novel and things were going great up until a week or so ago; you were making incredible progress. And then, everything just ground to a halt as you crept up onto that midway point that a lot of authors like to call the "muddle in the middle" (if you are having problems with the "muddle in the middle" see my previous posts on the Hero's Journey where I describe a solution to this... my take on the journey has no muddle in the middle. Instead, there is a midpoint Climax, giving you a goal to write to and away from).

Or maybe you have just plumb run out of original ideas and you need something more. Everything you're coming up with right now feels old and staid and stereotyped, as though you've seen it a thousand times.

Well, the solution might just lie in mind mapping. What is mind mapping? It's a relatively recent technique in radical thought development that allows you to free associate things very quickly. It does this by structurally laying out the information in a linear fashion where connections are formed between similar ideas. Because of the way the information in a mind map is stored, it is also a good method to store your notes from your research you do for your next novel.

A Google search on the web will uncover many mind mapping software products available, most for around a price of $200, but there are three that worth mentioning that are free. One is freemind (http://freemind.sourceforge.net/wiki/index.php) and the other is freeplane (http://freeplane.sourceforge.net/wiki/index/php). Freeplane seems to be an offshoot from freemind and has a few more bells and whistles, making it the better choice, I believe, although both programs seem pretty solid and are compatible with each other, so feel free to try them both out.

The third is a very interesting mind mapping tool I just stumbled across called Text2Mind. It is a completely online accessory that can be found at http://www.text2mindmap.com/#. You don't need to download a single thing. Just create the mind map in an outline mode and then, with just a push of a button, it outputs your map for you. It's a rather fun process and much simpler to use than the last two I just mentioned (although without near the power).

You don't need a computer program to mind map, though. You can do it the old fashioned way, with just a paper and a pen. Actually, different colored pens will come in handy if you have access to them. Mind maps are unique in that, when they are finished, they can almost resemble works of art.

The way you go about creating one is like this. First you come up with your initial idea. It doesn't have to be an incredibly great idea, just an idea you want to run with. For instance, this morning, while testing out the software programs I just described, I tried this procedure using the idea "superhero." So I wrote down the word "superhero" in the center of my paper and circled it. This was my root idea.

(Superhero)

Why don't you follow along and maybe even use the same root word I did? I'll wait while you find some paper. And while you're at it, grab a handful of colored pens or pencil crayons.

Now, as quickly as you can, you free associate any words that come to you based on the word "train." It doesn't matter if they don't really seem to have any connection to the initial word "superhero" at all (mine happened to, just because I picked such an easy word). Either way, you just write them down. In my case, the next word I thought of was "villain". So I wrote down "villain" as my next major node off of "Superhero." Now "villain" brought forth a lot of ideas; I quickly jotted down that he had been locked away up until recently but it was under public scrutiny for some reason. I thought, "Hey, maybe he just escaped from a lower security establishment. Perhaps an asylum he'd been moved to." So that went down. Then I thought of some sort of threat and the word "bomb," "National Bank," and "threatening city" all came to me at once. Because all of these things were associated with "villain " and not "Superhero" they get linked as child nodes to "villain."

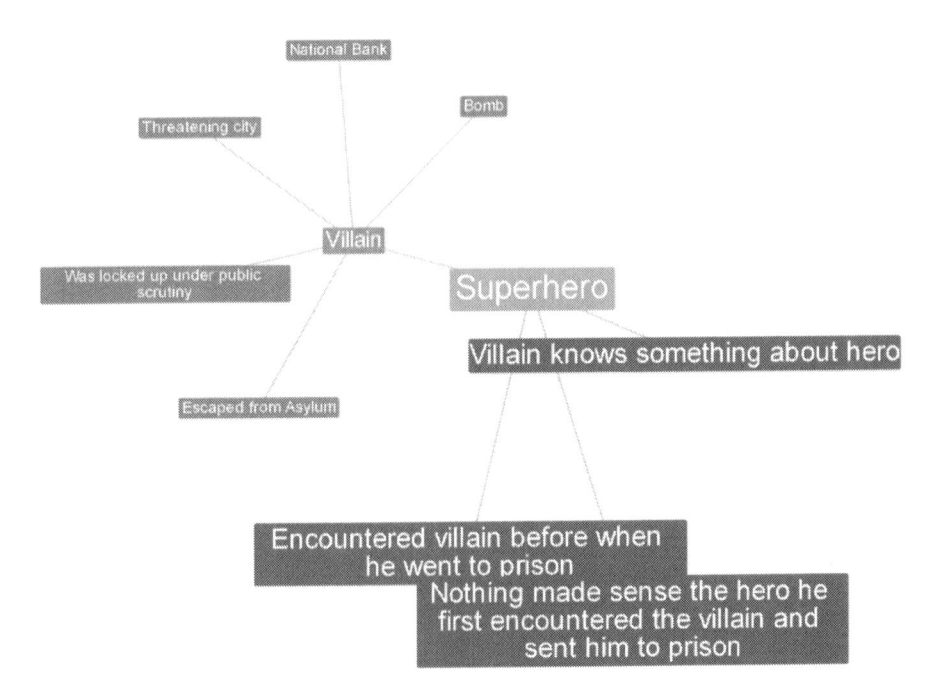

```
                National Bank
                      |
                      |    Bomb
    Threatening city  |   /
                \     |  /
                 \    | /
                  Villain
                 / |  \
                /  |   \
  Was locked   /   |    \      Superhero
  up under    /    |     \    /
  public    /      |      \  /
  scrutiny         |       \/
                   |       /\
                   |      /  \
              Escaped    /    Villain knows something about hero
              from      /
              Asylum   /
                      /
          Encountered villain before when
               he went to prison
          Nothing made sense the hero he
          first encountered the villain and
                sent him to prison
```

So, already I had the makings of a story. Then I started thinking about my superhero. Maybe it was he who put the villain behind bars in the first place. So I wrote that down in not so many words. I also alluded to their being something strange about that arrest and the hero has always wondered if the villain knows something secret about him. His real identity perhaps?

At this point, my mind map looked like the one above.

For the purpose of illustration, I am keeping things simple, but you can also have associations between child nodes, so there can be more than one tree leading to the same topic. For instance, "Was locked up under public scrutiny," might make sense to also connect to "Superhero" if he did indeed play a large part in locking the villain up.

Now the process simply continues. It's a lot like brainstorming, but comes much more naturally because this tree system is really the way your brain is set up. The neural net inside your head associates things in a way almost identical to what we're using here. In fact, the first five minutes you try to come up with free associations may be quite laborious, but keep at it because, it only takes a few more minutes until the dam suddenly breaks open and you can't stop the train of thoughts coming to you. They come at locomotive speeds, so fast it's hard to keep up sometimes. They key is to write everything down. Even if an idea seems stupid or not to match anything on your mind map, don't ignore it. It's coming to you for a reason.

So I added more nodes to my mind map and these came very fast. I even added a new major node, introducing a new character, as it were. A district attorney who came into office without much public support and so, in an effort to gain more support, decided to move the villain (whom the public thought should never have gone to prison due to insanity in the first place) from the penitentiary and into the asylum. It's shortly after this move that the villain manages to break out of the low security asylum. I've also added a few new nodes for my main subject. Now I have him working with the police to recapture the villain, only they don't manage to do it in time to save the National Bank from being blown up.

See how the story's coming together with very little actual involvement or straining of my brain? And it happens so quickly.

Have I used up all my ideas yet? I don't think so, they are still coming out of me like a fountain. So I keep adding them until the torrent stops.

Now I've gone ahead and added not only information about how the book will resolve with the villain's capture, but also I've even come up with ideas for the denouement. I won't go through all the intricacies of the story I've outlined here (and this really is an outline and it took a matter of fifteen minutes. I *told* you outlines don't have to be painful), those really aren't what's important. I'm sure you're much more interested in how this technique will help *you* build your ideas. Mind mapping is a very effective approach for doing a lot of things. Taking the place of brainstorming is only one of them.

In case you're wondering, this is the final map I came up with:

My ideas started slowing down at this point, so I called it done. It was enough (far more than enough, actually) to start writing a book if I so desired.

Notice my use of colors or, in this case, different shades of gray to differentiate the sections. Color can be very useful in mind maps. It helps you quickly see patterns for different sections of nodes and what they correspond to. Also, the mind reacts to color; color helps your brain remember things more easily. It's another mapping association layer it uses when searching for data it's filed away. So don't be afraid to use color or even different fonts for different sections.

You can also have more than one main idea on a mind map, if those ideas are similar. For instance, I could have another series of nodes starting with the words "alter ego" that mind maps the super-hero's life when he's not in costume. Or I could just make that a child node of the superhero tree I have already established here. Generally speaking, you're better off having completely separate maps for separate topics. Just make sure you label all your maps with codes explaining what project they are for and any other applicable information. If you're using mind maps to take notes, you may want one for every different reference material you read, or you could assign a different color to each piece of reference. The possibilities are literally endless.

How do you know when you're finished mind mapping? That's a question only you can answer. I map until the stream of ideas slows back down to what it was before it entered the frenzied period of intensity that it always does. But you don't have to stop there. You could put your map away for a day or two and then come back to it with a fresh mind and probably add a lot more detail and ideas.

While you are putting down words, you can reorganize the ones you have on the page, grouping like words together and connecting them interdependently of their child nodes or their parent nodes. Cross-referencing nodes is very powerful as it allows you to combine ideas under more than one heading. This is also another place where your different colored pens come in handy. With the software programs, you can automatically make every node a different color or, if you like, you can group nodes into "clouds"—bunches of nodes tied together. Clouds can be rendered any of a few different ways.

So what do you do once you're satisfied you have exhausted your mind of everything you can think of to do with your initial idea and all avenues leading off of it? You sit back, and start looking at the overall connections and how they lump together. Your mind has probably already started to see the problem in a different way. This is the power of mind maps; they make you think from different angles.

My story from the mind map I created doesn't require a lot of extra thought for interpretation. The story turned out to just wind up sitting right there on the map. I still need to flesh out some of the details, like what, exactly, is it the villain knows about the superhero and what effect does that have on the story, but for the most part my story is all there. This will happen more often than you would think. When it doesn't, you may have to keep looking at your mind map from different vantage points, trying to consider things metaphorically or on different levels. But, trust me, if you look hard enough, you'll find your story. It's there. And once you do, in a case like that, it might be time to mind map again, this time *knowing* what you're going for.

One last thing. You want to keep the ideas on the main nodes of the mind map simple. Don't write down full sentences. Try to keep it to single words, if at all possible. If you can't, make the phrases as short and concise as possible. Do use symbols and pictures if those help you. Don't forget to use colors. These all appeal to different parts of the imagination and will be of aid in generating ideas.

The main thing is not to take the process too seriously. Have fun with it. Whether you do it on paper or with one of the computer programs I described above, mind mapping is entertaining and enjoyable.

To recap, mind mapping a tremendous tool to get your creativity unstuck, but it's much more than just that. It's also a very good way to store your notes, as it replicates the same way information is stored in your brain. It makes it very quick and easy to find certain information once you get used to using it. It can also help you with study and memorization. This is especially true if you break different sections out into their own fonts and colors. The mind likes remembering different colors. And it's a fantastic planning tool because, being a tree structure, anything you may have missed while working out your initial plan should pop right out at you once you've structured your data into a mind map.

It definitely beats staring at that white screen of death on your computer monitor until one in the morning. Let me tell you that.

7. COMPOSITION

Scenes should not be full of exposition. We all fall into the trap of telling instead of showing, and it's a deadly trap to be stuck in. You should always try to have a hook at the beginning and end of your scene. Pull your readers into the narrative and leave them wanting to return to this portion of the story when the scene ends.

The hook at the beginning is where a lot of writers can fall into trouble. Feeling like there needs to be an adequate description of the location first, before talking about the characters; a writer may start his scenes slowly. That's the logical choice because we think in a linear fashion.

Watch out for this. Readers don't care about the natural order of things. They care about being intrigued.

Usually, if nothing else is working, I start a scene off with a piece of dialogue. Remember what I said about the first paragraph of your story having an interesting character doing something interesting in an interesting setting? And trying to get that down to the first line? The same holds true with each scene: give us an interesting character doing something interesting and make sure they're in an interesting setting. Don't be afraid to think up big set pieces for your books. Readers have good imaginations.

Dialogue is always a strong hook, because you can leave unanswered questions.

"What happened to your nose?" Frank asked me.

We were back in Pistillo's office. I sat in the armchair. Pistillo was cleaning the rifle again.

Is far better than:

We were back in Pistillo's office. I sat in the armchair in front of his desk. I noticed a marlin hanging on the wall I hadn't last time I was in here before. So, the man was a hunter and a fisherman. Pistillo himself was sitting in his chair. He had taken out the same rifle he had last time I was here and was cleaning it again.

"What happened to your nose?" he asked me.

The only interesting part about the second version is the "So, the man was a hunter *and* a fisherman," but surely we can drop that in as we go while still using the "lead-in by dialogue" version. Asking about the nose just grabs our attention more. We want to know about the nose.

You also want a good balance of setting and dialogue and no big exposition dumps. That's telling, not showing. But dialogue also has its drawbacks. It slows down the pace of a book. Read Hemingway. Lots of dialogue can stretch out scenes a long time, so you have to be choosy. Occasionally it's okay to throw in the odd two line summarization:

Take this passage, for example:

We drove to the mall, talking of all the summers we picked daisies in the park. Her memory was much better than mine.

Now, that could be written out so you actually hear the conversation, or it could be left as is. Which is better? That depends on where it's used. If it's in a place where this conversation isn't important and it's surrounded by a lot of showy scenes, then it's fine to summarize like this.

Always remember: form follows function. If you need to do something a certain way because the writing demands it, then do it that way.

It's the function of the writing that is of utmost importance. Story comes first. The mechanics always take backseat.

The only other thing I want to emphasize about scene construction is to check your pacing. Make sure you read your first drafts out loud to yourself. I tend to write mine so they are paced too quickly the first time around, but you will encounter your own idiosyncrasies about your own writing. Everyone is different.

Let's take one more run at scene composition with showing vs. telling in mind, because I do think this is vitally important and not something everyone gets so easily. Consider the following:

> *John got a date with Amelia tonight. He drove his car to her place and picked her up. After that, John and Amelia went dancing at that new club, Ringo's. John drank too much and got into a fight. He wound up in jail. Amelia had to bail him out the next morning. She wasn't too pleased.*

This isn't a scene; it's a synopsis. It contains an overview of a number of different scenes. Scenes are dramatic, meaning they contain drama. To write this dramatically requires you to unpack the details. How much of them you unpack is really up to you and, to some degree, defines your style and voice as a writer.

I will write just the first line of the above paragraph as a scene to give you an example of what I mean. Remember, this is how *I'd* do it. It's not necessarily the *best* way for you.

> *John came home from work late in a rather unpleasant mood. He'd had a fight with his boss and all he was thinking about was having dinner, putting up his feet, and watching the football game on television. Bedtime wouldn't come soon enough.*
>
> *That's when there was a knock on his door. He could tell just by the sound of the knock that it was Tim Jackson, his landlord. Shit, John thought. He'd forgotten to pay his rent.*
>
> *Tim knocked again right away. John knew he knew he was home; he could see his car in the driveway. Oh well, there was no point in postponing the inevitable. John answered the door.*
>
> *"Hi Tim," he said, scratching his head.*

"I need the rent, John," Tim said. Tim always reminded John of a reptile. It was something about the way his teeth were set in his mouth.

"Yeah. Okay if I get it for you tomorrow?"

"Why is it always tomorrow with you? Every month it's tomorrow." Those teeth looked ready to snap any minute.

"Sorry 'bout that, but I really don't have it on me. I'll have it tomorrow for sure."

Tim searched John's face as though trying to see whether or not to trust him. John didn't think Tim ever trusted him. "I'll be back tomorrow. If you don't have my money . . . " He never told John what would happen, just made it seem like it wouldn't be good.

"I'll have it. Jesus, Tim."

"Lots of people would love to live here, price I charge."

"I know. You're a saint."

Tim narrowed his eyes. John knew what he was doing. He was trying to tell if John was being sarcastic. Luckily he wasn't bright enough to pick up on sarcasm. "Just have my money."

John closed the door and sighed. He had no idea how he was going to come up with rent money in twenty-four hours. Not unless the rent fairy came and left him a check while he was sleeping. Could today get any worse?

As though reading his thoughts, John's telephone rang. John didn't even bother considering whether or not to answer it. At this point, he thought, just let the problems pile themselves up.

"Hello?" he answered.

"Hi, John? It's Amelia. We met a couple weeks ago at Shelly's birthday party."

Amelia. John remembered Amelia. Tall, blonde, curvy. Everyone at that party probably remembered Amelia. "Hi," John said, putting on an air of suaveness he didn't know he had.

"I was just wondering what you're doing tonight? My schedule sort of cleared up on me and I was wondering if you might want to go out? Maybe go dancing? I'd like to check out that new place. What's it called? Ringo's?"

Jack nearly stumbled over his own tongue. "Yeah, um, sure. Yeah! I'd love to. Want me to pick you up?"

"That sounds great!"

"Okay, hang on, let me get a pen." *He grabbed a pen and the envelope containing his overdue telephone bill.* "All right, give me your address." *John copied down her address as she told it to him.* "Okay, I'll see you in, say, an hour?"

"Sounds perfect."

John hung up the phone and smiled, wondering if maybe the rent fairy had come and just left him a present other than the rent money.

There, that's the first sentence of the paragraph above written out as a short scene. Now it's dramatic. You might think it sucks, and it probably does. I just wrote it off the top of my head. But it fulfills the job of the first sentence. Where the original sentence "told" us what happened ("John got a date with Amelia tonight"), the scene "shows" us him getting the date. It not only shows him getting the date, it also shows John's thoughts and feelings about it. There's also some added back and forth with his landlord that I seem to have arbitrarily added. Why did I do that? Because of something I already went over.
Conflict
The scene needed conflict.

Again, let me review: every scene has to have conflict. In a lot of ways, your scenes are three act structures squished into smaller time spaces. They should have virtually the same elements: a Setup, some sort of rising conflict and tension (and maybe suspense), and everything should eventually crescendo toward a climax and resolution.

Conflict is key. Conflict makes us interested and keeps us there. I added conflict by making John unable to pay his bills (I'm not sure how he's going to afford to pay for his date tonight, but somehow he gets drunk enough to get into that fight).

Remember, you want to keep the conflict and tension rising throughout your book, especially throughout that great expanse known as Act II, and the only way to do that is by writing highly charged scenes, with each one being a little more ramped up than the last. In reality, of course, you can't possibly have every single scene more conflicted than the one before it, but you do want to make sure you average a nice rising effect.

One last thing.

You want to come into scenes late and leave early. You want to start the scene at the latest possible time you can without losing any valuable information. It's a lot like starting your novel. You don't want to show your character from birth and you probably don't want to show him waking up and getting out of bed. You want to start on action. You want to pick up right where things get interesting. You want to hook the reader.

And you don't want to overstay your welcome. Again, here scenes are much like your novel as a whole—once you've finished showing the reader what is essential to the story, get out. You're done. If you have characters saying "Good-bye" a lot in your scenes, or getting into cars and driving down streets (although, sometimes getting into a car and driving away is a good way to end a scene) you're probably going on too long. You want to end on a hook or, in this case, you'd probably call it a cliffhanger.

Cliffhangers don't all have to be about Damsels in Distress tied to railroad tracks with trains chugging down the tracks toward them only yards away, mere seconds from running through them; they can also be little things. I'd consider the ending of the short scene I just wrote a mini-cliffhanger. It leaves the reader with at least a little bit of a question. Who is Amelia, anyway? What's going to happen on this date? Is John in over his head? It seems like nothing else in his life goes right . . . how is he going to botch tonight up?

It's really more in the phrasing than the content when it comes to ending scenes well. Although sometimes, especially when writing thrillers or mysteries, you really can end on a good cliffhanger. If you get the opportunity, by all means, pull out all the stops!

That about wraps it up for scene building. Just try to keep everything interesting with lots of conflict and tension and make sure you're showing more than you're telling. And always remember: the more you write, the better you get.

EXERCISES

1. Write a short one page scene involving a mother, father, and a four-year-old child at the beach. Put it in third person, but write it from the child's point of view. Don't make it too long; This is mainly a dialogue exercise, so be sure to include dialogue from each of the different characters.

2. Now rewrite that same scene from first person point of view, still using the child as your point of view character. Compare them when you are finished. The language in the narrative of the two should be very similar. Just because you're in third person, doesn't mean you shouldn't write it as though it's from the child's point of view. This is called "close third person," and is the third person method usually applied in commercial contemporary commercial novels.

3. Write another one page scene with two characters having an argument. Make sure they have different voices and, by that, I don't mean make one Italian and one Irish. We all have our own distinctive way of talking. You should be able to build that into your characters. If possible, get another writer or a good reader to look at it when you're finished and critique it. The argument shouldn't just go back and forth like a tennis game, but should be thoroughly steeped in setting and action.

4. Start a scene where the energy is very much shifted one direction and end it with the energy shifted completely the opposite direction. See what effect this has on your writing and how you write. Feel how the shift in energy gives you something to write toward and makes the scene development actually an easier process. Once you've done it one way, say, negative to positive,

write another scene doing it the other way, positive to negative. You should always try to have energy movement in every scene. Again, these scenes can be single page works.

5. Try mind mapping a book idea. Have fun with it. Use either one of the free programs I mentioned, or just good ol' pencil crayons and paper. Is the story you came up with better than the usual ideas you have? Is it something you might write one day? Either way, save the mind map somewhere safe. In an "ideas" folder is a good place. There's no need to write a summary of the idea (unless it's something obscure you got from using the mind map as a metaphor) as in most cases the mind map itself acts as a genuinely great outline.

KEY POINTS

- Unless you have good reason not to (perhaps because your entire book is told in first person from a particular character's point of view), always write your scenes from the point of view of the character with the most emotions at stake.
- Every scene should be filled with conflict. Conflict drives fiction.
- You can use index cards to keep track of scenes. They are fun and make it easy to rearrange the order of things quickly to see new combinations you might not otherwise have tried. Index cards can even replace an outline.
- Every scene has emotional energy. It's either positively or negatively charged. Your scenes should always move from one charge to the other; so if you start off positively charged, the scene should end negatively charged.
- Your outline doesn't have to be a huge weighty document describing everything down to meticulous detail. Sometimes, having the four cornerstones of the three act structure (the Inciting Event, the First Pivot Point, the Second Pivot Point, and the resolution of the Climax) is enough to get you started writing. Generally, once you know the resolution, the other three come much faster.
- You can use an "Evolving Outline" that changes as you write. Don't be afraid to veer off outline and go down tangents to see where you end up.
- The resolution and Denouement of your story in Act III are tied very closely to the Setup in Act I. If you find your ending doesn't work, try looking at the beginning.

- Mind mapping is a tremendous brainstorming tool that can also be used for other things like storing research information.
- Scenes should be constructed like mini-three act structures themselves. They should have a Setup, a period of rising tension and struggle, and a Climax with a resolution.
- Start scenes late and leave scenes early.
- Scenes should start with a hook and end with some sort of cliffhanger, or a hang of some sort.

CHAPTER THREE

Voice

Everyone who wills can hear the inner voice. It is within everyone.

—Mahatma Gandhi[15]

1. CHARACTER VOICE

When we talk about "voice" in writing, generally there are two different things we can be talking about—authorial voice or character voice. Authorial voice is the overall tone and style that comes through the use of your language to convey whatever story you're telling. Generally, authorial voice doesn't change. You can usually tell the same author from one story to the next, if he has a dominant voice. It didn't matter what sort of story Hemingway wrote, you always knew it was a Hemingway story because of his style and the way it "sounded." It had an openness to it that nobody could match, although many, many people tried.

Right now I'm going to discuss character voice: making your characters sound like human beings instead of stilted cardboard characters when they speak. So this section is about how to write good dialogue.

The first step is to know your characters. This should be an obvious consideration, but a lot of people just jump in without giving it a whole lot of thought. But really, who are these people that are talking, any-

---

[15] Mohandas Karamchand Gandhi (October 2, 1869 - January 30, 1948) was the preeminent leader of Indian nationalism in British-ruled India. Employing non-violent civil disobedience, Gandhi led India to independence.

way? If you were to walk into a bar or a café and put down a digital recorder without anyone in the place knowing and later played it back and listened to all the odd conversations around the room, I bet you'd be surprised by what you heard. First, you'd discover that no two people sound the same. Everyone talks differently. I'm not talking about accents and things like that, although that can come into play; I'm talking about phrasing and the way people use words to edge their opinions in to other people's sentences. Some people try to dominate discussions. Some hardly speak. Some just make guttural sounds. Many spend a lot of time gesturing with their hands and a lot less time making noise with their mouths.

All this should come into play when you write your dialogue if you want to write superb dialogue.

One of the best ways I know of to get to know your characters is to do exactly what I just said: throw them all in a bar together and have them start talking to each other. Just type and listen to them while they talk. Just start typing random conversations, trying not to think too much about what you're doing. If you can let go with your left brain, after you start to relax—say about twenty to thirty minutes into the process—you'll begin to figure out who's who.

Then you'll start to pick up on the differences between your characters, but that's only one piece of the puzzle. You still have to write dialogue well and writing good dialogue is a craft that some people seem to naturally possess and others have to struggle very hard with. The good news is, like everything else to do with writing, dialogue is a craft that can be learned. And once you've got it, you've got it for good.

Let's start by taking a look at some bad dialogue.

I'll set up the scene: Bill and Ted are meeting for lunch to discuss a business proposal that Ted is offering to bring Bill in on for a meager investment of five thousand dollars. Bill doesn't actually have that kind of money, but he doesn't want to let his friend know he's broke, so he's playing along that he's interested. I'm not going to take this scene very far, just long enough to use it as an example.

Here goes:

"Hi Bill," Ted said. "I want to thank you for meeting with me. I think you will like what I am going to show you."

"Well I don't know," Bill replied, laughing. "I'm pretty cynical when it comes to investing my money. I don't like to just throw it around."

Ted pulled out his laptop and a binder full of promotional material. He flashed Bill a smile. "Let me have a chance to show you what we have been up to. I think you might just change your mind."

"Okay," Bill said.

Ted ran through a PowerPoint presentation and discussed financial projections while Bill tried to feign interest. "So..." Ted asked when he was done, "what do you think, Bill?"

"Um... I'm sorry Ted, but I think I have to pass."

Ted's face fell. "Can I ask why?"

"I just don't feel comfortable investing in something with a friend for one thing. Also, like I said before, I'm pretty tight fisted with my money. Maybe you should talk to Dave at the office. This might be right up his alley."

Ted seemed a bit ticked off. He put his laptop back into his briefcase along with the binder. "Yeah, I will talk to Dave. Thanks for your time, Bill."

Okay, first let me start by saying this isn't really that bad. I was trying to make it horrible and found it hard to write horrible dialogue. This is part of the good news I told you about. Once you know how to write good dialogue, you naturally will continue to do so. Even when you attempt to go for stilted, you end up with just mediocre.

But let's see if we can do better. I don't want to restructure the actual stage direction of the scene too much, although, I will do a bit because what happens around the dialogue *is* part of the dialogue. Mainly, I want to concentrate on the words coming out of the character's mouths.

"Bill!" Ted said, taking Bill's hand. Bill had stood as Ted approached the table. Ted had arrived late, wearing a pressed suit and carrying a briefcase. He had his hair slicked back. Dave, on the other hand, was in dungarees and a T-shirt. "How the hell are ya, buddy?"

"I'm good, Ted," Bill muttered as they sat. "Pretty good."

"Been here long?"

"Not really." Bill looked down at his coffee cup, half empty.

"I need one of those," Ted said, looking for a waitress. He made eye contact with one and motioned for her to bring him a cup.

Ted placed his briefcase flat on the table in front of him and put both his palms on top. He stared right into Bill's eyes. "So . . . how's the wife?"

"She's . . . she's okay, Ted," Bill said quietly. "You know. Same old thing." He looked nervously across the restaurant to a bunch of people being seated.

"Glad to hear it." Ted smiled. He had impeccably white teeth, reminding Bill of a shark. "Still golfing?"

Bill looked away again. "Not really. Threw out my shoulder . . ."

"Ooh, sorry to hear that."

"Yeah . . ."

"Anyway-" The waitress arrived with Ted's coffee, cutting him off. She set it down on the table in front of him, making him have to move his briefcase.

"Well," Ted said, "What do you say we get right down to business?"

"Sure . . . " Bill said, tentatively. His hands felt clammy.

Ted popped the latches on his briefcase open. They seemed extra loud in the small restaurant. He pulled out a laptop and a binder stuffed with promotional material. He passed the binder over to Bill. "I think you're gonna love what I have to show you," Ted said.

"I don't know," Bill said, "Stacey and I are pretty tight when it comes to our money. It's more her than me."

Ted smiled. "She's got ya by the short hairs, hey? Well even she'll be impressed when you tell her about this."

With a bit of rearranging of coffee cups and chairs, Ted set his laptop up on the table so they could both see it and began running through a PowerPoint presentation describing his investment deal. Every so often, he'd stop and refer Bill to a page in the binder. The presentation was very professional and slick.

Bill felt very warm. A trickle of sweat ran down the side of his face.

The presentation came to an end. "So," Ted said, "what do you think? I can get you in for five thousand. That's a pretty sweet deal just for you. We've moved up to ten thousand for everyone else at this point. I'm only doing this because we're friends."

"Gee, I really appreciate the opportunity Ted . . ." Bill said, " . . . but I don't know. I think I'm gonna have to pass."

"Seriously? Can I ask why?"

Once again, Bill's gaze wandered across the room. "Like I said, Stacey and I are pretty tight with are finances. She doesn't like me to throw money around. I know this is a good deal. I can see how good it is."

"You bet it's good."

"I know. I can tell."

"Then what's the problem?"

"I just . . . I don't think she'll get it."

"Why don't you go home and talk it over with her?" Ted suggested.

"Okay," Bill said, with a sigh. "I'll do that."

"Good man!" Ted said, checking his watch.

He stood from the table. Awkwardly, Bill stood too and they both shook hands. "I've gotta take off," Ted said. "I have another appointment downtown in twenty minutes. Don't forget to talk to Stacey about the thing. I'll call you in a couple days. All right?"

"All right."

"And give her my love."

"I will."

Okay, now you're probably going to call foul and say I cheated because it's so much longer, but that is a little bit of the point. Real dialogue isn't condensed into a few lines; it meanders and goes on tangents. Things happen to interrupt it. That's also why there is more happening in the second scene; all of the extra stuff happens around the dialogue; it's part of the scene and really you have to think of it as being part of the dialogue.

There's also better characterization—we actually see that Bill is nervous–but that's part of good dialogue too. And notice the structure of the sentences. They aren't all the same length like they are in the first scene. They vary. Sometimes speakers go on for three or four sentences, in other cases, they say one word and get cut off or drift off. If you listen to real dialogue in real life, people rarely say a complete sentence and hardly ever say a complete sentence without a contraction. You should pretty much always use contractions in dialogue unless you have a good reason not to. Good reasons might be: the character speaking is Data from *Star Trek: The Next Generation*; he is a God of some sort; or he is some sort of being that speaks very formally. Without contractions, a certain level of stiltedness will automatically occur in your dialogue.

Another thing to watch for when you're writing dialogue is that you're not playing ping pong. Dialogue shouldn't just be back and forth, one speaker says something the other reacts with something the other reacts back, and so on. There are always multiple levels of things going on. We are always saying one thing and meaning something else. In other words, there is always subtext happening. Half the time, we are playing catch up, still talking about something referred to three lines of dialogue back while the person we are talking to is onto an entirely new topic.

Want to do a neat exercise? Do exactly what I mentioned hypothetically doing at the beginning of this section. Most smartphones have recording software. Next time you're at a gathering or a party or wherever you happen to be with a lot of people carrying on different conversations, place your smartphone in an inconspicuous spot with the recording feature active and just let it record. Then, later, listen to all of the talking. Sure, you might feel a bit like the CIA, but it will do wonders for your dialogue writing.

Better yet, transcribe the conversations you recorded. I actually wrote a short story this way once and it turned out to read very much like something that may have been written by J.D. Salinger.

Let me throw in a little disclaimer here. I have no idea what privacy laws you'll be breaking by doing this exercise. I just know it's a good exercise. If you end up in prison, though, you're on your own. I don't know nothing.

One last example. One of my latest novels, *Dream with Little Angels* (Kensington, 2013) is written in dialect. A lot of editors warn against writing in dialect, because you have to be dead on for it to work. I had no problem selling my book and I think the dialect helped. I'm about to present a scene from that book to give you an idea of how I handled the dialogue. Note that only the dialogue is in dialect, the rest of the prose is not, it's not exactly perfect English, but it's certainly not as southern as the dialogue.

There are also other interesting differences between the prose parts and the dialogue parts. The book is written in first person from the point of view of the eleven-year-old son of the detective solving a murder. Whenever he refers to his mom in dialogue, he calls her "mom," and whenever he refers to her in the narrative, it's always as "my mother." I do the same thing with the words "reckon" and "think". In this way, the narrative around the dialogue is elevated to a more literary level, even though the book retains the feeling of being placed firmly in southern Alabama.

In this scene, the protagonist (eleven-year-old Abe Teal) and his best friend Dewey (who is at least one burnt sienna short of a full box of Crayolas) are suspicious of Abe's neighbor. They have no idea what, precisely they suspect he might be doing, mind you, they're just suspicious. So the two of them follow him into town one Saturday morning on their bicycles.

> Dewey turned out to already be up. He answered the phone on the first ring, which was good, because I didn't want to wake up his ma. She would have her own concerns, although through the years I had discovered Dewey's mother didn't seem nearly as thorough as my own when it came to worrying about or monitoring her son's business.
>
> "I'll meet you outside on my bike in fifteen minutes," I whispered excitedly into the phone after telling him about what I saw.
>
> "Why was he dressed like a cowboy?" Dewey asked. I heard him yawn right before he said it. It annoyed me that he wasn't already off the phone and getting his shoes on.
>
> "How the heck should I know? Why is he walking down Cottonwood Lane before seven on a Saturday? And the biggest question is why is he carrying a shotgun with him?" I was getting frustrated, because it was questions like these that were exactly the reason we had to follow him. If we knew all the answers, we could just stay home and Dewey could go back to bed the way it sure seemed like he wanted to right now.
>
> "You said the box just looked like it could carry a shotgun," Dewey said.
>
> "Yeah, but what else would you put in a box like that? Come on, Dewey. It was a cardboard shotgun box if I ever seen one."
>
> "Have you ever seen one? I never even heard've one."
>
> I thought that over. "No, I suppose I haven't. Not until this morning, anyway."
>
> "I'm not sure I should leave," Dewey said. "My mom's still asleep."
>
> "Leave her a note. Tell her you'll be back before nine." I reminded him I now had my very own watch.
>
> "I'm still thinking that maybe we should wait . . ."
>
> "Wait for what? We've been watchin' his house going on . . . I don't even know how long. Now, out of nowhere, I actually see him leave and we have the opportunity to find out what he's really up to. And you're worried about your mom because she's sleepin'?"

"We know he ain't taking roadkill," Dewey said. "It came back, remember?"

"We know he ain't taking it no more," I corrected him. "We have no idea what he does. This is what we have to find out." I sighed, trying not to get too angry and raise my voice too loud. I didn't want to wake anybody.

Finally, I convinced Dewey that going after Mr. Wyatt Edward Farrow was not only the right thing to do; it was, by all intents, the only thing to do.

"All right," he said. "Give me twenty minutes."

"Twenty minutes? You already used up ten on the phone. We need to catch up with him. You got ten to get here."

"All right."

It took him more like seventeen. In fact, I was on the verge of calling him back when I saw his bike pull up outside my yard through that gap in them drapes. I already had my boots on and quietly headed outside using the backdoor, being careful to shut it slowly so it didn't slam the way it normally did. I grabbed my bike from beside the garage and pushed it gently down the driveway in the still quiet of the early morning.

"What took you so long?" I asked, still keeping my voice down.

"I was in my pajamas when you called."

"So was I."

"I was hungry."

I rolled my eyes. "Fine time to think about eating. Anyway, let's go before someone wakes up and finds us."

"Did you leave YOUR mom a note?" Dewey asked.

I nodded.

"What'd it say?"

"Said I was going biking with you and I'd be home by nine. What did yours say?"

Dewey's cheeks pinkened under the golden morning light. The sun twinkled off the chrome of his handle bars. A few puffy white clouds were stretched across an otherwise light blue sky the color of a dipped Easter egg. "I said we was going after your neighbor to see what it is he does on Saturday mornings dressed as a cowboy."

I stared at him for what felt like a full-on minute, wondering if he was pulling my leg. He wasn't. "Now why would you go say somethin' dumb like that?" I asked.

"Cuz it's the truth, ain't it?"

"So? What if your mom calls my mom?"

"I always tell the truth."

I bit my tongue and thought before responding. "I do too, but just because I left out part of the why doesn't mean I wasn't being truthful. Anyway, it's too late now to worry 'bout it; we ain't goin' back to your house to rewrite your note. Let's go, before we lose any chance of findin' him. Christ, Dewey, it's been nearly half an hour since he left."

We kicked off in the same direction Mr. Wyatt Edward Farrow had been walking. "I figure he's likely gone downtown," I said. "Although I doubt too many shops or anythin' is open so early on a Saturday morning." I said this, although I didn't rightly know whether or not it was true. Maybe all this time I'd been thinking I was one of the only people who woke up bright and early on Saturday mornings when the truth was it actually turned out most folk were just like me, and my mother and Carry were the exceptions. I guess me and Dewey were about to find out.

While we rode, I told Dewey about me and my mother finding Carry and her boyfriend the night before. Most of the story I went over rather quickly, but he made me slow down at several key areas. The first was when I described what Carry was wearing in the back of that car. I knew he'd be interested in hearing that, I just never realized how interested. He must have asked me nearly ten different things about it. Finally, I just got mad.

"She was in her bra. What else do you need to know? Why is this so important?"

Dewey shrugged. He was coasting beside me. "I dunno," he said.

"Well, let's get past it, then, all right? I mean heck, you can either imagine what she looked like, or you can't. I don't see how I can provide any more details than I already have."

He stopped me again when I got to the end and told him about how my mother pulled out her gun, pointed it straight at Carry's boyfriend, and—the most important part, I thought—used the word. Not once, but twice.

"Really?" Dewey asked. This interested him even more than Carry's undergarments. "Was the gun loaded?"

It was my turn to shrug. "I'm assuming so. My mom said it was."

"And she used all them words?"

I nodded. We both swerved around a parked Chevy truck. "I couldn't believe what I heard," I said. "She even said she was gonna blow his balls off, or something to that effect."

"Wow."

When Dewey was finally satisfied that he'd wrung every detail of the story he could from me, we fell into silence for a while. I rode the lead, taking us up to Main Street.

"How do you know this is the way Mr. Farrow went?" Dewey asked.

"I don't," I said. "I just figure if you're gonna go out on a Saturday morning and get dressed up, you're probably headed downtown. I doubt he was going to the swamp or any of the mud roads or anything like that. He certainly didn't look dressed for roadkill collectin'."

Dewey considered this and seemed to be satisfied that it made some sort of sense, because he never asked any more about it. "So," he said after a bit, "did your mom really arrest Mr. Garner?"

This question didn't sit well with me, but I answered the truth. "Yep. Far as I know, he's still in jail."

"You don't sound too happy about it," he said.

I hesitated. Truth was, I wasn't happy about it, but I didn't exactly know why. Something about the whole thing felt very wrong to me. Like there was something I should understand but didn't, or maybe something I should be remembering but forgot. "Tell me somethin', Dewey; you were there that afternoon in the rain when we went searching for Mary Ann Dailey. Remember all the stuff Mr. Robert Lee Garner said? Remember the way he talked about Ruby Mae Vickers? How he put flowers out for her?"

Dewey said he did. "He didn't seem as though he wanted to talk much 'bout them flowers, though."

I nodded. "But we saw more flowers that day we rode over to his ranch, remember?" I asked. "The day they found Mary Ann? Those flowers seemed fresh to me."

"Yup," Dewey said. "Me, too."

I backpedaled slightly, slowing a bit. "Dewey, do you think Mr. Garner could do something like this to Mary Ann?"

"If the police think so, I don't see why my opinion would rightly matter. I'm only eleven years old," he said. This was a slightly different opinion than the one he had expressed the night Mary Ann Dailey showed up dead and Mr. Garner was first taken into custody.

Notice the dialogue doesn't overwhelm the scene by taking up all the space nor does it get squeezed out of existence by exposition. Exposition, dialogue, and setting all have to exist together in balance for things to work properly.

I want to give you one more example by an author other than myself.

Lewis Carroll was a master at not just writing dialogue, but expressing things in a way that nobody else could ever possibly say them in. He could take scenes that really weren't filled with that much conflict, and *make* you *have* to read through them, simply by virtue of the *way* they are composed. He excelled at creating minor conflicts between characters and keeping them going almost like little tennis matches. Each tossed quirky lines back and forth, often misinterpreting what the other meant. And the whole time you read it, you get the feeling there's a lot more going on here than just a banal bit of speech.

This scene is a piece from *Alice's Adventures in Wonderland*—the first Alice book, where Alice attends the Mad Hatter's tea party. It takes place in chapter seven. Just read it for the dialogue and the way the characters play off one another and how the rest of the exposition is set between their speaking. Pay special attention to how Carroll cleverly constructs the scene.

Partial Chapter VII of Lewis Carroll's
Alice's Adventures in Wonderland

There was a table set out under a tree in front of the house, and the March Hare and the Hatter were having tea at it: a Dormouse was sitting between them, fast asleep, and the other two were using it as a cushion, resting their elbows on it, and talking over its head. 'Very uncomfortable for the Dormouse,' thought Alice; 'only, as it's asleep, I suppose it doesn't mind.'

The table was a large one, but the three were all crowded together at one corner of it: 'No room! No room!' they cried out when they saw Alice coming. 'There's *plenty* of room!' said Alice indignantly, and she sat down in a large arm-chair at one end of the table.

'Have some wine,' the March Hare said in an encouraging tone.

Alice looked all round the table, but there was nothing on it but tea. 'I don't see any wine,' she remarked.

'There isn't any,' said the March Hare.

'Then it wasn't very civil of you to offer it,' said Alice angrily.

'It wasn't very civil of you to sit down without being invited,' said the March Hare.

'I didn't know it was *your* table,' said Alice; 'it's laid for a great many more than three.'

Ill. 2-4: A scene from the Mad Hatter's Tea Party from Chapter VII in Lewis Carroll's Alice's Adventures in Wonderland

'Your hair wants cutting,' said the Hatter. He had been looking at Alice for some time with great curiosity, and this was his first speech.

'You should learn not to make personal remarks,' Alice said with some severity; 'it's very rude.'

The Hatter opened his eyes very wide on hearing this; but all he *said* was, 'Why is a raven like a writing-desk?' 'Come, we shall have some fun now!' thought Alice. 'I'm glad they've begun asking riddles.—I believe I can guess that,' she added aloud.

'Do you mean that you think you can find out the answer to it?' said the March Hare.

'Come, we shall have some fun now!' thought Alice. 'I'm glad they've begun asking riddles.—I believe I can guess that,' she added aloud.

'Do you mean that you think you can find out the answer to it?' said the March Hare.

'Exactly so,' said Alice.

'Then you should say what you mean,' the March Hare went on.

'I do,' Alice hastily replied; 'at least—at least I mean what I say—that's the same thing, you know.'

'Not the same thing a bit!' said the Hatter. 'You might just as well say that "I see what I eat" is the same thing as "I eat what I see"!'

'You might just as well say,' added the March Hare, 'that "I like what I get" is the same thing as "I get what I like"!'

'You might just as well say,' added the Dormouse, who seemed to be talking in his sleep, 'that "I breathe when I sleep" is the same thing as "I sleep when I breathe"!'

'It *is* the same thing with you,' said the Hatter, and here the conversation dropped, and the party sat silent for a minute, while Alice thought over all she could remember about ravens and writing-desks, which wasn't much.

The Hatter was the first to break the silence. 'What day of the month is it?' he said, turning to Alice: he had taken his watch out of his pocket, and was looking at it uneasily, shaking it every now and then, and holding it to his ear.

Alice considered a little, and then said 'The fourth.'

'Two days wrong!' sighed the Hatter. 'I told you butter wouldn't suit the works!' he added looking angrily at the March Hare.

'It was the *best* butter,' the March Hare meekly replied.

'Yes, but some crumbs must have got in as well,' the Hatter grumbled: 'you shouldn't have put it in with the bread-knife.'

The March Hare took the watch and looked at it gloomily: then he dipped it into his cup of tea, and looked at it again: but he could think of nothing better to say than his first remark, 'It was the *best* butter, you know.'

Alice had been looking over his shoulder with some curiosity. 'What a funny watch!' she remarked. 'It tells the day of the month, and doesn't tell what o'clock it is!'

'Why should it?' muttered the Hatter. 'Does *your* watch tell you what year it is?'

'Of course not,' Alice replied very readily: 'but that's because it stays the same year for such a long time together.'

'Which is just the case with *mine*,' said the Hatter.

Alice felt dreadfully puzzled. The Hatter's remark seemed to have no sort of meaning in it, and yet it was certainly English. 'I don't quite understand you,' she said, as politely as she could.

'The Dormouse is asleep again,' said the Hatter, and he poured a little hot tea upon its nose.

Ill. 2-5: A scene from the Mad Hatter's Tea Party from Chapter VII in Lewis Carroll's Alice's Adventures in Wonderland

The Dormouse shook its head impatiently, and said, without opening its eyes, 'Of course, of course; just what I was going to remark myself.'

'Have you guessed the riddle yet?' the Hatter said, turning to Alice again.

'No, I give it up,' Alice replied: 'what's the answer?'

'I haven't the slightest idea,' said the Hatter.

'Nor I,' said the March Hare.

Alice sighed wearily. 'I think you might do something better with the time,' she said, 'than waste it in asking riddles that have no answers.'

'If you knew Time as well as I do,' said the Hatter, 'you wouldn't talk about wasting *it*. It's *him*.'

'I don't know what you mean,' said Alice.

'Of course you don't!' the Hatter said, tossing his head contemptuously. 'I dare say you never even spoke to Time!'

'Perhaps not,' Alice cautiously replied: 'but I know I have to beat time when I learn music.'

'Ah! that accounts for it,' said the Hatter. 'He won't stand beating. Now, if you only kept on good terms with him, he'd do almost anything you liked with the clock. For instance, suppose it were nine o'clock in the morning, just time to begin lessons: you'd only have to whisper a hint to Time, and round goes the clock in a twinkling! Half-past one, time for dinner!'

('I only wish it was,' the March Hare said to itself in a whisper.)

'That would be grand, certainly,' said Alice thoughtfully: 'but then—I shouldn't be hungry for it, you know.'

'Not at first, perhaps,' said the Hatter: 'but you could keep it to half-past one as long as you liked.'

'Is that the way *you* manage?' Alice asked.

The Hatter shook his head mournfully. 'Not I!' he replied. 'We quarrelled last March—just before *he* went mad, you know—' (pointing with his tea spoon at the March Hare,) '—it was at the great concert given by the Queen of Hearts, and I had to sing

> "Twinkle, twinkle, little bat!
> How I wonder what you're at!"

You know the song, perhaps?'

'I've heard something like it,' said Alice.

'It goes on, you know,' the Hatter continued, 'in this way:—

> "Up above the world you fly,
> Like a tea-tray in the sky.
> Twinkle, twinkle—"'

Here the Dormouse shook itself, and began singing in its sleep 'Twinkle, twinkle, twinkle, twinkle—' and went on so long that they had to pinch it to make it stop.

'Well, I'd hardly finished the first verse,' said the Hatter, 'when the Queen jumped up and bawled out, "He's murdering the time! Off with his head!"'

'How dreadfully savage!' exclaimed Alice.

'And ever since that,' the Hatter went on in a mournful tone, 'he won't do a thing I ask! It's always six o'clock now.'

A bright idea came into Alice's head. 'Is that the reason so many tea-things are put out here?' she asked.

'Yes, that's it,' said the Hatter with a sigh: 'it's always tea-time, and we've no time to wash the things between whiles.'

'Then you keep moving round, I suppose?' said Alice.

'Exactly so,' said the Hatter: 'as the things get used up.'

'But what happens when you come to the beginning again?' Alice ventured to ask.

'Suppose we change the subject,' the March Hare interrupted, yawning. 'I'm getting tired of this. I vote the young lady tells us a story.'

'I'm afraid I don't know one,' said Alice, rather alarmed at the proposal.

JOURNEYS UNDER THE MOON

'Then the Dormouse shall!' they both cried. 'Wake up, Dormouse!' And they pinched it on both sides at once.

The Dormouse slowly opened his eyes. 'I wasn't asleep,' he said in a hoarse, feeble voice: 'I heard every word you fellows were saying.'

'Tell us a story!' said the March Hare.

'Yes, please do!' pleaded Alice.

'And be quick about it,' added the Hatter, 'or you'll be asleep again before it's done.'

'Once upon a time there were three little sisters,' the Dormouse began in a great hurry; 'and their names were Elsie, Lacie, and Tillie; and they lived at the bottom of a well—'

'What did they live on?' said Alice, who always took a great interest in questions of eating and drinking.

'They lived on treacle,' said the Dormouse, after thinking a minute or two.

'They couldn't have done that, you know,' Alice gently remarked; 'they'd have been ill.'

'So they were,' said the Dormouse; '*very* ill.'

Alice tried to fancy to herself what such an extraordinary ways of living would be like, but it puzzled her too much, so she went on: 'But why did they live at the bottom of a well?'

'Take some more tea,' the March Hare said to Alice, very earnestly.

'I've had nothing yet,' Alice replied in an offended tone, 'so I can't take more.'

'You mean you can't take *less*,' said the Hatter: 'it's very easy to take *more* than nothing.'

'Nobody asked *your* opinion,' said Alice.

That's only the first bit of the chapter, but isn't it amazing how Lewis Carroll's brilliance shines through even such a simple scene like this? The reader feels more spinny reading the dialogue than Alice seems to and she's actually there. I love the way each character has his or her own voice. You can tell whose talking, simply from what they say and how they say it and, indeed, very little of the dialogue's actually tagged. The Hatter actually makes what I feel to be an editorial point on the entire chapter when he tells Alice that they keep moving round and round, because that's exactly what's happening in the dialogue and yet, at the same time, there *is* some forward momentum. The scene does progress.

Just remember, there are three keys to making your dialogue great: listen to other people talk, read a lot of books by authors who write dialogue that you like, and by far, the most important thing is to practice, practice, and practice.

2. AUTHORIAL VOICE

Authorial voice is the "you" that shines through in your writing. It's the reason you can read a few pages of prose and just know Stephen King wrote them, or know they were penned by Hemingway, or by Dean Koontz, or Kurt Vonnegut. Or by Jeffery Deaver. All of these authors have one thing in common: they all have very distinct authorial voices. Does it mean their stories all sound the same? Well, the answer to that is tricky. It's sort of a yes and no thing.

Developing your authorial voice is the best thing you can do for your career, especially if your voice is unique and compelling. When you first start writing, it's actually beneficial from a voice development point of view to try and emulate other authors. This little exercise will help you learn what it means to write with a voice. Then, once you leave the nest and write with your own voice, you'll know what you're doing.

The key to developing your voice is to not try too hard. Relax, and write almost as though you were talking to your readers. Especially on initial drafts, don't even worry about grammar or syntax or punctuation, just tell your story as though you were sitting around a campfire trying to enthrall a bunch of friends on a cozy summer's night. The thing is, you already have a voice. The key is finding it. And it's not very hard to find, because you use it every day. The hard part is learning how to let go and just write with it.

This is not to say you can't wax poetic from time to time. You won't always write with the same words you use when you normally speak, but you should still write in the same manner you speak. Or maybe, to be more precise, I should be telling you to write in the same manner in which you normally think. When you think to yourself using words, what do those words sound like? They are probably slightly different than the ones that come out when you open your mouth and actually speak. They probably have a more eloquent quality to them. It's that voice that is yours and yours alone. It's that voice that's going to make you stand out from the rest of the crowd of writers floundering to put down sentences any way they can.

Once you've started finding your voice, there are some qualities you should work on perfecting. It must be confident and strong. It should not be transparent in the writing. Your characters should all sound different, and each of your stories should have their own tone depending on how they're set, but the voice behind that tone and those characters should be unarguably yours. You will find, as you develop this voice that it might change as it grows stronger and gains conviction. As long as you like the changes you're experiencing, roll with them.

What do you do if you absolutely hate the voice you find yourself naturally writing in? Well, this is where the exercise of trying to copy other author voices comes in handy. Find authors who have strong voices that you admire and teach yourself to write in a voice style similar to theirs. Do not take their style verbatim, though. You do not want to be seen as a copycat of any particular writer. This will do your career no good.

You may have the opposite problem. You may find your natural voice is very similar to a well-known published author. If this is the case, I wouldn't fret too much, providing you're not actively trying to simulate that writer. My advice would be to stop reading his work, though. The more you read of a single writer's work, the more your own voice will naturally get pulled in the direction of that writer's voice.

The biggest problem facing you while finding your authorial voice is that it takes courage because you have to let go of the handrails and walk across the tightrope without a net. Once you start writing with your own voice, you are truly out on your own. Your writing suddenly belongs to you in a way it never did before. It's like giving up your last vestige of security because now it's all you and nobody else. And when you get critiqued (and of course, you're still going to get critiqued just as badly as you were before), it's going to feel even more personal because, especially at first, it will feel like you've put yourself all over those pages. There will be a strong temptation to feel personally attacked.

Don't let yourself be. Try to keep an emotional distance from your writing. Always. You will write better, you will be able to see your own flaws better, and you will take criticism better. Criticism is good. People are doing you a favor by telling you what you are doing badly. Always try to remember that.

Even after all this, the tradeoffs for writing with your own voice are by far worth it. Your writing skill will improve much more quickly, and soon your work will take on a more professional form than it had before.

Finding your own unique authorial voice is a huge step toward publishing your first book. Editors and agents are always looking for new, original voices. It's original and fresh voices that sell books.

And we all want to sell books.

EXERCISES

1. Write a scene where one character is from one part of the world, say England, and the other is from somewhere else, say, Boston. Try to write the dialogue in dialect. Remember, don't overdo it. It's easy to go overboard and overwhelm the reader. Remember, this is an exercise in dialogue, so have them in discussion.

2. Now write a scene with two characters that aren't so diversified. Maybe one is from the bad part of town and grew up in a poor family and the other is in college. Again, this is an exercise in dialogue, so have them in discussion. The voices should be discernably different without having to look at the attribution.

3. Write a scene between an adult and a twelve-year-old child arguing over something the child wants the adult to buy for him. Put them in a crowded retail store. This is another dialogue exercise so make it a dialogue intensive scene. The voices should be discernably different without having to look at the attribution.

KEY POINTS

- When it comes to character dialogue, remember that everyone has a different way of speaking, not just people from foreign countries. Some gesture more, some stutter, some have bigger vocabularies than others. Some people aren't well educated. Some will use catch phrases. Your characters should be discernable through their speech.
- Everything happening around the dialogue is actually part of the dialogue. The gestures and other habits we see add characterization to your book.
- If you write in dialect, remember that less is more. The same thing goes for writing from a different time period or a country where they don't speak English. Throw in the odd medieval word for a story set in the south of France during the Middle Ages, and when your characters speak, occasionally use a French word (that would've been in use at the time). Otherwise, avoid trying to write in Old English or anything like that. Nobody will understand your characters and it's the mark of an amateur. Leave out the thys and thous. Try not to use any slang that wasn't in use during the time period in question, but otherwise just write English. If you *are* writing for the Middle Ages, you may want to avoid contractions in speech, because nobody used them. This will make your characters sound more pompous, however. Just be sure you don't wind up with a bunch of characters talking like they're at a renaissance fair.
- Some of the best conflict comes through clever dialogue.
- While developing your authorial voice, read many books by writers who write with authorial voices you love. It's even better if you can hear the words being spoken to you, so pick up some audiobooks.

- You already have a unique voice inside you, it's just a matter of getting it to come out onto the page. This is another problem with an untamed Internal Editor—he gets in the way. So put him out of business during your first drafts.

CHAPTER FOUR

ACTION

Do you want to know who you are? Don't ask. Act! Action will delineate and define you.

—Thomas Jefferson[16]

1. ACTIVE VOICE VERSUS PASSIVE VOICE

Everyone's had it hammered into their skulls by now: "Write with active voice!" But, really, should you always do that? The answer is, most decidedly, no.

It's advice given, like most writerly advice, to beginners because it will immediately make their writing better. Most beginning writers start out automatically writing in the passive voice, in which the subject of a sentence is being acted upon rather than taking the action directly. "Batman was stabbed by the criminal" is a sentence written in passive voice. If you rearrange it like this: "The criminal stabbed Batman," it's in active voice.

Beginning writers also tend to write using static verbs that don't really punch up a sentence very well at all. This could be out of laziness, but I think it's more because their minds are so full of worrying about other aspects of the craft that the last thing they're thinking about is their verb choices.

---

[16] Thomas Jefferson (April 13, 1743 - July 4, 1826) was an American Founding Father, the principal author of the Declaration of Independence (1776) and the President of the United States. He served in the Continental Congress, representing Virginia at the beginning of the American Revolution.

For instance, take the example of: Randolph was driving his car to the store. "Was driving" is a very inactive verb form. Want to make it more exciting? How about this: Randolph hurtled his car toward the store. Or: Randolph's car fishtailed down the street, racing for the store. There are many ways you can pack a wallop into your verbs.

Making dynamic verbs a part of your writing style is integral to becoming a great author. Now, your first draft will probably be littered with static verbs even once you've done this for a while and that's fine. That's the whole point of second drafts. If there's one thing I've been trying to get through to you, it's not to worry about what you put down on paper the first time around. It's during the second revision where you go in and change it. Just get your story out there and finished, because that puts you far ahead of the game. Anyone can change Bill's airplane was falling out of the sky very fast to: Bill clung to his seat as his plane dove straight for the ground at an astronomical speed, but not everybody can finish a book.

When it comes to finding good dynamic verbs, I really find that the thesaurus can be your best friend. I own two. By the way, I'm one of those "book" guys. I know you can do the whole dictionary and thesaurus thing online these days, but I still have them all in book form. I use Webster's Third International and Webster's Eleventh for my dictionaries and for thesauruses, I have Merriam-Webster's Collegiate Thesaurus as well as Roget's International Thesaurus. The two thesauruses are completely different. The Webster's one allows you to look up words alphabetically, whereas the Roget's has you look up words by category which is really kind of cool. So you search through the index for VISION, for example, and then they have two sections, NOUNS and VERBS. Those then contain all the words associated with vision. I find I use both books equally.

What you really want to watch out for when it comes to dull verbs versus dynamic verbs are forms of the verb "be." For example: "The boy is eating an ice cream cone" contains a "to be" verb, "is." To remedy this, we could rewrite this sentence in a different manner. "Ice cream drips down the boys hands with each lick he takes of his cone."

Let's try an example paragraph. I'll write a first draft of something, not caring about my verb choices, and then go back and revise it into something that is (hopefully) better.

> It was nearly noon under the hot California sun. Children were out in the streets, playing. Some were skipping rope while others played hopscotch. An old lady was walking her dog down the sidewalk as the paperboy rode past and waved hello. *This is a perfect neighborhood*, she thought. She was very happy her and her husband had moved in to their new place. So far everything was perfect. It was much hotter than where they used to live in Colorado, and there was a lot less rain. She didn't really mind the rain, but now that she was here in Southern California, she decided she liked the sun better.

Okay, so there we have a completely fine first draft paragraph. It makes sense, it has characterization, internalization, and it even tells us a bit about the old lady's history. But those verbs really don't pop. Let's see if we can do better.

> At noon under the hot San Mateo sky, the sun hung low and hammered down onto the streets below. It reflected off the windshields of cars and the white concrete sidewalks. On either side of the street, children, squealing and laughing, engaged in skipping rope games, singing songs of boys and girls sitting in trees and kissing and little girls with axes giving their mother forty whacks. Some jumped on hopscotch squares drawn in pink and white chalk. Walking listlessly through the lush grass growing along the edge of the street, an old lady with her terrier watched the children play. Her face formed a creased smile. As the paperboy pedaled toward her, she expected him to make her move out of his way, but instead he veered around her, waving hello as he went by. *Oh, how much happier she was here than back in Colorado.* Glancing down the street at her brand new house, she couldn't believe she used to think she would never find a better neighborhood than the one they had in Colorado. Less than two weeks ago she still lived up there and she had thought all that rain had been romantic. She thought it made her happy. Now she knew nothing could be happier than all this radiant sunshine.

See the difference? I not only changed a lot of my verb choices, I changed a lot of everything else, too. The second version is far more powerful than the first. But take a look at the verb differences. First, I got rid of most of the "to be" verbs. There were some that I left, but very few. Look at some of the more powerful verbs now being used in the new version: hung, hammered, squealing, laughing, kissing, giving, jumped, formed, pedaled, veered, and glancing.

Also notice that the sentences are composed of different types in the second version. In the first version, most of the sentences are in subject-verb-noun form, and nearly all the same length. In the second version, I've broken this up and made the sentences different from each other and different lengths, giving the paragraph a much more interesting rhythm.

I started this chapter by saying you don't *always* have to write in active voice and, indeed, it isn't always in your best interest. As usual, this is a case of form following function. For instance, I write a series of mystery novels that take place in Southern Alabama and are told, primarily, in the first person from the point of view of an eleven year old boy. Now, it would seem out of place if, in this laid back little town I've created, I always had everyone speaking in active voice all the time. Southern people tend to drawl, hence the term "southern drawl." They ain't known for their activeness so much.

Let me give you an example from my newest book that will be out in spring of 2014. It's called *Close to the Broken Hearted* and is the sequel to my first book in the series *Dream with Little Angels*.

This is the prologue to the book, which, as you will see, builds up in intensity and, at the same time, builds up in its use of active verbs:

> *The spring sun is low in the sky outside the single-paned windows of the kitchen in the small farmhouse where the family has gathered to eat. Upon the table sits a roast chicken ready to be carved, a plate of mashed potatoes, and a bowl of peas and corn, both harvested last year but kept frozen through the winter months. The light falling in through the windows is a deep orange, almost red, as the father, Tom Carson, stands to say grace. His hat sits on the top newel of the short run of stairs that separates this room from the living room below.*

The table, like the house, was built by his father. The chicken and the vegetables came from the farm. Unlike the house, the rest of the farm had once all belonged to his father's father. Tom Carson is a proud man even though he lives a modest life. He is proud of his work in the fields that starts at daybreak and ends at supper. He is proud of his two children: Caleb, barely three, with black hair and fair skin like his father and Sylvie, five and a half, with blonde hair like her mother used to have. They are good kids. Respectful kids. Long ago they learned not to make noise or fuss about while their father says grace. Soon Caleb will start working with his father little by little out on the farm. Sylvie already does some jobs with her mother around the home.

Each of the kids clutch their mother's hands. Mother closes her eyes. She is a good woman. Tom is lucky to have all he has. He notices wrinkles around his wife's eyes he hasn't noticed before, and wonders how hard this life has been on her. It's a thought that hasn't occurred to him until now.

In his cracked voice, he delivers the blessing, thanking the Lord Jesus for this wonderful bounty He has bestowed upon their family. The Lord Jesus has been good to Tom Carson.

Tom finishes and takes his chair at the table, folding his napkin onto his lap. Mother's fingers let go of the children's hands. Her gray eyes open and she smiles across the table at Tom. Tom reaches for the platter of chicken so that he may start to carve.

Across the room, there's a loud knock at the door.

Mother jumps.

"Who would be knockin' aroun' here at supper time?" she asks.

"Dunno," Tom Carson says gruffly. He gently lifts the napkin from his lap and begins to rise from the table when the door swings open with a squeak. It wasn't locked. Tom and his family never lock their doors. Nobody around these parts ever lock their doors.

Tom freezes, half out of his chair, as Preacher Eli Brown steps into his home. The preacher man is dressed in a white shirt with black trousers and vest. Muddy boots cover his feet. His thin face is fixed and stern, but what's caught Tom's attention is the gun the preacher holds in his right hand. It is pointed at the floor, being held as though it wasn't there at all.

"Preacher Eli," Tom says, trying to keep his voice calm. "What brings you 'round here? We's just 'bout to sit down to supper as you can see." He sits back down.

The preacher says nothing, just stomps across Tom's living room leaving a trail of dried mud on the wooden floor. He comes up the few stairs toward the small kitchen where the family squeezes around the table. With each of the man's footsteps, Caleb wiggles out of his chair and crawls under the table where he seeks out the safety of his father's legs.

Preacher Eli dangles over the rail along the top of the stairs, the gun hand waving conspicuously in the air as he speaks with a low slow drawl. "Tom. You and I have quite a land dispute goin' on. This thing oughta be worked out soon or there could be some trouble comin'."

Tom Carson looks down at his empty plate. "There ain't no dispute, Eli. The land's mine. It belonged to my father, just as it belonged to his father. Been in my family at least three generations. Maybe even more."

"The church disagrees with you."

Tom turned back to the preacher, his face red. "The church has no jurisdiction here, preacher. If the land belonged to you, you'd have a title to it. If you got a title, produce it. But you can't do that, cuz you ain't got one, and since you ain't got no title, you ain't got no land."

"The title is <u>missing</u>. You can't produce one either."

"Yes, well, the title seems to have <u>gone</u> missing." Tom clears his throat. "I'd say you had somethin' to do with that. Doesn't matter, Eli. Everyone knows the land belongs to me."

"You wanna start asking folk?"

"No. Folk is 'fraid of you."

Preacher Eli Brown's teeth form a thin V of a smile. They are more brown than white and less than straight.

"That how the church doin' things these days, Eli? Bit of a step backwards, ain't it?" Tom nods at the gun. "That why you here? To scare me into giving you my land so you can build your new 'facility' on it? I got news for you, Eli. I ain't afraid of you or your 'church'"

This time it's Preacher Eli who reddens. "Well you oughta be. You oughta be very 'fraid. It is a spiteful and vengeful God you forsake. One does not just turn his back on the will of the Lord Jesus without severe repercussions." His bony voice grows in anger and volume. From under the table, Caleb climbs up onto his father's lap.

For a minute, Tom Carson says nothing; just stares pathetically back at the tall preacher who looks somehow scarecrow-like bathed in the red-orange light of dusk. "You are a fool, Eli. Who said anything about forsakin' God? I ain't turned my back on the Lord Jesus. Your church has nothing to do with neither God nor Jesus. Least if it does, it sure ain't my Jesus. If it were, heaven help us all. There is absolutely nothing holy about your affairs, Eli. You oughta be ashamed of callin' yourself a man of the cloth. You've made a mockery of everything folk hold sacred."

Tom turns back to the chicken. He's done talking to the preacher. He's given this man too much time in his house already. But as soon as he picks up the knife to begin carving the bird, a strange feeling comes over him, and he hesitates, glancing back at the man with the gun.

Preacher Eli's eye twitches. His facial muscles tighten. When he talks again, it's with the same commanding voice he uses from the pulpit. "How dare you speak to me with such irreverence? It is <u>you</u>..." His hand holding the gun shakes. "<u>You</u> Tom Carson. You who must... who <u>will</u> answer for your sins."

Something flashes in the preacher man's eyes: a flicker of insanity.

Tom Carson has never been much of a gambler, but in that instant when he sees that look in Preacher Eli's eyes, he knows he's made a grave mistake. Until now, Tom had thought Eli Brown was many things, but a killer was definitely not one of them. Sure, the man had brought a gun into his home, but Tom had never really been scared. At no time did he think he or his family were in jeopardy of being hurt. Tom had chalked the weapon up to being part of the preacher's game--part of his ploy to scare him into giving up what rightfully belonged to him. Tom had decided almost immediately after the man entered that he wouldn't let himself be so easily duped.

Only now, in this split second, Tom knows he's played his cards all wrong. Everything is over. It's all about to come to an end at the hands of a madman he grossly underestimated.

That thought's the last thing to go through Tom's mind as Eli raises the gun and pulls the trigger.

The small room, suddenly gone dark, fills with the sound of a gunshot. It echoes off the wooden walls and floor like a thunderous death knell. Tom hears nothing else, only that deadly explosion. It seems to last an eternity and fills everything, even his mind.

In fact, Tom has been so focused on Preacher Eli, he hadn't noticed when Caleb made his way up his pant legs onto his lap minutes ago.

Now, as the sound dies away, leaving only the smell of gunpowder in its wake, Tom looks down, expecting to see his own stomach blown open; expecting to see himself dying.

What he sees is far, far worse.

There in his lap lay what remains of his little boy.

His perfect little man who just turned three years old barely two weeks ago lies with half his head on Tom's leg, and one arm wrapped around his waist.

Tom's eyes fill with tears as he takes in the blood splattered across the table, the floor, the counters, and most of this side of the kitchen. Tom himself is covered in it. He begins to shake. He rubs his son's arm as the world grows very small, and he looks back up to the preacher. It takes a minute for the words to come. When they do, they barely escape his lips. "What... what have you done?" he asks quietly.

The preacher's eyes widen in surprise as he steps slowly back down the stairs. His hand holding the gun falls to his side, the weapon slipping off his fingers and falling to the floor. His head shakes. "No..." he says. "No."

Across the table, Mother begins screaming, "My baby! My baby!" She comes around to where Caleb lies dead in a bundle in his father's lap. "My poor sweet baby."

Her daughter Sylvie remains quiet. She just pulls her feet up onto her chair and, wrapping her arms around her knees, tries to make herself as small as possible. She watches her mother and father cry over their dead son. She sees the preacher man who came in right before supper and killed her baby brother in the name of Jesus leave by the same door he came in through. She watches it all like a movie, unable to really comprehend what it means. It's so emotionally confusing, she feels almost nothing.

Just an emptiness inside. All empty and hollow.

She begins rocking back and forth on the wooden chair, her long blonde pigtails swinging against her face. In her mind, a voice screams "No! No! No!" over and over, but it's only in her head. On the outside, she's quiet. In fact, she doesn't even hear her parents crying anymore. She sees them, but she doesn't really process what she's looking at.

Nothing makes any sense.

When she woke up this morning, she had been a happy five-year-old girl with a good family and a good life. For the last year, she always told her mom her biggest wish was to raise horses and have babies when she grew up. Three babies.

Those had been her dreams. Horses and babies.

Now, sitting in that kitchen of death, Sylvie Carson no longer cares about the horses or the babies. She no longer cares about life. Preacher Eli killed her baby brother and he also killed her dreams. And none of it made any sense.

What Sylvie doesn't know is that this is only the beginning.

Because for her, the world will never make sense ever again.

Notice there are a lot of "to be" verbs here, especially at the beginning, but where it's important, I switch to active voice: "Mother jumps" "There in his lap lay what remains of his little boy" "Across the table, Mother begins screaming" "The preacher's eyes widen in surprise as he steps slowly back down the stairs" and so on.

It's important to start using active verbs in your writing as much as possible. Once you do, you will automatically get a feel for when you should use them and when you should pull back a bit. If you're writing a suspense thriller, you're going to use them a lot more, especially during the high-tension suspense scenes.

2. Beware Needless Stage Direction

Quite often on first drafts, I will find myself writing needless stage direction that serves only to bog down my prose. It's important that, as writers, we are aware of these tendencies and get rid of such things on second draft.

Here's an example:

> *She watched as Fiona and Jessica fought in the parking lot.*

The phrase "she watched" is unneeded in this sentence. You may feel you need <u>some</u> stage direction, such as:

> *She turned. In the parking lot, Fiona and Jessica were fighting.*

This is slightly better.

But, by far, the best way to handle this is to simply do away with the direction entirely. The audience knows the action is being filtered through your point of view character already, so you don't need to remind them. Something like this is by far the best way to handle a situation of this type:

> *In the parking lot, Fiona took a swing at Jessica. Jessica ducked, but came around with a left of her own.*

Always remove phrases like "she saw" and "she noticed" in favor of direct presentation.

Exercises

1. Take something you've previously written (a page or two, no more) and go through it and try to punch it up by using active verbs. Don't be afraid to pull out that thesaurus. If you don't feel right doing it with your own work right now, or have nothing available to "punch up", see what you can do with this one:

Bill and Shelly arrived late to the baby shower. As usual, it had been Shelly's fault. She just could not leave the house on time. Ever. She was constantly doing her makeup or fixing her hair or applying just "one more dab of this." "Come on!" Bill had called from the door, jacket already on, keys already in hand. I'm supposed to meet the guys at Tucker's for a beer to watch the game in five minutes.

Nine minutes later they were finally in Bill's car and Bill was mad. Lisa lived over ten miles away on the other side of town and he knew Phil and the rest of the gang wouldn't have waited for him. Why would they? He wouldn't wait for them if the situation was reversed. Luckily, he knew all the back roads where there was very little traffic.

Coming down Hawthorne, Bill turned hard onto Second and then made a quick left onto Gabaldi. He was doing twenty miles an hour over the speed limit, but he didn't care. All he could think about was beer and basketball.

That's when the blue and lights of the cop car lit up the road behind him.

"Oh dear," Shelly said, hardly even annoyed. It just made Bill Madder.

"Screw this," he said. "I drive a four liter Mustang. Let's see what that piece of Pontiac junk he's driving can do."

Slowly, Bill's foot lowered onto the gas pedal and he felt the car speed up. Pretty soon trees were going past his windows in a blur. The speedometer read one hundred and thirty miles per hour.

Bill turned out to be right. The cop couldn't keep up, but no doubt he was calling the incident in. There'd be roadblocks ahead.

But Bill knew other backstreets. Pulling on the emergency brake so his brake lights wouldn't flash, Bill turned down a narrow alley, his speed once again resuming way above the hundred mark.

"Are you crazy?" Shelly asked, her knuckles white on the hand grip.

"Your fault for taking so long," Bill said and smiled.

Two more dark alleys later, Bill made the main highway. From there it was just one street over to Lisa's baby shower. They turned out to be only eight minutes late and the guys hadn't even left yet.

2. Now it's your turn. Try to write something that isn't so active and then rewrite it so that it really pops off the page. Keep things moving as much as possible. The scene I chose earlier in the chapter wasn't even really a scene that lent itself well to verb usage. You could pick something with a lot more dynamics to it, like a plane crashing or an earthquake.

3. Make a list of all the common verbs you use all the time that you would do well to find replacement words for. Then brainstorm a bunch of other words you can use instead of those words (or look them up in a thesaurus) and start a notebook to keep handy by your computer while you're writing. Good common verbs to watch for are things like: walk, run, drive, go, went, smiled, sighed, and laughed. I'm sure you have your own list.

KEY POINTS

- Try to keep your writing as active as possible by not only writing in active voice, but by making sure all your verbs really pop. Use a thesaurus if you need to.
- Break up your sentence structures so they aren't all the same. It's easy to get in the habit of writing every sentence in subject-verb-noun form. Don't do this all the time. Also make sure your writing has a rhythm to it and that your sentences vary in length.
- There are some cases when you don't want to write with high-action verbs. For instance, you may want to set a very stoic scene that leads up to a dramatic climax. In that case, the beginning half of the scene would be written using dull and unassuming verbs, with the intention of taking the reader by surprise when you finally kick it into high gear.
- Watch out for needless stage direction. *Mary looked at the chipmunks fighting over the acorn in the bush* should be changed to simply: *Three chipmunks leapt on each other, quarrelling over a lone acorn they'd discovered in a thorny bramble.* By context and the previous text, the reader already knows it's Mary doing the looking. Or if that isn't the case, maybe change it to: *Mary heard a strange scuffling. In the brambles, three chipmunks leapt upon each other, struggling to be the first to reach a lonely acorn.*

CHAPTER FIVE

Description & Setting

> Men shut their doors against a setting sun.
> –William Shakespeare[17]

1. BE SPECIFIC

Supplying details is one of the most important jobs you have as a writer. Details and how they are used are what decide whether or not your readers are able to suspend disbelief while reading your books. You have to make sure you give them enough details to put them in the story, although it is possible to go overboard. Some authors are very good at description and can get away with giving out a lot more of it than others. This is something you will have to figure out for yourself.

But for my books, set in a small mythological town in Southern Alabama, I want to make sure my readers see the streets, the road signs, the stores, the early morning papers being delivered, the kids waiting at the bus stop to go to school. I want to show the season, so I mention the trees and the leaves and how hot the sun is, although it's always pretty darn hot in Southern Alabama.

Occasionally, I'll throw in a bird or a specific tree or group of trees if my characters are driving by a forest. But I make sure the bird and the

---

[17] William Shakespeare (April 26, 1564 - April 23, 1616) was an English poet and playwright. Quote citation: "Timon of Athens" Scene II.

tree are indigenous to the area my book is taking place in first, of course.

You can also add details through inferring things by character internalization. What I mean by this is if your character is considering making her daughter a costume for a Halloween party and is all anxious about it and we can see her thoughts, you've effectively told us the time of year.

Two rules of thumb when it comes to details:

- A detail is concrete if it appeals to one of our senses.
- A detail is significant if it conveys a judgment or an idea or both at the same time that it appeals to our senses.

So, in the second case, you're relying on the reader to make a connection, or a leap, if you will, between what you're saying and what you want him to take away from it.

For example:

Concrete detail: The leaves of the maple had begun to look burnt by the sun.

Significant and concrete detail: The leaves of the maple had begun to look burnt by the sun and many had fallen, leaving its branches bare like the arms of some frightened stick man.

The first example suggests that it's late summer or early fall.

The second example suggests that all the leaves are dying and that winter's coming, but it's up to the reader to make this judgment call.

Make sure you select only those details that are significant to the story. These are things that are essential to an understanding of character, setting, time, or mood. Everything, ultimately, has to be about the story.

Here's an example from the prologue of my novel *Dream with Little Angels*. This is *all* setting.

> *The grass is tall, painted gold by the setting autumn sun. Soft wind blows through the tips as it slopes up a small hill. Near the top of the hill, the blades shorten, finally*

breaking to dirt upon which stands a willow. Its roots, twisted with Spanish moss, split and dig into the loam like fingers. The splintery muscles of one gnarled arm bulge high above the ground, hiding the small body, naked and pink, on the other side. Fetal positioned, her back touches the knotted trunk. Her eyes are closed. Above her, the small leaves shake together as their thin branches shiver in the cold breeze. The red and silver sky gently touches her face. Her breath is gone. The backs of her arms, the tops of her feet, are blue. She's too small for this hill, too small for this tree.

She's too small to be left alone under all this sky.

2. ADJECTIVES, ADVERBS, AND CONCRETE NOUNS

Most writers are comfortable using adjectives and adverbs for describing things, sometimes to their own detriment. Too many adverbs can be a bad thing, just as too many adjectives lined up in front of a noun is almost always the mark of an amateur writer.

Far better, I think, it is to use a combination of adjectives and precise concrete nouns for description. The use of adverbs is generally considered bad form, so try to use them sparingly. Other than this, it's simply a matter of reading a lot of good writing and a whole lot of practice.

Consider the following passage where I've boldfaced all the words relating to description:

> Aurora, who considers herself a well-to-do **vampire**, wears a **black cloak** with **red lining**, a **gold coronet** edged with **lozenge-shaped rubies** in **gold mounts**, slick black **pants**, silvery chain **mail**, and a couple of ancient weighty **medallions** suspended from a heavy silver **neck chain**. On her head she wears a **carcanet** inset with a **blood red ruby rose**. She hasn't changed much in the last two hundred years. Her **black hair** is slicked back with a **silver stripe** running through it. She has a **shark-toothed smile** that displays four **sharp fangs**. When satisfied, she enjoys smiling, and her **eyes** will often open wide in **pleasure**. In those **eyes**, one can see the vastness of the **universe and stars**, but usually her **eyes** are narrowed; they hide much and they watch, waiting for her chance to pounce.

You get a full description of Aurora, without any overdoing it of adjectives and absolutely no dreaded adverbs. Just a precise description of exactly what the reader needs to know, explained by using mainly concrete nouns with some supporting adjectives both of which are boldfaced above.

Notice that I haven't used any highbrow nouns, either? It's important when you're writing that you keep your words as simple as possible. George Orwell had a rule: always write your sentences as short as they need to be, and never use a complicated word if a simpler one will suffice.

3. WHEN TO USE DESCRIPTION

Description should be used when it is appropriate. There are general usage rules you can follow by looking at commercial fiction but really it's up to the author to decide where to place description and setting and how much of it is too much or not enough.

Generally, I like to start my scenes with my characters doing something and then have some description of the environment the scene is taking place in. If a new character enters the story or a scene that hasn't been introduced before, you should probably have a quick description of that character either at that point or as soon as possible afterward.

For instance:

Frank walked down the sidewalk along Franklin Street toward Beckett's place, making sure his gun was easily accessible. He wasn't about to screw this one up. Even though the case appeared to be cut and dried, he'd been a detective long enough to know you had to prepare for the worst, and this was one of those times that the worst could be something pretty bad.

He'd parked his car a block away from Beckett's on the side of the road so Beckett wouldn't see it. There was a natural bend in the road as Frank followed it inwards. Along the sidewalk's edge were woods. Mostly birch and hemlock, but Frank noticed farther back the woods grew denser with oak and ash. Thick trunks that pushed together, giving Frank the feeling he was staring into the black pools of Hell as he looked deeper into those woods.

He kept walking toward Beckett's house. Above his head, boughs of thick leaves overhung the sidewalk, blocking out the sun, low in the western sky.

Finally Beckett's house came into view. Frank was closer than he thought. It had been right around the corner.

Beckett lived in a ranch style home; it was mostly white with stone trim. Despite being only one level, it looked pricey. And it looked new. But then, should that surprise Frank? Beckett had to be making dough like crazy, even if he was trying to hide that little tidbit of info. Frank wondered if old Beckett cooked the drugs up here in the house or had some other place he did it. Or, quite possibly, he paid some other guy to do it for him. That was probably more in line with a guy like Beckett's style.

A brand new red convertible sat in the driveway. The plates matched the ones Frank had run for Beckett. That meant he was probably home. Frank sighed. Like it or not, this was probably going down and it was going down now and he was doing it by himself.

Walking past the nice trimmed lawn and the short hedgerow, he came to the cobblestone walkway that ran along the front of the house to the door. Frank decided his best approach was to try the easy way first: just go up and knock. Who knew what would happen? The navy blue curtains across the picture window were drawn shut as he went past and ascended the four brick steps to the porch before knocking on the thick wooden door.

Frank waited. Nobody answered. Right before Frank was about to knock again, he noticed the light in the peephole go dark. Someone was on the other side. Here we go, *thought Frank. His fingers went to the handle of his forty caliber Smith & Wesson he had beneath his coat.*

To Frank's surprise, Beckett opened the door with no sign of being armed. At least Frank figured it was Beckett. He'd never actually seen the man before.

"You Calvin Beckett?" Frank asked.

"Yeah," Beckett replied. "Who the hell are you?"

The man standing in front of Frank was taller than him by at least four inches. He probably stood six-two. He wore a white wife-beater that needed to be washed and hung half-tucked into denim jeans that were about an inch too short. He wore no socks on. His right eye was messed up, almost like he'd taken a gunshot to the face. He had a scar below his other eye. His face had more stubble on it than Frank could grow in a week. All Frank could think was: This is Calvin Beckett? *He was nothing like Frank had expected.*

Calvin Beckett looked like a man who'd been through a war and somehow managed to come back alive. He seemed like a survivor—that was the best way to describe Frank's initial estimate of him.

Seeing Beckett didn't help Frank's state of mind much. The last thing he wanted was to go up against someone who looked like a survivor. In Frank's experience, survivors did just that: they generally survived.

This shows the way *I* do description and setting and mix it with my dialogue. Basically, I describe things as they need to be described, giving the reader as much internalization as needed to move the story along, but not so much that it bogs things to a halt.

One last note about description. Kristine Kathryn Rusch, good friend and amazingly talented (not to mention prolific) writer, once told me that you should hit all five of the reader's senses every two pages. I have trouble making that mark. I usually shoot for every four pages. But this could be why she's won so many awards that I haven't.

For a final example, I'm going to give you one from Mark Twain. This is part of chapter three of *The Adventures of Tom Sawyer*. Twain writes amazing description and setting, as anyone who's read his work knows. He also writes amazing dialect, so this is a great lesson in both.

A Portion of Chapter Three of Mark Twain's
The Adventures of Tom Sawyer

Tom skirted the block, and came round into a muddy alley that led by the back of his aunt's cow-stable. He presently got safely beyond the reach of capture and punishment, and hastened toward the public square of the village, where two "military" companies of boys had met for conflict, according to previous appointment. Tom was General of one of these armies, Joe Harper (a bosom friend) General of the other. These two great commanders did not condescend to fight in person—that being better suited to the still smaller fry—but sat together on an eminence and conducted the field operations by orders delivered through aides-de-camp. Tom's army won a great victory, after a long and hard-fought battle. Then the dead were counted, prisoners exchanged, the terms of the next disagreement agreed upon, and the day for the necessary battle appointed; after which the armies fell into line and marched away, and Tom turned homeward alone.

As he was passing by the house where Jeff Thatcher lived, he saw a new girl in the garden—a lovely little blue-eyed creature with yellow hair plaited into two long-tails, white summer frock and embroidered pantalets. The fresh-crowned hero fell without firing a shot. A certain Amy Lawrence vanished out of his heart and left not even a memory of herself behind. He had thought he loved her to distraction; he had regarded his passion as adoration; and behold it was only a poor little evanescent partiality. He had been months winning her; she had confessed hardly a week ago; he had been the happiest and the proudest boy in the world only seven short days, and here in one instant of time she had gone out of his heart like a casual stranger whose visit is done.

He worshipped this new angel with furtive eye, till he saw that she had discovered him; then he pretended he did not know she was present, and began to "show off" in all sorts of absurd boyish ways, in order to win her admiration. He kept up this grotesque foolishness for some time; but by-and-by, while he was in the midst of some dangerous gymnastic performances, he glanced aside and saw that the little girl was wending her way toward the house. Tom came up to the fence and leaned on it, grieving, and hoping she would tarry yet awhile longer. She halted a moment on the steps and then moved toward the door. Tom heaved a great sigh as she put her foot on the threshold. But his face lit up, right away, for she tossed a pansy over the fence a moment before she disappeared.

The boy ran around and stopped within a foot or two of the flower, and then shaded his eyes with his hand and began to look down street as if he had discovered something of interest going on in that direction. Presently he picked up a straw and began trying to balance it on his nose, with his head tilted far back; and as he moved from side to side, in his efforts, he edged nearer and nearer toward the pansy; finally his bare foot rested upon it, his pliant toes closed upon it, and he hopped away with the treasure and disappeared round the corner. But only for a minute—only while he could button the flower inside his jacket, next his heart—or next his stomach, possibly, for he was not much posted in anatomy, and not hypercritical, anyway.

He returned, now, and hung about the fence till nightfall, "showing off," as before; but the girl never exhibited herself again, though Tom comforted himself a little with the hope that she had been near some window, meantime, and been aware of his attentions. Finally he strode home reluctantly, with his poor head full of visions.

All through supper his spirits were so high that his aunt wondered "what had got into the child." He took a good scolding about clodding Sid, and did not seem to mind it in the least. He tried to steal sugar under his aunt's very nose, and got his knuckles rapped for it. He said:

"Aunt, you don't whack Sid when he takes it."

"Well, Sid don't torment a body the way you do. You'd be always into that sugar if I warn't watching you."

Presently she stepped into the kitchen, and Sid, happy in his immunity, reached for the sugar-bowl—a sort of glorying over Tom which was wellnigh unbearable. But Sid's fingers slipped and the bowl dropped and broke. Tom was in ecstasies. In such ecstasies that he even controlled his tongue and was silent. He said to himself that he would not speak a word, even when his aunt came in, but would sit perfectly still till she asked who did the mischief; and then he would tell, and there would be nothing so good in the world as to see that pet model "catch it." He was so brimful of exultation that he could hardly hold himself when the old lady came back and stood above the wreck discharging lightnings of wrath from over her spectacles.

• ──────────────── •

You can't ask for a better example than that. Even though it's just a small portion of the chapter, you can see how Mark Twain paints a picture of the scene as though you were looking at a photograph. He manages to pick out just the important details and give them to you in a way that is poetic yet doesn't interfere with the story at all. It's the way all description should be.

Description and setting is an art in itself. It's something you have to practice, and, like everything else, the more you do it the better you get. Here's some advice: read a lot of books by writers who handle description and setting the way you would like to handle it and try to emulate them. That's one way of accelerating the process.

EXERCISES

1. Take the sentence: **The man drove the car down the road**. Now, describe the man. This is the only change allowed. You may replace the word man with a different word if you wish. or you may add description another way. This rule applies to all the following examples.

2. Now describe the car. Again this is the only change allowed.

3. Finally, describe the road. In case I need to remind you, this is the only change you may make, other than the two you have already made.

4. Now describe how the man drove the car down the road.

5. Now give the sentence a setting.

6. Give the sentence an observer of the man driving the car.

7. Describe how the observer feels about the man driving the car down the road. Show the reader; don't tell.

KEY POINTS

- Be specific when describing something. Instead of saying *The car drove down the road*, say *The old Buick with the light blue trim on the hood and the doors, roared down Main Street kicking up dust in its path.*
- A detail is concrete if it appeals to one of our senses. A detail is significant if it conveys a judgment of an idea or both at once that appeals to our senses.
- Try to avoid adverbs unless it's absolutely necessary. Use a good mix of adjectives and concrete nouns for your descriptions.
- Don't just dump heaps of description on your readers. Spoon it out gradually, as the scene progresses.
- Try to hit all five of your reader's senses every two pages. Sometimes you can get multiple hits from a single description: *The icy air whistling through the pier was cold and held the saltiness and smell of the sea before which I stood* hits touch, hearing, sight, taste, and smell. All five in a single sentence. So it really isn't as tough as it sounds.

Part III

Archetypes

The creation of something new is not accomplished by the intellect but by the play instinct acting from inner necessity. The creative mind plays with the objects it loves.

–Carl Jung[18]

---

[18] Carl Gustav Jung (July 26, 1875 - June 6, 1961) was a Swiss psychotherapist and psychiatrist who founded analytical psychology. He developed the concepts of extraverted and introverted personalities.

CHAPTER ONE

How to Use Archetypes

> Today you are You, that is truer than true. There is no one alive who is Youer than You.
>
> –Dr. Seuss[19]

1. WHAT ARE ARCHETYPES?

Archetypes are psychological representations of all that we encounter in the physical universe. This includes fundamental definitions of everything, including things like chairs and tables, and books, as well as things like personality traits and the roles people play in our lives and our culture.

The concept of the archetype has been around at least as long as Plato, although the term, which is Greek, was not in use then. Most of the research on archetypes that we rely upon today was done by the psychologist Carl Jung who discovered the fascinating fact that archetypes are not something we learn, but are actually something we are born already knowing. Archetypes are embedded into our psyche. They are part of what Jung called the "collective unconscious," and can be found nearly everywhere on Earth, across every culture and continent, and even existed across societies before those societies had any contact with other cultures.

---

[19] Ted Geisel (March 2, 1904 - September 24, 1991 was an American writer, poet and cartoonist, probably best known for his books *Green Eggs and Ham* and *The Cat in the Hat.*)

In other words, everyone has the same library of archetypes at their disposal. This is what makes them such a powerful tool to use in your writing—you can tap into this very primal source of energy that is common across cultures and people. You can leverage it in your storytelling, using tropes that will ring true on a guttural level for nearly all your readers. They won't simply understand the basic nature of your stories, they will actually expect certain story beats to be there and resonate with them.

The power of archetypes and archetypal themes is phenomenal.

It's as though we all have an encyclopedia set in our brains telling us exactly the way the *real* things are and everything else we see around us are just reasonable facsimiles of these perfect forms. That was precisely Plato's take on it. Jung wasn't quite so cut and dried. He found that the psyche basically mapped out different roles that people and things fulfilled and would act them out in various ways. In this case, I'm talking about human archetypes, what have come to be called Jungian archetypes, which are what this chapter will be discussing. Chapter three deals with animal archetypes, another concept Jung investigated thoroughly.

These "roles" or "figures" would automatically appear in our stories and our dreams and, especially, our religions. Our religions are full of archetypal symbols, many of which are the same from one religion to the next in varying degrees.

This explains why we see so many commonalities between all these things across all cultures throughout the world. Archetypes define ancient patterns of personality that are part of the shared heritage of the human race and they're amazingly constant throughout all times.

Jung also found that if an archetype was suppressed, it led to it being acted out in dysfunctional ways. For instance, two archetypes we all share are called the Anima and the Animus. The Anima is the unconscious feminine personality inside of the male psyche and the animus is the unconscious masculine personality inside of the female psyche. These particular archetypes are often suppressed due to stigma, cultural fear, and other reasons and the results can be devastating. According to Carl Jung's research, such suppression can lead to such aggressive behavior as serial killing, mass murdering, and other nasty things.

At worst, we tend to carry around anima or animus energy depicting what we consider our perfect mate and we can unexpectedly project that image onto some poor person of the opposite sex. We may end up in relationships where we never actually see our partners for who they really are, as we never see past the anima or animus energy we've reflected onto them from our subconscious.

This is the kind of power we're talking about drawing from when we refer to the primal power of archetypes and archetypal storytelling. Not that you're going to make anyone go on a killing spree (we hope), but you can definitely tap into some emotions.

The concept of archetypes is an indispensible tool for understanding the purpose of a character in a story. If you grasp the function of your character's archetype, then you can determine if that character is being used to his full potential. Or, if you need a character for a role and have a list of archetypes handy, it's much better to pull one from a stack of interesting multi-dimensional beings then to throw in some cardboard cut-out stereotypical character everyone's going to expect just because he was the first thing that popped into your head.

Joseph Campbell said archetypes were biological; that they were built into the wiring of every human being. Good storytellers instinctively choose archetypes to create dramatic experiences that are recognizable by everyone.

Archetypes can also be thought of as masks. A character doesn't have to remain the same archetype throughout a story. He may come into your tale performing the function of, say, a Herald, then switch masks to function as a Trickster, or a Mentor, or a Shadow.

There are many, many archetypes. Literally thousands. Probably hundreds of thousands. I'm going to go over a few common ones here in detail and then give you a list of a bunch more in less detail because you should have the knack of how to use them from the descriptions I've given of the few.

A little research on the Internet will allow you to uncover many others if you are interested in learning more about archetypes. There are also piles of books available devoted to the study of archetypes. Most of these are psychology texts, but it's amazing how much they pertain to writing.

2. ARCHETYPES ARE NOT STEREOTYPES

It's important to know that archetypes are not stereotypes. There is a huge difference. You do not want to use stereotypes in your writing. They are over-used, they are boring, and they are clichéd. The difference between an archetype and a stereotype is the difference between creating a cake from a box of cake mix you buy from the store and just add water, eggs, and stir to making the cake from scratch with all your own ingredients.

Archetypes are *foundations* for characters. They provide a framework. A *structure*. Characters are then assembled on that structure. What you benefit from is that the structure comes with certain expectations that each different archetype will fulfill. If you think of archetypes as masks that your characters can put on and take off throughout your story, it is easier to understand them. Or, at times, a character may even wear multiple masks.

3. LIGHT SIDES AND SHADOW SIDES

Almost every archetype has a shadow side and a light side. To put it in terms of morality, one might say the shadow side is the evil or dark side of the personality, and the light is the good aspect of the personality, although neither side is really good or evil, they are just different. An archetype is capable of showing both shadow aspects and light aspects at the same time, the same way people are capable of showing two different sides of themselves at the same time.

4. CHARACTERS MAY HAVE MULTIPLE ARCHETYPES

In reality, people are archetypes, but none of us are made up of just a single one. According to Caroline Myss, author of *Sacred Contracts*, we each have twelve different archetypes; there are four that we all share and then eight that are private only to ourselves.

Your characters in your story probably don't need to be this complex, but they could be if you wanted them to be. I find, especially by mixing shadow and light personality traits, that giving each character a single archetype is enough. But you may find it useful to map multiple archetypes to a single character simultaneously.

5. SOME BASIC ARCHETYPES

Herald

Almost always, a Herald appears in Act I and brings news of some sort of event or challenge to the protagonist. The Inciting Event is generally brought in the form of the Herald. The Herald doesn't have to be a person. It can be a news announcement that the stock market just crashed. It can be a letter from the bank telling the protagonist that his great Aunt Lindsay that he didn't even know he had just died and left him 1.5 million dollars. The Herald manifests itself in thousands of different ways. The declaration of war is a Herald used in many books and movies.

Or, of course, it can also be a real Herald. Someone showing up with a horn and a scroll giving the protagonist news of something special.

Whatever it is, the Herald motivates the protagonist and gets the story rolling.

The Herald mask may be worn temporarily by another archetype. A Mentor frequently acts as a herald who issues challenges to the Hero.

Like nearly every aspect of the three act structure, the Herald is flexible and may enter the story at any point, but most frequently he shows up in Act I. Whether it's an inner call to adventure, an external event or issuance, or news of some sort, every story needs the energy of the Herald.

The Herald is one of those few archetypes that doesn't really have much contrast between his dark shadow side and his light side. The Shadow Herald may occasionally make announcements or cause events that are misleading to take the protagonist down the wrong path, but this is uncommon.

Hero

The Hero is the ultimate archetype. He is the final manifestation of your protagonist if he proceeds along his journey. Most protagonists, upon becoming Hero's, have a short journey home before reaping the benefits of their quest. They bask in their Elixir. They marry the fair maiden. Heroes generally end their days victorious and win the hands of princesses after slaying dragons and live out the rest of their lives in the peacefulness of their new found kingdoms.

Although rare, there are shadow traits to a Hero archetype. Shadow Heroes shut themselves off from the rest of the world and become paranoid of their success. They begin to think others are out to take away what is rightfully theirs. Usually, Shadow Heroes suffer a decline in their health and become old and decrepit, mere shells of their former selves.

Mentor

The Mentor archetype is usually a positive figure who trains or aids the Hero. Joseph Campbell calls it the Wise Old Man.

Mentors often speak the words of God, or are inspired by divine wisdom. They may be Heroes who have gone through the ordeal themselves once. Indeed, Mentors may serve as role models for what the protagonist may become, if he stays on the path.

The Mentor archetype is closely related to the image of the parent. One primary purpose of the Mentor is to provide the protagonist with the tools and training he'll need to succeed on his quest. Training is a key role of the Mentor. Another important function of the Mentor is just to motivate the protagonist. This is especially true during Act I, when the protagonist may be reluctant to answer the call to adventure. The Mentor can help him overcome his fear.

Ill. 3-1: *In Arthurian legend, Merlin was a Mentor archetype. He also, at times, played role of a Shapeshifter. And, of course, he was the classic Wizard.*

The protagonist may encounter the shadow side of the Mentor as the "fallen Mentor"—Mentors that are still on their own journeys. They may be experiencing a crisis of faith. The protagonist needs these Mentors to pull themselves together one last time in order to help them get through their ordeal. Such a Mentor may follow the protagonist right through the entire Hero's Journey and find his own path to becoming a Hero.

Mentors are useful for giving characters a swift kick in the rear and getting stories going. This is why you'll often see them enter the story in Act I. Remember, though, form follows function. If you need them placed elsewhere in the story, then place them elsewhere. Anytime your protagonist needs someone to show him the ropes or give him a series of tests or award him with an item he will use later to defeat the antagonist, don't be afraid to pull in a Mentor archetype.

Mentors are one of the most powerful of all archetypes that you have at your fingertips. They are incredibly flexible. Very often you will see the Mentor mixed with other archetypes.

Threshold Guardian

At each entrance into a new world (in other words, at each Pivot Point), there may be powerful guardians at the threshold, put there to stop the protagonist from going any farther. They seem to be an overwhelming force, but if handled properly, they can be defeated by the protagonist or just simply bypassed.

Threshold Guardians are usually not the story's main antagonists, but often they might be the antagonist's henchmen. They may also be neutral characters—part of the new unknown world the protagonist is venturing into. Threshold Guardians are generally working in the shadow side of their archetype. On very rare occasions, the protagonist may encounter light side Threshold Guardians that turn out to be secret helpers, placed in the protagonist's path to test his willingness and skill, usually put there by Mentors. Or, sometimes, they might actually *be* Mentors.

Usually, to get past a Threshold Guardian, the protagonist must solve a puzzle or pass a test, like the Sphinx who presents Oedipus with a riddle before he can continue his journey.

Threshold Guardians are actually doing the protagonist a favor. They're making certain he is prepared mentally and physically for the journey that lies before him. They are making testing his courage t and preparation for change by forcing him to have the strength to stand up against them.

Protagonists must recognize the strength in the resistance of Threshold Guardians. It is far better to take their energy and use it so it doesn't harm them then try to attack them. It's like hitting one bottle with another—it's always the moving bottle that breaks. There are many ways for the protagonist to react to Threshold Guardians. Everything from running away, to attacking, to trying to lie his way past them. The protagonist might even offer him treasure or promises of gold on his way back from his journey. The best way to beat a Threshold Guardian is for the protagonist to absorb him into his nature and, in that sense, he makes the protagonist stronger. Protagonists soon learn to watch out for the little tricks of Threshold Guardians and find ways of avoiding them. Advanced Protagonists transcend rather than destroy these kind of foes.

In stories, Threshold Guardians may be gargoyles, guards, knights— anybody who watches over passages and makes sure nobody gets by without having his wherewithal tested first.

Shadow

The Shadow archetype represents the antagonist. He is the villain in the story. He isn't necessarily a person, he can be a team of evil monsters, or a dark force, or a thing, or even a concept. Often, it's suppressed dark energy from the inner world of the protagonist's subconscious. This is especially true in horror stories. Shadows can be everything protagonists hate about themselves—all their dark secrets that they won't admit to anyone.

Shadows challenge protagonists. Unlike heroes, Shadows are Shadows at the beginning of stories. They don't grow into Shadows through a journey. Having said that, it is vitally important that you make your Shadow characters realistic by making them fallible and especially by humanizing them.

Even the most evil of people don't actually believe, in their own heart of hearts, that they're evil. They think they're acting out of the right reasons. Give your Shadow archetypes the right motivations to do the wrong things, and make them flawed. We have talked a lot about making sure your protagonist is flawed. Well. it's just as important to make sure your Shadow characters are flawed, too.

Shadows create conflict and bring out the best in protagonists by putting them in life-threatening situations. It has often been said that a story is only as good as its villain because a strong enemy forces the protagonist to rise to the challenge.

The Shadow archetype can be expressed in a single character but it may also be a mask worn by any of the characters at any time. The Shadow can even overtake the Hero when he is crippled by doubt or guilt, acts selfishly, or abuses his power. The third *Spiderman* movie (Sam Raimi, director) is a perfect example of this. When Spiderman binds with Venom and begins to struggle with the evil inside of his own soul that the "suit" activates. Venom, one could say, represents Peter Parker's Shadow side.

A Shadow may also wear other masks. As I've already said, you aren't confined to having only one archetype per character at a time. Hannibal Lechter in *Silence of the Lambs* is a Shadow wearing the mask of a Mentor as he helps Clarice Starling hunt down Buffalo Bill.

And again, I can't stress enough: Shadows should not be completely evil. They should be humanized by a touch of goodness or some other admirable quality. Make them vulnerable so that killing them becomes a moral dilemma for your protagonist if the occasion arises that he gets the chance.

There are both internal Shadows and external Shadows. External Shadows are villains the Hero must physically fight. They may be concepts or things, but they are external to the Hero himself. Internal

Shadows exist inside the Hero himself. He may be fighting his own mind. He may be up against his own demons. Nicolas Cage lost to an internal Shadow in the film *Leaving Las Vegas* when he gave in to his alcohol addiction and let it kill him.

By the end of your story, your protagonist must destroy or vanquish external Shadows. Internal Shadows must be disempowered by bringing them into consciousness. The psychological concept of the Shadow archetype is a useful metaphor for understanding the unexpressed, ignored, or deeply hidden aspects of your protagonist's psyches.

Warrior

Warriors are strong with skill and determination in battle. They live for the fight and like fierce competition. Their toughness of will is only matched by their heroism and ability for self-sacrifice.

It might be the Warrior who goes up against the dragon. Warriors are fierce and brave and strong of heart. They have fire in their blood and live to battle. Their goal is victory. They strive to win the Elixir, whether that prize be jewels, or gold, or the hand of the princess.

Shadow Warriors can be blood-thirsty and kill just for the thrill of killing. They lose sight of the goal and go on rampages. They can become ego-obsessed and prey on those weaker than them. They might also connive and plot to overthrow kings and anyone with power greater than them, for if they can't get power through fighting, they will try to achieve it any way possible.

An example of the Warrior archetype is the Greek god Ares.

KEY POINTS

- Archetypes are psychological representations of the universe around us. They are primal, and have existed in our minds before birth.
- Archetypes can be found nearly everywhere on Earth and cross cultural and even continental boundaries.
- By using archetypes in your writing, you are tapping into this vast communal resource of commonalities everyone shares. Archetypes make your stories powerful.
- Archetypes are not stereotypes. Archetypes are a structural foundation for you to build a character upon. A stereotype is a ready-made character based on clichés that you can just plunk into your story and expect readers not to notice your lack of originality.
- Every archetype has a light side and a shadow side.
- Archetypes are like masks being worn by a character.
- Characters may have multiple archetypes, making them more complex.
- Characters may take off the mask of one archetype during a story and slip on the mask of another for a time.
- Some basic and common archetypes are: the Herald, the Hero, the Mentor, Threshold Guardians, the Shadow, and the Warrior.
- Don't be afraid to turn the function of the Archetype on its head and have him act differently than the reader will expect. Many stories have done this successfully.

CHAPTER TWO

Getting More Out of Archetypes

> *By three methods we may learn wisdom: First, by reflection, which is noblest; Second, by imitation, which is easiest; and third by experience, which is the bitterest.*
>
> —Confucius[20]

1. A JOURNEY THROUGH ARCHETYPES: ANOTHER VIEW OF MYTHIC STRUCTURE

Now I want to delve a little more closely into archetypes and show you how it connects to the Hero's Journey. In particular, I want to focus on seven Jungian archetypes. These are:

- The Initiate
- The Apprentice
- The Nonbeliever
- The Athlete
- The Warrior
- The Mother
- The Spirit

---

[20] Confucius (551 - 479 BCE) was a Chinese teacher, editor, politician, and philosopher. His philosophy emphasized personal and governmental morality and justice. It was later developed into a system known as Confucianism.

The best way to approach this discussion is to just give a very brief description of each of these archetypes in order. I'll concentrate on their light—their *normal*—attributes.

The Initiate

The Initiate is what the Taoists would call "The Uncarved Block." He is ignorant. Not by choice, but by circumstance. He simply has no idea about the rest of the world or his potential within it. He only knows what he knows and all he has known up to this point in his life. He may have secrets lying deep within him waiting to be tapped that he is completely oblivious to, but he doesn't care about those.

In fact, he is happy in his ignorance. Blissfully happy. Blissfully ignorant. He is, in some ways, the young boy, still bound to his mother.

The Apprentice

By nature, an apprentice is someone with a mentor. He is in the process of being trained in methods he may not fully understand, but he is being trained nonetheless. In the case of the Apprentice archetype, the Mentor training him doesn't necessarily have to be a real person. It can be the memory of a dead father haunting him and forcing him to learn new ways that his father had always told him he would need to learn in order to survive.

These new ways are usually learned in order to tackle a new world with new rules that he will soon encounter but he probably doesn't yet fully understand or even have a proper concept of. What drives the Apprentice is the Mentor, not the need to survive. In the process, he builds skills he doesn't even realize he's attaining.

The Nonbeliever

The Nonbeliever archetype is usually an archetype that has shifted masks from an Apprentice archetype and believes he has done so too early. One of two things happen. He either begins to encounter this new world he's been warned about and feels he's inadequately prepared and. He feels he still doesn't fully understand everything about it or the new rules he must learn to follow. Or else he might become convinced the new world doesn't even exist. If this happens, he questions whether he wasted his time ever wearing the mask of the Apprentice archetype.

Whichever it is, the nonbeliever has a crisis in faith. He questions his progress. He begins rethinking all his archetype shifts and wonders if things might have been better before, back when he wore the mask of the Initiate.

The Athlete

When a character puts on the mask of the Athlete archetype, his focus becomes entirely on his physical body and achieving physical goals. All of his emphasis is put on how he looks and how he performs. He believes there is nothing he can't overcome and no training he cannot complete through pure physical activities. In essence, he attempts to become a superhero.

The Warrior

I'm doing these archetypes in order for a reason. I want you to assume this is one character wearing all these different archetypal masks in order and, as the Athlete archetype takes off his mask and exchanges it for the mask of the Warrior, his focus once again shifts. Now he wants to compete and defeat his opponent every opportunity he gets. He lives to collect prizes and rewards. Life becomes a game of non-stop competitions that he must win at all costs.

It is during this archetypal phase that leadership qualities will stand out. Whatever drive the character has will be very pronounced and relentless. He is the Warrior. For a more detailed explanation of the Warrior archetype, see the previous chapter.

The Mother

The Mother archetype emphasizes fulfilling the desire of others. Characters wearing this mask nurture others, asking them, "How may I serve you?" He will care dearly for the people close to him and the people that need him. Instinctively, he will protect those around him.

This archetype also longs to see others excel within themselves. The Mother tries to build self-esteem and self-confidence and show the innate potential everyone has available to them.

When Carl Jung originally introduced archetypes into modern psychology, he didn't want them to become some abstract intellectual idea, so he advanced various mythic images to illustrate them. Most of these he pulled from Greek mythology. For instance, in this case, he used the Goddess Demeter to represent the archetypal mother. In the same way, Zeus was introduced as the archetypal father.

Demeter's character as mother-goddess is identified in the second element of her name "meter" derived from the Proto-Indo-European *méhtēr (mother). There are different explanations for the first part of her name. It's possible that it comes from the old form of "earth," designating Demeter as "Mother-Earth."

The Spirit

When a character slips on the mask of the Spirit archetype, the realization of the difference between being "in" this world and "of" this world becomes obvious. This archetype is the God archetype. His actions will be nearly inseparable from the divine. Given the right circumstances, Spirit archetypes will give their lives for the betterment of mankind without question.

Characters who have achieved this archetype understand the Circle of Life, to coin a corny phrase, in its totality. They have the wisdom of the sages. And once they've come this far, there is no going back. They may shift masks to other archetypes, but they will always know that, underneath, they truly are the God archetype and nothing else.

Relating this to the Hero's Journey

The astute of you have probably already figured this out.

These seven archetypes I just listed, the Initiate, the Apprentice, the Nonbeliever, the Athlete, the Warrior, the Mother, and the Spirit, are exactly the Hero's Journey in that order. They describe precisely what your protagonist goes through–on an archetypal level–throughout your story. So, this shows you the power of archetypes. It also shows you the flexibility of Mythic Structure. It also shows you something else.

And that is this: what I just explained, along with the Hero's Journey, is a complete metaphor for life.

There's a reason why this is all embedded into our psyches. Writers didn't make it up. It's stuff we're born with. We dream in three act structures and Jungian archetypes. We automatically write in it. It's the way the universe works. Everything around us happens in three acts. Everything starts off as the Initiate, goes through a stage of questions and struggles, and finally, if all goes well, successfully reaches the ultimate stage of becoming one with the divine.

The Hero's Journey is man's quest to become God. The story of Jesus is pure Mythic Structure. Most religions are. That's why there's so much similarity between them and why they all ring so true for us. They're primal.

You want to write primal stories that ring true for your readers. You want to use archetypes. You want to write myths that will move your readers beyond anything they've ever read before.

There are thousands of Archetypes. Possibly hundreds of thousands. Lots of research has been done on them and luckily, even for the layman, most of that research is accessible. Usually, you won't find it with writing references. Jungian Archetypes fall under psychoanalysis, but don't let that scare you off. Buy some books and start studying on your own. Collect them. I've already given you the most common wants to start with. Let me flesh that out a bit with some of the more esoteric ones.

2. More Esoteric Archetypes

Artist

The Artist archetype constantly strives to beseech others to see the beauty in life. He expresses himself with an intensity and vigor that goes well beyond the passion of most people. His art exemplifies the world through all of life's senses, but seems to reach just beyond, touching something divine. He inspires a wish in others to witness the glory of life and all its symbolism.

There is a shadow side to the Artist archetype, though. He can use his talents as an excuse to hurt other people, mistreating them in ways that benefit himself. He might also take on the role of the "starving artist," playing the Pity Card to try and acquire attention. He may also become a cliché of himself, indulging in eccentricities and the like.

The god Poseidon is an example of the Artist archetype.

Ill. 3-2: *The god Poseidon is an example of the Artist archetype.*

Bully

Despite how it sounds, The Bully archetype isn't necessarily a bad one. Bullies do tend to intimidate others, but that's generally because of their confidence and assuredness, not because they really pick on anyone else. What they do bully is their inner fears that plague them. By confronting those fears, they're able to dispel them, and this is the source of their confidence.

However, there is a shadow side to the Bully. When it is present, Bullies become abusive, both physical and verbal, and they do this to hide the fact that they honestly have deep fear about their lives. The Bully actually masks the Coward who lurks just beneath him.

Businessman

The Businessman archetype wants clear definitions about things. He is drawn to a master skill and values order and harmony. Always the intellectual, he refuses to look beneath the surface of things, preferring everyday appearances and appreciating the sense of order and moderation they bring. He likes unemotional perfection.

The shadow side of the Businessman is that he may become overly dominant. If this happens, there is a break in the psyche and he becomes the Traitor. The Traitor displays an isolation from the feminine.

Ill. 3-3: The god Apollo is an example of the Businessman

Apollo is a primary example of the Businessman archetype.

Damsel

The classic Damsel is the Damsel in Distress—always vulnerable and in need of rescue, preferably by a knight in shining armor. Most Damsels need to get over their secret wish that someone's going to come along and pull them out of their life and ride away with them into a better one. To do this, they must become empowered and inspired to learn to be independent and to rely upon themselves. Part of that is discovering what makes for a healthy romance and not one where one partner is revered.

The shadow side of the Damsel manifests when the Damsel never gets past her constant waiting for her knight in shining armor to come and provide her with everything she's ever wished for in life. She's stuck in a fairytale illusion.

Sleeping Beauty is an example of a Damsel in Distress. She is in need of a prince to come and kiss her and wake her from her endless sleep.

Destroyer

The Destroyer is constantly tearing down or demolishing everything around him. He is driven to destroy, and sometimes with an urge to rebuild. Destroyers have their place in society. They can make good psychoanalysts or function well in any capacity where it is good to "destroy" someone's delusions. Sometimes, they can destroy to make way for new growth. But, generally, they are detrimental, hurting themselves as often as anyone else—destroying their own relationships, their jobs, and so on.

When the Destroyer's shadow side manifests, he can become overwhelmed with his own power and prey on other people's hopes and dreams, dashing their potential. If he is in a position of power, he may cause wars, or destroy the environment. Sauron from *Lord of the Rings* is a good example of a shadow Destroyer.

Father

The Father has untouchable qualities of leadership and displays fearlessness to his family. He has inner courage and enforces family structure, yet not at the expense of being gentle, kind, and fair. He has tremendous patience.

The shadow side of the father is that he may become a Tyrant. He can begin to feel his rule is absolute and try to destroy those who resist him. When acting like this, he uses his family as pawns to attain his own goals. He slips into allowing himself the enjoyment of any vices he pleases to indulge in.

Zeus, the king of the gods, is the quintessential Father archetype as described by Carl Jung.

Fool/Wanderer

The Fool is also usually the Wanderer. He can be a thief and a messenger, but always he is up to some inane shenanigans. He always has a good time. He is the master of wit with eclectic taste and knowledge of worldly things. The reason he is the Wanderer is that he hates to be in one place too long.

Many times, the Fool appears in a story to supply comic relief after a very tense scene, much like the Trickster does.

The Fool is terrible at making plans and often unreliable. This archetype relates very well to children since, like Peter Pan, he refuses to grow up. In fact, Peter Pan is a great example of this archetype.

On the shadow side, the Fool gives in to his lackadaisical side and begins to plot while still outwards jesting. Then his greatest asset is being under-estimated by his opponents, who simply write him off as a joke. This gives the Fool leverage, should he require it.

He is a master of disguise and can easily slip on the mask of the Shapeshifter.

The Greek god Hermes is a perfect example of the Fool/Wanderer in action because he shows that the archetype is capable of being combined with many other archetypes. There are a multitude of stories about Hermes wearing the mask of the Fool/Wanderer along with other archetype masks.

For example, the mother goddess Demeter's virgin daughter, Persephone, was once abducted by Hades. Demeter searched for her in vain until Zeus sent Hermes to the Underworld to retrieve her. Hades agreed, but gave Persephone a pomegranate that, when she ate it, she became bound to Hades for 1/3 of the year.

Persephone's time in the Underworld reflects those times on the ancient Greek calendar when the seasons are unfruitful. But she always reappears each spring.

In this case Hermes was acting as both a Fool/Wanderer and a Herald at the same time.

During the *Odyssey* by Homer (the sequel to the *Iliad*), Hermes helps Odysseus by informing him of the fate of his companions who have been transformed into animals through the power of Circe. He instructs Odysseus to chew on a magical herb that will protect him.

Here, Hermes combines his normal archetype with the archetype of the Informant.

Hermes is also the one Zeus ordered to go to Calypso and demand she release Odysseus from her island imprisonment where she had him held captivated by her singing for ten years so that Odysseus could continue his journey home and finally reunite with his wife.

This is yet another case of Hermes combining archetypes, keeping his Wanderer aspect and adding the Herald.

When Odysseus killed his wife's suitors, it was Hermes who led their souls to Hades, combining his normal archetype with the archetype of the Guide.

It is quite for archetypes to wear multiple masks simultaneously, and Hermes illustrates some perfect examples.

Hermit

The Hermit has all the knowledge at hand that ever was since the beginning of time, for he has spent his days alone in meditation, seeking transcendence. The realm in which he resides is constantly expanding to include not only our own world but other worlds as well. He is feared by others, for he is associated with death. Usually he stays hidden in his cave, away from others.

In his shadow state, he can be moved to vengeance and use all the knowledge at his disposal to plot revenge. But his anger never shows, for he is patient and thoughtful and cunning in his planning. Through his manipulation of information his powers seem almost magical. He employs both subterfuge and stealth.

Ill. 3-4: Hades and Cerberus, the hound who guards the underworld.

Like the artist, the Hermit lives in his own world. His is based on secret facts. He is the Sage. The gaining of knowledge of the innerworkings of the world is his primary concern.

An example of this archetype is the Greek god Hades.

Messiah/Punisher (Male)

The Messiah archetype is almost like a sub-archetype. Any of the other archetypes can provide a framework within which the Messiah archetype can grow. There are two aspects key to the Messiah archetype: the pursuit of some higher purpose and the ability to bring out the best in others. Other than his divine roles in life, everything else comes last. He has given himself to the greater good and a higher power. Indeed, anyone he encounters who doesn't have something to do with this higher purpose is not even worth recognizing.

But this Messiah archetype has a shadow side and that is the Punisher. The Punisher avoids physical combat, if possible, instead trying to preach to the people, using his words to tear down and destroy. Winning over the hearts of the people to his maligned ways becomes his primary purpose and his weapon.

The god Osiris is an example of the Messiah/Punisher archetype.

Osiris was the Egyptian god of the underworld and the afterlife. Even though he was ruler of the dead, often he was referred to as "king of the living" because the Egyptians considered the blessed dead "the living ones."

All people, not just pharaohs, were believed to be associated with Osiris at death. In union with him, they

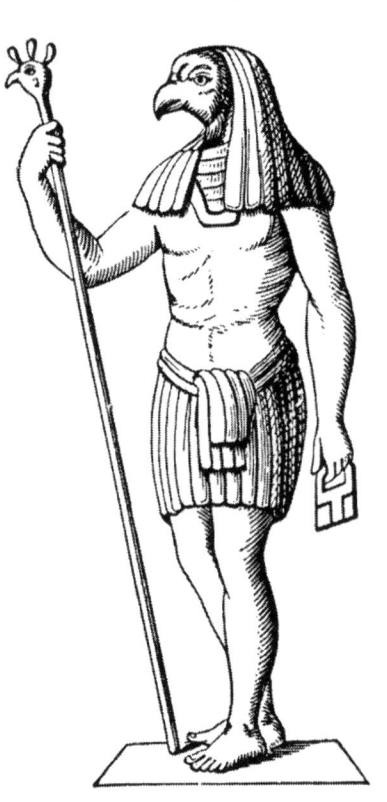

Ill. 3-5: The Egyptian god of the underworld and the afterlife, Osiris, is an example of the Messiah/Punisher archetype.

would inherit life through a process of imitative magic. Osiris was also associated with the cycles of nature.

Messiah/Destroyer (Female)

This is the feminine version of the Messiah archetype and she is similar to the male described above only that she is more aggressive in her mission to both save (on the light side) and destroy (on the shadow side). While the male Messiah punishes preferring to use his words, the female destroys any way she can. She will develop vast armies and take their lead to keep the charge going in both the light and shadow states. She is the holy warrior, like Joan of Arc.

The goddess Isis is an example of the Messiah/Destroyer archetype.

Isis was an ancient Egyptian goddess whose worship spread throughout the world. She is often depicted as Horus, the hawk-headed god of war and protection. She is also known as the Protector of the Dead.

She married her brother, Osiris, and conceived Horus with him. She was instrumental in Osiris's resurrection when he was murdered by Set. She gathered up all his body parts that had been strewn across the earth and, using her magical abilities, restored them back together again.

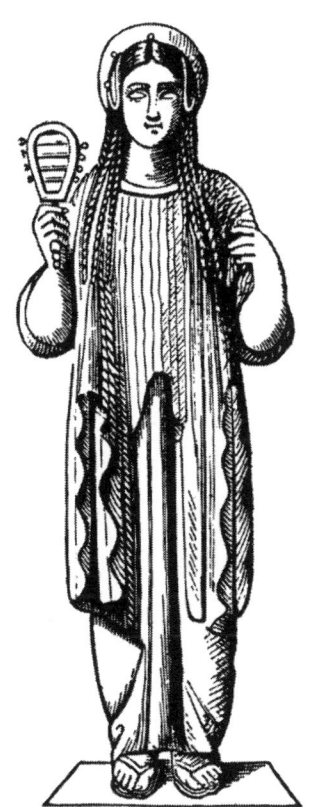

Ill. 3-6: The Egyptian goddess Isis, worshipped for war and protection, is a Messiah/Destroyer archetype.

Mystic

Mysterious and wise, the Mystic is an odd combination of an old soul and a young girl combined into one. She can be a Shapeshifter, but regardless of what form she takes, her hidden wisdom makes her a dangerous adversary. To get what she wants, she is capable of manipulating things so subtly behind the scenes. It's sometimes impossible to tell the Mystic's done anything unscrupulous at all.

She likes to pretend innocence and influence with an invisible persuasion that's always there. She may appear as an old crone, a strange child, or an enchanted druid, but behind the Shapeshifting mask, she's always the same and holds the energy of acceptance and peace.

Like the Artist and the Hermit, she lives in her own world and is most comfortable there.

An example of the mystic archetype is the goddess Hestia.

Shapeshifter

The Shapeshifters appearance changes as soon as you start to examine it closely. It is sometimes difficult to understand, but it's worth the effort because it can be an asset in your writer's toolbox.

Shapeshifters often appear in stories as characters the opposite sex from the protagonist. You can spot a Shapeshifter because, from the protagonist's point of view, they appear to always be changing. Sometimes it might even be the love interest who turns out to be a Shapeshifter—if the story has a love interest. They can never be trusted to be the same person from one moment to the next.

Fatal Attraction is the classic example of a movie with a Shapeshifter in it. Glenn Close changed from Michael Douglas's lover into his would-be assassin.

I already briefly discussed the feminine and masculine personality archetypes known as the anima and the animus. Well, a psychological purpose of the Shapeshifter archetype is to express the energy of these personality traits.

Shapeshifters bring questions into stories. Some questions, like, "Is she who we think she is?" asked by the reader, or others asked by the protagonist, such as: "Does he love me? Is he telling me the truth?" Naturally lead one to believe a Shapeshifter is at work in the book.

A Femme Fatale is a type of Shapeshifter; a sort of sub-archetype that Joseph Campbell called The Woman as Temptress. Like Sharon Stone in *Basic Instinct*, protagonists are betrayed by such women, misled into thinking they're lovers when, in fact, they're killers. The "fatale" aspect of the archetype isn't essential, though; Shapeshifters might only be there to confuse readers and/or protagonists.

Shapeshifters aren't always women. They can be manifested by either women or men.

Other archetypes can wear the mask of the Shapeshifter temporarily. For instance, Mentors and Tricksters are natural Shapeshifters. Shadows (or Villains) and their henchmen might become Shapeshifters to mislead the protagonist like the Wicked Queen did to Snow White so she could trick her into biting the poisoned apple.

Sometimes even the protagonist will become a Shapeshifter if it's needed. In *Sister Act*, Whoopi Goldberg dresses up like a nun to escape from the mob.

As you can see, Shapeshifters are very versatile and can be quite useful in different situations.

Slave

The Slave archetype isn't a slave to any person in this world, but a slave to what he or she considers to be "God". Slaves surrender their power of choice to the divine, trusting in it blindly and completely. Note that what they consider to be "God" doesn't have to be an actual "god." It can be something representative of God, such as an establishment, or a movement, or some sort of political faction. In extreme cases, it might even be a single person.

The shadow attributes of the Slave archetype is that they will give away their willpower to any external authority out of fear of making any choice on their own. This can lead to things like massive political regimes and crowd mentalities.

Trickster

The Trickster archetype transcends convention and stuffiness and doesn't like to play by the established rules. Usually, they exist for the purpose of comic relief, by breaking up unresolved tension and suspense for a while, but they also have other uses. They can, for example, give questionable gifts to the protagonist like the fairy folk in Irish folklore are said to do. Or they might offer advice or directions that the protagonist must weigh whether or not is safe to take.

Tricksters might be servants or friends working for the protagonist or the Shadow, or they could just as well be independent with their own agenda. They're behavior is usually unpredictable. If they are not working with the protagonist, they may try to manipulate things to get their own way.

Often, Tricksters will stir things up just for the sake of stirring things up. They are at times catalyst characters, affecting the lives of those around them but remaining unchanged themselves.

There are classic trickster characters, especially in the animal/totem archetypes. The Native Americans say the raven and the coyote are both tricksters.

EXERCISES

1. Take one of the archetypes, preferably the Fool/Wanderer, that I've described in these chapters and create a character based on that archetype. Write up a single page description of the character and include things like how he would react under pressure and to certain circumstances.

2. Now take another archetype, preferably the Mentor, and do the same thing. Put the two characters in a tavern and have them talking to one another. Maybe have the conversation grow into an argument. See how the dialogue between the two is different. How do their mannerisms change? Your scene should be no longer than a page.

3. Take the first character you created and develop a new character based on that same archetype, only make the new character from a completely different era. If your original character was a wise old fool/wanderer from ages past, make your new character a modern high school kid who's always getting into trouble for doing dumb things and following with the wrong crowd.

4. Put both your characters that are based on the same archetype into a scene and have them carry on a conversation together. Notice that they still have different mannerisms and speech patterns. This is what makes archetypes different from stereotypes. Archetypes form the foundation for character development; they do not give you a ready to go character. You still have to do the work. What you gain is the knowledge that

the character you've created is going to act in appropriate ways to their inner selves. Once again, this scene should be no more than a page.

5. Try these exercises with numerous archetypes until you are comfortable using archetypes as the basis of character development. Archetypes are a very valuable tool for your craft and can't be practiced enough.

6. Create a character that changes archetypes throughout a scene. Have him start out wearing the mask of the Herald and then slip on the mask of the Shapeshifter instead. Again, put him in a scene where he converses with one of the characters you created previously and see how the transformation affects the character's mannerisms, dialogues, actions, and demeanor.

7. Create a character developed from a combination of two or more archetypes. Feel free to use a combination of two that you've already used. Put this complex character into a scene where he is interfacing with at least two other characters (these can be stock characters, or even characters from fiction that you know well) and see how easy or difficult it is to deal with the extra attributes that the other archetypes bring.

KEY POINTS

- You can view the Hero's Journey through archetypal roles that the protagonist takes on during the journey. Looking at the structure this way enables you to see it from an emotional level.
- More esoteric archetypes consist of the Artist, the Bully, the Businessman, the Damsel, the Destroyer, the Father, the Fool/Wanderer, the Hermit, the Male Messiah/Punisher, the Female Messiah/Destroyer, the Mystic, the Shapeshifter, the Slave, and the Trickster.
- There are sub-archetypes which exist beneath the main archetype. For instance, the Damsel In Distress is a sub-archetype of the Damsel and the Femme Fatale is a sub-archetype of the Shapeshifter.
- There are thousands of other archetypes that you can find with a minimal amount of research.

CHAPTER THREE

Animal Archetypes

If there were only one truth, you couldn't paint a hundred canvases on the same theme.

–Pablo Picasso[21]

1. Finding Your Story's Theme

I've already discussed Jungian archetypes as far as human roles go and how they can improve the characterization of your writing by helping you develop well-rounded characters. What I haven't discussed is animal archetypes. The ancient shaman of the world knew about animal archetypes and the powers of the animal totem. Even Carl Jung saw that each animal represented an archetype that humans had some degree of natural connection with, sometimes to one or more different animals. Unlike the "humanized" archetypes, the animal archetypes seemed to be even further beyond conscious awareness.

In Shamanism, a totem (which can be an animal or a plant) is perceived to have a direct relationship with a particular person. The person is not associated to one specific totem but to the entire species—or, in our case, the archetype as a whole. Individual totems were simply thought of as individual physical manifestations of the general archetype).

---

[21] Pablo Picasso (October 25, 1881 - April 8, 1973) was a Spanish painter, sculptor, printmaker, ceramicist, and stage designer of the 20th century. He is most widely known for co-founding a movement called Cubist. His most famous work is probably the proto-Cubist *Les Demoiselles d'Avignon* (1907).

You could use the animal archetypes I list here the same way I've taught you to use the archetypes in the previous chapters as the basis for character development; however, I think there's a much more powerful use for animal archetypes, and that is in developing an archetypal story lesson for your character to follow. Because your story is derived from the animal archetype it will transcend the primal power of the archetype and bring with it a very strong literary punch.

Let me try to explain this more clearly.

Each animal archetype, like the human archetypes, represents a set of its own attributes and, taken metaphorically, these attributes can be translated into an archetypal theme for stories. Sometimes you have to sort of look at them backward to see the lesson in them, but it's always there. You'll see what I mean once we start going through them. This "lesson" becomes the theme for your story.

Having an archetypal theme for your story is good because it gives it a primal foundation. It makes it ring true on a subconscious level. It gives your story that sense of "wonderment" we're all looking for when we read.

Stories, like all mythology, and all art for that matter, are just metaphors. They are attempts to know the unknowable through a language that falls short of being able to explain it. Poetry probably comes closest. We want to experience the eternal in a world where time gets in the way because, as Joseph Campbell likes to put it, time and the eternal are opposites. Time sweeps away the eternal. The eternal can only exist now and it can only exist everywhere and nowhere. Time exists then and there. There is no eternal in time. So, in giving your stories an archetypal theme, you're trying to give your readers a glimpse into the eternal.

When you start writing a new book, or just after you've finished your outline based on the scaled back three act structure I presented earlier, you should ask yourself: Does my story have an archetypal theme? If it doesn't, *should* it? If it possibly can, the answer is probably yes. In fact, giving it a theme might make your storytelling job a lot easier. If you find a theme after you've nailed down your story's cornerstones but before you've gone any further, it might even make the job of filling in the rest of the three act structure that much easier.

If you do decide you need a theme, there's a good chance you'll be able to find one through an animal archetype that plays well against your Hero's Journey. The theme is basically the lesson that the hero will learn throughout the story. Having this theme doesn't change anything we've talked about. In fact, we've already touched on it, in a way, by saying the protagonist and the world at the beginning of the story must be flawed and, by the end of the story, they either must be flawed differently or no longer flawed. This change is the theme of your story. What you want to do is make this theme, or lesson, as archetypal (or primal, or as humanly subconscious) as possible.

So let's look at a few animal archetypes and the themes they bring to mind. Remember when reading the attributes of the archetype that we're talking in metaphor. Generally speaking, these archetypes reflect the way your protagonist will be at the end of your story, so you would want to start the story with your would-be Hero flawed against the traits described in the archetype.

There are many, many animal archetypes to draw on, each one offering a different archetypal lesson, and you can find a lot on your own through researching via the Internet (do a Google search on "animal archetypes" or "animal totems"). I have only listed a little more than a couple of dozen here. I've mixed male and female pronouns in these descriptions, but any of these archetypes can work with either gender of protagonist. The important part to learn here is to see how I am interpreting a story from the metaphorical attributes of the animal archetype.

Ant

Basic Archetype Description

Ants are hard workers who work well with others. They are willing to sacrifice their lives for the good of the community. They are industrious.

Theme Revealed

The theme I associate with the archetype of the ant is the story of a the misanthropic protagonist who starts the story almost unable to function in day to day life situations. Probably something in the near past has caused him to go into a tailspin and he's lost his job and maybe his girlfriend. He's on the verge of losing his apartment because he can't make rent, and he no longer has any friends because he's systematically gotten drunk with each one of them and told them all off. Your Setup, then, is to show the protagonist in this state, basically having a pity party for himself. You know what his character arc is going to be: he's going to be reintegrated back into society, but not *just* reintegrated. Read the description. He's going to be willing to sacrifice himself for the lives of others if it's good for the community. That's about as far away from a pity party as you can get, so you desperately want to show this disparity.

You probably feel that you've read this story before. Probably more than once. That's because you have. It's a theme we see again and again because it's an archetypal theme. I'm not suggesting it's contrived—you won't be simply rehashing some old tale and just adding some new polish here and there—you're using a *theme*. You're taking a basic building block and using it to create a primal story on top of what you know will work on a guttural level because it's proven to be true.

Bear

Archetype Description

The Bear is a protective mother with hidden strength. She has the solar qualities of power and courage and the lunar qualities of intuition. She is patient and can hibernate through winter storms. She looks inward to seek answers and learns to know herself.

Theme Revealed

Right away, when I read this description of the bear, the movie *Three Men and a Baby* comes into my mind. That movie used the bear theme did it not? Three men began the movie without a clue as to how to look after a child and having their doubts if they even wanted to and, through the course of the movie they learned to become "protective mothers" with "hidden strengths."

The part about looking inwards makes me think the character will find those strengths inside himself—sort of like Dorothy in the Wizard of Oz. When Dorothy asked Glenda what she needed to do to go home, Glenda told her, but then she also said the power was inside Dorothy all along.

From reading the archetypal description, I think the theme of the bear is one of becoming a protective mother through discovering power you hadn't known existed inside you all along.

Again, this theme probably feels familiar. That's because it's archetypal. It's not stereotypical. Don't get the two confused. There's a huge difference. This is a foundation for a story to be developed onto, not a recipe where you just plug characters into a sequence of plot events.

Bee

Archetype Description

The Bee shares a connection to the Goddess Diana. She has a full understanding of the female warrior energy that bond brings. Her journeys take her close to the land of the non-living; she can communicate with the dead and help earth-bound spirits move on to their proper places. She may also play a role in reincarnation. The Bee has great concentration and a penchant for prosperity.

Theme Revealed

This is a tragic theme of death and loss. It is a protagonist unable to move on past the death of a loved one and it's only through questing on her own Hero's Journey that she can find the energy inside her and understand her connection to the divine—in this case, her connection with the Goddess Diana in order to move on with her own life.

This may involve some sort of "communication" with the deceased, either metaphorically, or—as in the movie *Ghost* with Patrick Swayze and Demi Moore—literally. Either way, something extraordinary must happen that allows the protagonist to finally let the deceased and herself come to find rest.

And, in doing so, she becomes the Hero she set out to become at the beginning of her journey.

Beetle

Archetype Description

The beetle understands past lives and can see into them and draw energy from them. He carries the Golden Strand that leads to the Center of the Universe which is a bridge to spiritual enlightenment. The Beetle is an archetype steeped in the cycle of death and rebirth; he relies heavily upon the resurrection.

Theme Revealed

This is the classic Hero's Journey. The quest to the divine. The protagonist becomes a Hero by going through a resurrection and may draw on the symbolic power of "past lives." Indeed, once he's gone through the All is Lost stage, he's driven by forces and strengths that come from a place he doesn't necessarily understand.

Butterfly/Caterpillar

Archetype Description

The Butterfly transforms into a thing of almost divine grace. She becomes balanced and develops the ability to fly. What starts off as slow and grounded winds up as a thing of utter beauty and fragility? Butterflies stay focused on the outcome and the process. They are associated with reincarnation, transformation, and transmutation.

Theme Revealed

This is the same theme as the ugly duckling, or the geeky girl who writes depressing poetry about death, feels confined to the small town (especially living in her double wide trailer out in the middle of Redneckville) and has only one real friend. She generally thinks life is nothing but a tragedy only to discover, after three hundred odd pages, that there is beauty and wonder in the world she never dared imagine.

Usually that wonder and beauty come in the form of a love interest at first, but, by the end of the story, goes well beyond that. The protagonist learns to love herself and the world on her own and in her own way. She quite literally develops wings and takes flights (okay, maybe not literally... well, maybe in *some* stories).

By the time she's finished her journey and transformed into a Hero, her world has changed completely. This theme is similar to the "coming-of-age" theme, but not quite the same.

Cougar

Archetype Description

The Cougar has strong leadership skills and has moved beyond his ego. He moves with grace and speed and often makes his way with unseen intention. Self-confident and cunning, he has achieved balance in his power and strength and has also attained self-assurance.

Theme Revealed

This theme is the path of the warrior. If the protagonist begins the story very young, it could be a story about fulfilling his destiny to fight a certain battle. Or, if he begins the story already grown up, his confidence may be shaken from a recent incident and he needs to retrain because he's full of self-doubt. Many, many variations spring to mind when I read this archetype description and every one is a viable basis for a story because they're all anchored to the points of this archetypal form.

Coyote

Archetype Description

The coyote holds a child-like trust in truth. He is intelligent and able to laugh at his own mistake. He can be a Shapeshifter. The coyote understands that all things in the universe are sacred and yet, at the same time, nothing is sacred. He is also a teacher. He can teach the balance between risk and safety and that it's only when we've let go of all our pretenses that we can truly connect with the divine source.

Theme Revealed

The key to this theme is the understanding that simultaneously all things are sacred and yet, at the same time, nothing is sacred. The protagonist learns that he has been hiding behind a mask, protecting himself from a world he did not need protection from. That mask may take the form of an inappropriate sense of humor, an inability to let people get close to him, or an unwillingness to show anyone who he truly is.

His journey takes him inwards, back to a child-like state, when he used to trust the world. And it's in that state that he realizes what the event was that sparked his sudden distrust of everything. By bringing this event under the light of consciousness, the power of the event is taken away, and the protagonist is able to dispel it completely.

Once he's completed his ordeal and become a Hero, he has the power to take what he learned along the way and teach it to others.

Crab

Archetype Description

The crab is the dancer. He understands the power of the dance. He also has the ability to find uses for things that seem completely useless to others and to escape disaster by moving sideways. Movement is a big aspect of the Crab, whether it is away from danger or through water and emotions. If his home space is threatened, the Crab will defend and protect it.

Theme Revealed

This is the theme of the flighty protagonist nobody takes seriously. She focuses her energies on strange things, perhaps her passion is creating art from other people's trash, or coming up with exquisite dance steps she never intends anyone to see but her cat.

The protagonist's world is tipped upside-down, however, when the Inciting Event forcers her to change. Maybe her parents demand that she move out of their basement and get a real job, or perhaps her mother dies. Whatever it is, something happens to disturb her normal way of life that she finds comfort in no matter how odd it may appear from the outside, and suddenly she is thrust into the unknown path of Act II—a journey full of trials and tests she thinks she is completely unprepared for.

In the end, though, she finds the magic really was in the dance, or in her art, or wherever her passion that everyone else found so strange happened to lie. It was that seemingly useless and benign creative energy she'd been expending before that ultimately saves her.

In the end, she comes full circle, "moving sideways to escape." Only now, she has the experience that makes her a true Hero.

Dog

Archetype Description

The Dog loves unconditionally. She forgives freely. She seeks companionship and love, and serves selflessly.

Theme Revealed

The theme of unconditional love and forgiveness is one that comes up over and over again in stories. It is a universal theme that rings so true, it never fails to bring in at least one summer blockbuster every year. You always know the one. It's the girlie movie where all the guys in the theatre are crying by the end of it.

Start any protagonist off in your setup as an unloving, uncaring, unforgiving person, who will automatically be lonely because of it—which you won't really have to go so hard to show. And slowly, through Act II, have them go up against a barrage of trials and tests that makes them reassess the way they treat other people and realize they need to find forgiveness for something in their past before they can move on. Then, finally, have them come to that one big test where they encounter that one person or incident that breaks through and they start to show unconditional love for the first time. That should happen right before you start to head into the Darkness Closes In Point of Act II. Then, in your Climax, have the person they love either die or almost die and just watch how quickly you turn on the faucets of your readers.

This theme is a powerhouse.

Donkey

Archetype Description

The Donkey is characterized by his stubbornness, but he has good skills at decision-making. He is pretty well armored against other people's opinions about himself or anything else, for that matter. He believes what he wants to believe and will only change his belief when he feels it is right to do so. If he feels it isn't right, he will not change. When the Donkey is on someone's side, he is a devout and loyal friend, protective and helpful.

Theme Revealed

The Donkey archetype as it stands nearly exactly describes a story theme outright. Here's one that comes to mind based on this theme.

Your protagonist begins as a stubborn, boorish man, refusing to move on anything, even when he knows he's wrong—the opposite of what he'll end up being once his journey is complete.

Perhaps the Inciting Event in the story is that his father's died and he's inherited his father's business. His father was a successful and prosperous business man who spent most of his time at work and never passed down any of his knowledge to his son. So the protagonist is immediately out of his depth, especially given his characteristics. Because of how he acts toward people, business begins to plummet and profits take a dive. Investors worry about a hostile takeover. The board demands he step down as CEO, and they put someone else temporarily in his place. This someone else will become the Shadow figure in the story, secretly wanting the power of the corporation to be his instead of the protagonist who is its rightful heir.

Throughout Act II, the protagonist wanders unemployed through his father's old house, looking through boxes of old books and ledgers. He finds notes and knickknacks and begins to learn things about his father he never knew. His father was good at business because his whole life was about business.

During this process, the protagonist discovers he hasn't really gotten over his father's death. He still has his ashes and decides to go on a road trip and spread them around the places he *does* remember being taken to as a child. There were *some* good times they spent together, after all. This turns the story in a sad, heart-breaking way.

Meanwhile, the new "temporary" CEO is putting things in place to make sure his position is permanent. He's bad-mouthed the protagonist and character-assassinated him as much as possible. He's even set things up so that it looks as though the protagonist was going to try and embezzle company funds.

But the protagonist returns from his road trip, which is his journey through Act II, a changed man. He's read all his father's notes and ledgers and even a book he wrote about business. He feels like he really knows his father now; he knows how he thought. He knows business now.

But the protagonist still must face his final showdown against the antagonist. He bursts into a director's meeting where he is not allowed and the new CEO immediately begins shouting to have him removed. But before that happens, the protagonist begins making a speech.

It's a speech pulled from the annals of his father's books and ledgers. Our protagonist has read them all so many times, he knows most of his father's thoughts on business by heart. He understands his father on a level he never did when he was alive and feels closer to him now than ever. He knows what made him successful at business.

His heartfelt speech has echoes of his father's voice in it, a man the board members respected dearly.

When security comes to take him out of the room, the head of the board stands and says, "No. Let him finish."

And he does. When he's finally done, he turns and starts walking out. He knows he can't win his job back, but at least he got to have his say.

Only, behind him, one by one, the members of the board begin to stand and clap, giving him a standing ovation, much to the disappointment of the temporary CEO whose job now really is only temporary.

With the Climax over, it's just a matter of showing the Denouement: the protagonist as Hero leading the successful company with a big picture of his father on the wall behind him.

Goat

Archetype Description

The Goat knows how to build strong foundations. He is sure of foot, agile, and independent. He has great willpower. He helps others get over their insecurities. The Goat is the self-help guru.

Theme Revealed

This theme only works if you start your story off with your protagonist delusional and thinking he's independent and "sure of foot" when he actually isn't. He likes to solve everyone else's problems without even recognizing his own. His character arc is learning that he's not the "self-help guru" he thinks he is, and that he needs more help than anyone. In coming to this revelation, he manages to find his independence and build his foundation so that, by the end of your story, he actually is the man he thought he was at the beginning.

Hawk

Archetype Description

The Hawk can move between the divine and the present world freely. Observant and wise, he knows the Truth. He can see beyond the veil of the eternal. The Hawk is one with the Spirit and can see past lives. He awakens us to our creativity and our life purpose.

Theme Revealed

You can go a lot of different directions with an archetype like this. You could almost take the attributes literally if you were writing a fantasy story and have a mystic character searching through different realms to find his life's purpose. It would be almost like a basic coming-of-age story.

You could use this archetype as a launch pad for a mini-brainstorming session and come up with a sort of tangential idea like having a protagonist who's stuck in a rut in her life and doesn't really know where she's headed. She goes to see a psychic who tells her something that sets her off on her journey into Act II. Ultimately, the protagonist discovers she has some talent doing something creative, like painting or sculpting, and it's in that where she finds life's ultimate purpose. Sort of saying "God is in the details."

Lion

Archetype Description

The Lion has tremendous leadership qualities. Having let go of all his stress, he displays fearlessness and courage. He enforces structure within the family, yet is gentle and fair. He shows great patience.

Theme Revealed

This theme is the obvious doubtful father who needs to find his way back to his family. Maybe he spends too much time at the office. Maybe he's missed too many ball games. Maybe his kids are getting into trouble. Something wakes him up to the fact that he's not doing his job, and it sets him off on his journey to become a better parent. Since he ends the journey with great patience, I would start the journey by showing the protagonist in the Setup without great patience ... either with how he deals with his kids, or the people he works with, or maybe just with other people in general.

Llama

Archetype Description

The Llama's journey usually involves overcoming materialism and moving over hurdles. She is good at comforting others and withstanding the cold. Once she's abandoned attachment to possessions, the Llama is able to achieve divine enlightenment. The Llama is the archetype of the Buddhist Bodhisattva.

Theme Revealed

This is the theme of someone moving from the world of the materialistic into that of the missionary. In Buddhism, this is referred to as the path of the Bodhisattva.

Although your story doesn't have to have *that* much of a dichotomy between the Hero state at the end of the book and the Initiate state at the beginning. Your protagonist won't necessarily go from being a materialistic bastard to Mother Theresa. This is one of those cases where there is a lot of gray area to play with. That's why it's such a common basis for stories.

We've all seen this theme used many times, to great effect. The classic example is Charles Dickens's *A Christmas Carol* where Ebenezer Scrooge takes the complete journey of the Llama, starting out a belligerent, materialistic curmudgeon who detests mankind in general and winds up becoming a truly generous soul with a heart full of love, who comforts others and wishes no ill will on anyone. Of course, he has to go through an Act II full of tension while three spirits drag him through his past, present, and possible bleak future to get there.

Monkey

Archetype Description

The Monkey acts in unpredictable ways but always with a certain power and grace that is true only to him. He has superb observational clarity and can see things that are hidden from others. Monkeys form families and get along well in communities.

Theme Revealed

This is the "romantic comedy funny guy integrating with single mother and her kids" theme. The monkey is the protagonist, probably your goofy guy, trying to get the girl who has a child or two at home. Because of her kids, she's hesitant about dating. But he assures her, he's great with kids. He is a bit of a funny guy. Think: Steve Carell.

The plot probably follows your standard boy meets girl, boy loses girl, boy gets girl back with a few scenes thrown in with the kids either liking him or hating him. If they like him, they can help him get back with her, if they hate him, there can be funny scenes with them trying to sabotage his attempts.

In the end, of course, he succeeds. He becomes part of the family. But he's still the funny monkey-guy he was at the beginning of the story.

Moose

Archetype Description

The moose has a strong connection with the soul which exists in the void, or soul world. He can move between the real world and the world of the soul. He is able to detect energy that allows him to find parts of the soul that were previously hidden away or use that energy to acknowledge truths that have been denied by the soul. He can move unseen in his travels. Full of strength and wisdom, he builds self-respect among his peers and acts as a bridge between them and the elder members of the herd.

Theme Revealed

The moose theme is the fallen Hero suffering a crisis of faith. Something has caused the protagonist to lose sight of who he truly is and the worst part is he doesn't even realize it's happened.

The Inciting Event occurs, launching the protagonist on an adventure that slowly brings his problem to light. In the Climax of the story, he discovers the truth—that parts of his soul have been hidden away. This likely happened subconsciously, as a defense mechanism to some tragedy he went through in the past. He may have suppressed the event entirely, but now it comes into consciousness, and by bringing both the problem and the event into the light of wisdom, he is able to regain those portions of himself that were missing from him. In doing so, he regains the position in life he once held and becomes, once again, the Hero.

Owl

Archetype Description

The Owl is wise. Silent and swift, he can shed insight on issues for others. If you want your secrets kept, tell them to the Owl. Generally, the Owl prefers to be alone, but will come to the aid of others when required. He has the ability to see into the shadows. He has complete freedom.

Theme Revealed

This is basically the theme of the Hermit. Your protagonist may start off the story exactly fitting the description of the archetype, but perhaps less willing to come to the aid of others when required than stated. He doesn't like to be bothered by anyone.

Then something happens that drives him out of reclusion and he must face civilization. The dichotomy between his hermetic life and the fast-paced world of humanity and the ongoing questions about who to talk to and who to trust and who to help become the trials and tests of Act II until he is pulled into a Climactic finale in Act III where he has to decide, ultimately, which life he really wants to lead. Does he return his life of desolation and loneliness that he had thought he loved? Or does he remain among these people he has now learned to call friends?

Rabbit

Archetype Description

The Rabbit is full of paradox and contradiction. He is a puzzle. Yet, at the same time, he's quick thinking and able to live by his own intuitive actions. Some say he receives hidden teachings. He can be full of guile but also display humility. If he displays fear, it is not for long, for it soon passes.

Theme Revealed

The rabbit archetype suggests the theme of a journey toward fearlessness, humility, and the ironic. As always, your protagonist should begin the story with his personality set as dramatically contrasted as possible from what it will end up like once his journey is complete and he returns a Hero. In the case of the Rabbit theme, you want a protagonist paralyzed by fear. Someone so scared of life and everything around him that it interferes with his ability to think on his feet. He should probably be smart, though, just unable to use that intelligence properly because of the fear blocking him. In fact, he may even be smart to an ironic flaw, like Russell Crowe in *A Beautiful Mind*, a movie which illustrates this theme quite well.

This isn't an easy theme to pull off because your ending tends to be ambiguous.

Raven

Archetype Description

The Raven is the explorer of the unknown. He has the ability to find light in the darkness and is the wildcard of the animal kingdom, surrounded by mystery. He is at once, both destroyer and rebuilder. He has the courage of self-reflection. Sometimes he can have elements of the Trickster archetype. When the Raven speaks, it is often in riddles, but with the feeling that he is very learned, most likely from direct experience with the unknown.

Theme Revealed

When I read the description of this archetype, the movie *The Crow* immediately comes to my mind. It's a tough theme because the archetype is more the sort of character you would normally see playing opposite the protagonist or as a subsidiary character. I think any book using this theme would have a very unusual plot. Not that that's a *bad* thing. Like I said, it reminds me of *The Crow*, which is a fabulous movie.

Scorpion

Archetype Description

The Scorpion teaches constant vigilance and how to deal with intensity, whether it is environmental, physical, or spiritual. She is a master of self-defense and is always prepared for battle. Her size is misleading, for, although she is a small creature, her ability to "slip through the cracks" allows her many advantages. She works well as a spy or a secret agent.

Theme Revealed

This one should be obvious; it practically tells a story in the description. You could go a few ways with it, though. It could be the story of a young girl being trained for a secret mission she'll perform when she's a certain age; it could be the story of the person giving the training; it could be the story of someone already trained and going out on a mission that is against her spiritual beliefs and she must struggle with the morality of it. I'm sure you can come up with many more.

Skunk

Archetype Description

The Skunk archetype is all about having a good reputation, whatever it takes to get one, he'll do it, providing it doesn't come at the expense of his self-respect. He generally shows a lot of willpower and courage and displays much self-confidence, although at times it can be simple bravado. Skunks like to think they exude a lot of sensuality. But above all, reputation rules. It's all about understanding how to "walk the talk" so to speak.

Theme Revealed

This theme has been used many, many times in countless books and movies. It's the story of an Initiate, generally still wet behind the ears, learning to cope in the real word. And not just cope, but become an integral member of some sort of establishment. Many times it's a team or a gang. Other times it's learning how to overcome a certain foe or win a championship even though all the odds are against him. Movies like *Million Dollar Baby*, *The Karate Kid*, and *Grease* are just a few examples of stories based on this theme of building a reputation, finding self-respect and courage and the will-power and self-confidence it takes to "walk the talk."

You'll also see this theme used in a lot of mob movies and gangster films. The *Sopranos* used it a lot for many of their subplots.

Snake

Archetype Description

The Snake is associated with rebirth; the shedding of one's skin and it coming back; also, the symbol of the snake swallowing its own tail makes the circle which is the perfect symbol of life and regeneration. Elusive, the Snake is able to see the truth in people. She is the guardian of sacred places and the keeper of hidden knowledge. She represents power and life force. She is able to directly use the energies of the earth. She has protection from religious persecution.

Theme Revealed

Traditionally, the Snake is the Shadow figure in most religious stories. She was the one who suggested the woman eat from the Tree of Knowledge in the Garden of Eden. She is seen in a similar light in the religions of other cultures.

And yet, in other stories, the snake is seen as sacred. The snake swallowing her tail is the symbol of life and regeneration. The perfect image of reincarnation.

Her archetype suggests a theme of loss and gain—perhaps a tale of losing one's spirituality, only to find it again in the most unusual of places. Or it could be the story of lost love found again; the death of a loved one leads the protagonist to think they'll never be happy again and then, when things look their worst, they fall in love once more, with the one person they never expected to, or at the one time they never expected it to take place, or in the one way it couldn't possibly ever happen.

Any story of opposites coming together is one suggested by the theme of the snake. The snake shows a continuous circle; the cycle of life that goes round and round that doesn't ever end. Death and rebirth. Loss and discovery. Tears and joy. Despair and hope.

Spider

Archetype Description

The Spider is the weaver of the fate of the universe. Full of wisdom and creativity, she works with divine intervention, understanding the basic underlying concepts of the patterns of life's illusion. She can be a Shapeshifter and can use her energy to move and transform the creative force of life.

Theme Revealed

This is another archetype that suggests a character who is not the protagonist but plays a major role in the story. Some sort of subsidiary character that drives the plot.

The theme of having someone responsible for "weaving the fate of the universe" is not new. It is generally reserved for fantasy and science fiction works, though.

The archetype suggests a connection of the patterns of the illusions of life. If I were to use this theme, I would introduce this element into the story as a Mentor archetype working closely with the protagonist, perhaps also wearing the mask of a Shapeshifter, so the reader wasn't really sure whether the Mentor was acting in the protagonist's best interests or not. You could also consider combining this archetype with any of a number of different ones.

Swan

Archetype Description

The Swan shows tremendous grace while dealing with others. She has the skill of divination and can see into the future. With a great understanding of spiritual evolution, she recognizes the symbols in dreams. Swan archetypes can develop empathic abilities and awaken their inner power.

Theme Revealed

This is another theme that is almost exclusive to a certain type of story. It's certainly asking to be used in a metaphysical context.

Here's an example.

The protagonist starts the story not knowing she has latent spiritual abilities (perhaps she can see into the future) and it's the awakening of this power, caused by some external Inciting Event, that kicks the story into action.

Act II is full of sudden questions like: What is real and what isn't? Perhaps there's an antagonist in the form of a dark power on the other side of the veil; perhaps it's a human antagonist, someone like herself, who has felt the protagonist's powers "go live" and now considers her a threat.

The protagonist must be given a goal of some sort. Maybe she dreams of someone in danger; perhaps it's a little girl with abilities like herself being held captive by the antagonist and the protagonist must then set out to find her and set her free. The story then turns into a metaphysical mystery.

Tiger

Archetype Description

The Tiger has extreme focus and patience. He has the ability to look inwards and possibly act as a healer (the Tiger's orange coloring symbolizes vitality and regeneration). He has courage, power, strength, willpower, and is an extreme source of energy. He is able to use tactics to his advantage. He can quickly perform action without analysis.

Theme Revealed

This is the theme of the true commander. He knows when to strike, and he knows when to wait. Like all themes, when using this one, start your protagonist at the other end of the spectrum. Have him coming back from a tour of duty where everything went wrong. He lost five men he shouldn't have lost. He now doubts his ability to command.

Through the story's journey, he learns to trust himself again and regains his courage and, with it, his power and his strength. He again starts to display his ability to act strategically.

But it's all in simulations. He still hasn't gone back into real war.

Then it happens. He's called back into action.

And the doubts return.

Next thing you know, he's in charge of a squadron of men, and he's having flashbacks to what happened before. It's all too similar. He can't hold it together. But somehow, something allows him to dig deep down inside himself and find the strength to pull it off. Maybe it's the dog tags of one of the dead men from the original squadron that he's always kept with him that bring him back to reality.

Whatever it is, something turns around the bleak moment at the end of Act II and allows him to conquer the Climax he faces in Act III and come out once again the Hero.

Warthog

Archetype Description

The Warthog has the ability to dig up the truth under most circumstances. He can sense when danger is near and wears a fierce mask. He is the protector of evil and displays courage against his foes.

Theme Revealed

This is the theme of many superhero movies. *Batman* comes to mind as a primary example. The protagonist wears a "fearsome mask." In the case of *Batman*, this is a literal mask, but, of course, it doesn't have to be. It can be a metaphorical mask, too. And he fights for the truth and to protect the people of Gotham.

In stories like these, there is generally less of a character arc than in other Hero's Journeys. This isn't necessarily a good thing, but, in the case of superhero stories it's almost a necessity. The story starts with the protagonist already a Hero, so his journey has to be to something else. Good superhero movies have managed to find good journeys. Dark Knight was still a journey to the divine. Batman gave up his right to be a citizen of Gotham in order to save it. In the end, he looked like the villain. Spiderman 2 was a journey about Peter Parker finding out who he really was, but even more than that, the theme of identity was so prevalent in that movie it was repeated in nearly every major character and every major scene. It was by far the best of the three Sam Raimi Spiderman flicks.

Generally, though, these sorts of stories are more about the conflict between the Hero and the Shadow than anything else, so you have to make sure their encounters are exceptionally exciting, clever, and fresh and that they continue to increase the stakes and raise the tension as the story progresses.

Wolf

Archetype Description

The wolf is the Teacher archetype. He guards you as he teaches you, sometimes strongly, sometimes gently, but always with love. He can teach you about rituals, how to establish order and harmony within your own life. Instinctive and intelligent, he is able to heal.

The Wolf knows that discipline within a group creates true freedom. He knows how to find new paths and take new journeys. He is able to maintain perfect balance. He is loyal, and independent. Although he prefers to be alone, he is able to aid others when the need arises.

Theme Revealed

Again, the Wolf suggests a theme for a story where the Wolf is a major subsidiary character and not the protagonist himself.

He appears to be the quintessential Mentor, with an Eastern philosophical slant. Although he shows many of the same attributes as the standard Mentor archetype, I've included him because he's more specific in what he does. He teaches "gently" and "with love" and knows that "discipline within a group creates true freedom."

All of these things are archetypal concepts that go straight to the heart.

I'm sure I could go through an animal encyclopedia and keep adding more and more animals forever, but the challenge lies in researching the archetype behind the animals. It's important to find out what the values of the animals really mean. These aren't just made up, these are the actual archetypes that Shamans have known about for thousands of years. They call them "animal totems." The work done by Carl Jung showed that what the Shamans had been saying was right; there was a connection between humans and these animals—an association between their traits and behavior expectations in our psyche that are embedded before birth. Furthermore, these expectations and this base of knowledge is surprisingly similar across cultures, time, and distance. So much so, Jung coined the phrase "collective unconscious" to explain it.

Each of these animal archetypes bring with them an archetypal message or lesson that is truly primal. It is something that, if your Hero learns it from example, will ring true with your readers on a psychic level. Because that's where the strength of the archetype lies. In the subconscious. And, as Joseph Campbell would say, in the eternal.

Knowing this, you can be certain that you are writing to your readers on a subconscious level. It's almost like playing on a non-level playing field, but your readers will love you for it. It's the primal stories that give them that feeling of "Ahh!" when they come to the final page of your book, and you leave them wanting more.

2. Combining Themes

Themes can be easily combined. Components from one can be added or taken away from another. Don't be afraid to mix things up a bit. Remember, all the parts are what is archetypal about them, so you can mix and match and still be writing archetypal themes.

And they'll all plug in neatly to the three act structure we discussed earlier.

As I already said a few times. The structure is infinitely flexible, and supports a huge amount of variety. Take advantage of it. Use it. It works. Use archetypes in your writing. They work. Write thematically with archetypal themes. They're powerful and will bring out the power in your own craft.

EXERCISES

1. Try to quickly sketch out your own theme idea based around the theme of the Hawk. If the Hawk doesn't appeal to you, feel free to choose another animal. Your idea should be in point form (or it could be done through mind mapping) and no more than a page long.

   Remember, the archetype is providing only a metaphor for the theme, not a map of how to write the story. This cannot be said enough. When you talk about Archetypes, there's a strong desire to consider them stereotypes and, if anything, they are the opposite of stereotypes. Also, read the description of the animal's attribute and don't rely heavily on interpretation of the theme. The interpretation is a metaphor that you may interpret much different than I do. The key is to make sure you stay true to the attributes of the animal. That's what will make your story archetypal.

2. Now put the theme you just came up with and brainstorm or mind map a story to build upon it. It doesn't have to be Hemingway, it only has to be a viable story; that is a story with a beginning, a middle, and an end. In fact, just shoot for the four cornerstones of the three act structure: the Inciting Event, the First Pivot Point, the Second Pivot Point, and the resolution of the Climax. Get yourself used to thinking in stories this way. If you do, soon, you'll find your "outlining" process is nearly automatic and just falls out of the idea.

   Give a rough sketch of your story in whatever form you like. No more than a page long. A mind map is fine. If you do just go along with the four cornerstones, be sure to include any details that are important to this particular theme as well.

No matter what theme you follow, your stories will all be original because the theme is just a foundation—in no way does it provide you with a recipe for a finished story. You still need to do the hard work and build a story on top of it. The theme only ensures your story is archetypal.

3. Try combining the themes you came up with in Exercise 1 with a new animal theme of your choice and make a new single theme out of it. What do you gain by doing this? Does it add to the complexity of the theme or simplify it? How much fresher and more original does this make the theme from either of the two you had come up with before this step? How do you think it would affect the story generated from it?

4. Just like you did in Exercise 2, take this new combination theme and roughly build a story upon it. Again, no more than a page r a mind map is enough. Be sure to include the four cornerstones of the three act structure along with anything relative to the theme itself. Did this combined theme make it easier or harder to generate a story? Is the story more complex? Do either of the stories point to using certain Archetype characters in them already, even from just the skeletal notes you've written down?

KEY POINTS

- Giving your story an archetypal theme makes it powerful and gives it the ability to resonate with people in a far greater way than it would otherwise.
- You can develop archetypal themes by looking at animal archetypes or what is known is Shamanism as a "totem,"
- To develop the theme, you review the attributes of the animal archetype on a metaphorical level. The theme you come up with then provides you a solid foundation for building your story upon.
- There is nothing formulaic or stereotypical about this process. You are not writing using a cookie cutter method or anything like that. You are finding a powerful theme to use as the basis for an original story.
- The themes I came up with for the animals I listed in this chapter aren't the only themes you could find. Because you examine the animal's attributes metaphorically, there is room for many variations on theme.
- You can find many other animal archetypes with an explanation of their attributes on the web. Just Google "animal archetypes" or "animal totems."

Appendices

There is no real ending. It's just the place where you stop the story.

–Frank Herbert[22]

I Bibliography

II Glossary

III Contact

---

[22] Frank Herbert (October 8, 1920 - February 11, 1986) was an American science fiction author, best known for his series *Dune.*

APPENDIX I

Bibliography

There are many, many books on writing out there. I probably personally own over two hundred of them myself and I doubt I have even made a dent in the heap that's available. I am proud to say, however, that of my two hundred, I have read every single one. And there is one thing I can say about writing books: they are not all created equally.

There's actually another thing I can say about them as well: Everyone has their own taste when it comes to books on writing. I have read books that make me wonder why they were ever published that other authors I know, and respect, rave on and on about. I just don't get it. But then, I'm sure they feel the same way about some of my personal favorites.

I have tried to keep this little tome as clear and concise as possible without meandering off into anything that I don't consider extremely practical and important when it comes to taking your writing to the next level and making it as polished and professional as you can in as little time as possible.

Anyway, with my little caveat about everyone not liking the same books, I list here what I consider my favorite books on writing. These are my "I couldn't live without them" books and most of them are on structure and other things discussed in this little tome. All the ones on structure offer a more complex version of the Hero's Journey than I've included in this book. If you're the kind of person who likes things complex, you may find these books of tremendous value. I purposely scaled the three act structure I provided here down to what I considered the bare minimum so that:

a) People would actually memorize and *use* it instead of feeling overwhelmed by it
b) People might actually *outline* the key points if there weren't too many too outline

I think both these points are essential parts of the novel writing process. But there's nothing wrong with the versions found in other books. There's definitely some merit in knowing the little nuances I left out, especially once you've mastered the techniques I've laid down here.

You will notice many of the books I've listed are actually screenwriting books. Don't let that scare you away from them. Screenwriting books are just as valuable for the novel writer as they are for the person penning a movie script. You can learn a *lot* from the way movies are written because movies have to be done well. They have to be tight. There is hardly any margin for error. All the techniques that apply to screenwriting also apply to novel writing. I think I've gotten more out of those particular books than the ones written specifically for novelists.

Some of the books and DVD sets, like those by Joseph Campbell, are on general mythology and can actually be pretty deep. If you want to avoid reading Campbell's *The Hero with a Thousand Faces*, the I suggest picking up a copy of Christopher Vogler's *The Writer's Journey*. Vogler basically took Campbell's book and distilled the essence down to what is meaningful for the writing process. Even still, the Campbell book *is* a fantastic read.

I've also listed two books that are more "grammar related" than "writing related" just in case you need to brush up in that area. I find myself constantly going back and rereading grammar books, just to make sure I keep my chops up. Anyway, the two I put down here are personal favorites. They aren't heavy, and they're actually quite fun to read.

The books are listed by author name, not in order of how good they are. As I said, it's my "I couldn't live without them" list, so they're all equally precious to me.

Bradbury, Ray. *Zen in the Art of Writing.* Joshua Odell Editions, Santa Barbara, 1944.

Bell, James Scott. *Plot & Structure.* Writer's Digest Books, Cincinnati, 2004.

Bonnet, James. *Stealing Fire from the Gods.* Michael Wiese Productions, Studio City, 1999.

Campbell, Joseph. *The Hero with a Thousand Faces.* MJF Books, New York, 1949.

Campbell, Joseph. *The Power of Myth (2 disc DVD set interview with Bill Moyers).* Apostrophe S Productions, 1999.

Field, Syd. *Screenplay.* Bantam Dell, New York, 2005.

Field, Syd. *The Screenwriter's Problem Solver.* Bantam Dell, New York, 1998.

Field, Syd. *The Screenwriter's Workbook.* Bantam Dell, New York, 2006.

George, Elizabeth. *Write Away.* HarperCollins, New York, 2004.

Gordon, Karen Elizabeth. *The Deluxe Transitive Vampire: The Ultimate Handbook of Grammar for the Innocent, the Eager, and the Doomed.* Pantheon Books, Toronto, 1993.

Hale, Constance. *Sin and Syntax: How to Craft Wickedly Effective Prose.* Three Rivers Press, New York, 1999.

King, Stephen. *On Writing.* Scribner, New York, 2000.

Kress, Nancy. *Beginnings, Middles & Ends.* Writer's Digest Books, Cincinnati, 1999.

McKee, Robert. *Story: Substance, Structure, Style, and the Principles of Screenwriting.* HarperCollins, New York, 1997.

Snyder, Blake. *Save the Cat!* Michael Wiese Productions, Studio City, 2005.

Snyder, Blake. *Save the Cat! Goes to the Movies.* Michael Wiese Productions, Studio City, 2007

Snyder, Blake. *Save the Cat! Strikes Back.* Michael Wiese Productions, Studio City, 2009

Vogler, Christopher. *The Writer's Journey.* Michael Wiese Productions, Studio City, 1998.

Voytilla, Stuart. *Myth and the Movies.* Michael Wiese Productions, Studio City, 1999.

Wellman, Wendell. *A Writer's Roadmap.* 1st Books Library, Bloomington, 2002.

APPENDIX II

GLOSSARY

This is a glossary of terms used inside this book that you may not be familiar with. I list them here for convenience. Italics denote words that appear elsewhere in the Glossary.

Act II Midpoint

    The middle of Act II—which should also pretty much be the middle of your book. It is here where your story usually comes to a *pseudo climax*, much like your real *Climax*, only not as big.

All is Lost

    A "false defeat" point near the end of Act II where the protagonist feels he can't go any further. He's doomed. All hope is lost. And during this stage, he must, in some way, experience a death of some sort, either literal or metaphorical. With this death dies all of the protagonist's old ways of thinking along with his old world. It clears the way for him to become the *Hero* during the *Resurrection* in the resolution of the story's *Climax*.

Anima

    The unconscious feminine personality inside of the male psyche. The energy of the *Anima* and the *Animus* shows up in the *Shapeshifter archetype*, among other place.

Animal Archetype

    An *archetype* based on ancient shamanic animal totems that can be used as metaphors to build story themes.

Animus

> The unconscious male personality inside of the female psyche. The energy of the *Animus* and the *Anima* shows up in the *Shapeshifter archetype*, among other places.

Archetypal Symbol

> A symbol primal to the subconscious that is instinctively mapped to a built-in emotion. The Blood of Christ is such a symbol.

Archetypal Theme

> Like the *archetypal symbol*, the *archetypal theme* is a theme which instinctively rings true on a primal level in our subconscious mind. In the same way, there are built-in emotions that go along with it. Writing with *archetypal themes* guarantees your writing will be solid and powerful.

Archetype(s)

> A psychological representation of things we encounter in the physical universe including personality traits and the roles people play in our lives. *Archetypes* are primal and become part of our psyche before we are born. They are amazingly constant across time and cultures and hold a lot of power. They show up in our dreams, our stories, our myths, and our religions, among other places.

Character Arc

> The change the protagonist (or any character) goes through between the beginning of the story (as shown in the *Setup*) and the end of the story (as shown in the *Denouement*). The greater the change, the more dramatic and more powerful the story. Stories are all about change.

Climax

> The point in the third act that the entire story builds toward. It's the ultimate showdown between the protagonist and the antagonist. It's where the protagonist ultimately goes through his *resurrection* and becomes a *Hero* and returns home with the *Elixir*.

Cornerstones

The four foundation points of your story that must be solid in order for your story to function properly. They are: the beginning (see *Inciting Event*), the resolution (see *Climax*), and the entryway between Act I and Act II and Act II and Act III (see *Pivot Point*).

Dark Night before Dawn

The final part of Act II where the protagonist musters every last ounce of energy he has and reaches way down deep and discovers he has nothing left. It's the point where you show your readers your protagonist's humility—he's been beat and he knows it. He will learn from this lesson.

Darkness Closes In

A point shortly after the *Act II Midpoint* where the protagonist has been doing quite well and it's time to put a stop to that. So, the bad guys begin rallying and things start turning badly. This is the first of three major bad plot points for the protagonist that drops him into Act III. The other two are *All is Lost* and *Dark Night before Dawn*.

Denouement

This is the final pages of the book, after the protagonist has gone through the Climax and Resurrection and returned as the Hero with the Elixir where you show him back in the normal world again. The scene exists as an antithesis to the Setup scene in Act I—you want to show how much things have changed due to the ordeal he went through during his journey. The greater the change, the more powerful the story.

Elixir

The ultimate boon for the *Hero*. His real final goal in the story. It might be the keys to the kingdom, it might be the princess's hand in marriage, it might be a treasure chest of gold. It might even simply just be the knowledge that this special world he experienced existed. Whatever it is, he returns home with it once he becomes a *Hero* and, in doing so, the world (which was flawed when he left) either becomes repaired or is now flawed in a different way. Whichever it is, the world is a better place for the *Hero* having faced the antagonist and returned victorious.

Hero

The archetype of your protagonist once he has gone through a transcendence in the resolution of the Climax. It is what he ultimately wishes to achieve.

Hero's Journey

The journey your protagonist takes from that leads him from an ordinary flawed character of the *Initiate archetype* through a sequence of trials and tests that build to a *Climax* where he has his final showdown against the antagonist and, hopefully, returns home a victorious *Hero* with the Elixir. It is a journey made up of three acts, a beginning consisting of a *Setup* and an *Inciting Event*, a middle consisting of a series of ordeals with a *Midpoint Climax*, and an ending consisting of a *Climax* and a *Denouement*.

Inciting Event

The main event that happens in the first act that kicks your story into action. Generally it is an external event, brought to the protagonist's attention by a Herald *archetype*. The Herald doesn't have to be a person; it can be a thing (like an announcement of war) or even the antagonist calling the protagonist out. In the latter case, the antagonist (which is the archetypal Shadow) would be temporarily wearing the mask of the Herald *archetype*.

Initiate

The *archetype* representing your protagonist at the beginning of his *Hero's Journey*. He is inexperienced and not yet ready to face all of the trials that lay before him. But he will learn the way as he goes.

Midpoint Climax

See *Act II Midpoint*.

Mythic Structure

See Hero's Journey.

Pivot Point

The point between acts; either the threshold right before leaving Act I and entering Act II or the threshold right before leaving Act II and entering Act III. These are very emotionally charged moments for your protagonist and should be well-considered during writing. See *Cornerstones*.

Pseudo Climax

See Act II Midpoint.

Resurrection

This is a point, generally near the resolution of your *Climax* or directly following it or even during it, where your protagonist goes through a transcendence of some sort. He is resurrected in a way that corresponds to the "death" he experienced during the *All is Lost* stage at the end of Act II. It is during this *resurrection*, that he truly becomes the *Hero*.

Setup

The first stage of Act I spent showing your protagonist at the start of the story—as a flawed character in a flawed world. The *Setup* should be short, because your story doesn't really start until the *Inciting Event*.

Shadow

The *archetype* of your villain or your antagonist.

Shapeshifter

The *shapeshifter* is an *archetype* who is hard to pin down because it keeps changing. Often this archetype manifests as a woman, but it can just as easily be a man. It will usually carry the energy of the Anima and the Animus and wear many masks. It brings questions into stories and offers a range of *sub-archetypes*, such as the "Femme Fatale."

Sub-Archetypes

A *sub-archetype* is an *archetype* derived from another *archetype*. For instance, the "Femme Fatale" is an *archetype* derived from *Shapeshifter*. The "Damsel in Distress" is an *archetype* derived from the Damsel and, really, the Damsel is an *archetype* derived from the Maiden.

Subplot(s)

A subsidiary plot to the main plot. *Subplots* are generally referred to by letters with your "A" Plot being your main plot and your "B" Plot being your first subplot. Other plotlines continue being lettered in ascending order. There's no rule for how many *subplots* a book has to have. You can have none or you can have five or six. Traditionally, the "B" Plot is the plotline featuring the romantic interest of the protagonist, but it certainly doesn't have to be. *Subplots* generally weave in and out of the main "A Plot" until finally coming back together and rejoining it again, usually at the beginning of Act III.

Three Act Structure

See *Hero's Journey*.

Threshold Guardian

A type of *archetype* that usually guards passages, primarily entrances between acts. Your protagonist will encounter them at a *Pivot Point*. They may be sentinels, or guards, or knights, or bouncers in bars. Whoever they are, their primary function is to stop the protagonist from proceeding any further. They may work for the antagonist, or they may have their own agendas.

APPENDIX III

Contact

Feel free to contact me if you have any questions, comments, critique, or anything else you wish to say about this book or writing in general. I would love to see you at one of my workshops!

I can be contacted in any of the following ways:

Email:	michael.hiebert@aol.com
Twitter:	@Hiebert_M
Website:	www.michaelhiebert.com

My website features my blog which I update on a fairly regular basis. You can usually find some good writing tips on it. A lot of this book originally appeared as blog posts, so some of it will feel a bit familiar to you already.

I also have the rest of my available books listed on my blog with links to where they're for sale, if that interests you.

Thank you for your interest and your support.

Made in the USA
Charleston, SC
26 June 2013